CENTER FOR THE SMALL CITY
University of Wisconsin - Stevens Point
Stevens Point, Wisconsin 54481

NONMETROPOLITAN INDUSTRIALIZATION

SCRIPTA SERIES IN GEOGRAPHY

Series Editors
Richard E. Lonsdale • Antony R. Orme • Theodore Shabad

NONMETROPOLITAN INDUSTRIALIZATION

Richard E. Lonsdale
University of Nebraska
and
H. L. Seyler
Kansas State University

1979

V. H. WINSTON & SONS
Washington, D.C.

A HALSTED PRESS BOOK

JOHN WILEY & SONS

New York   Toronto   London   Sydney

V. H. Winston & Sons, a Division of Scripta Technica, Inc., Publishers
1511 K Street, N.W., Washington, D.C. 20005

Distributed solely by Halsted Press, a Division of John Wiley & Sons, Inc.

Library of Congress Cataloging in Publication Data:

Main entry under title:

Nonmetropolitan industrialization.

(Scripta series in geography)
Includes index.
1. Industries, Location of–United States. 2. Community development–United States. 3. United States–Rural conditions. I. Lonsdale, Richard E. II. Seyler, H. L. III. Series.
HC110.D5N66   338'.0973   78–20887
ISBN 0-470-26631-7

CONTENTS

PART II. THE IMPACT OF NONMETROPOLITAN
INDUSTRIALIZATION

CONTRIBUTORS

Beck, E. M., Associate Professor of Sociology at the University of Georgia, Athens. His Ph.D. is from the University of Tennessee. His current research concerns poverty and racial discrimination.

Doering, Thomas R., Research Economist with the Nebraska Department of Economic Development, Lincoln. He holds a Ph.D. in geography from the University of Nebraska. Apart from his research on the community satisfactions of nonmetropolitan manufacturers, he is interested in the developmental aspects of recreation and tourism.

Erickson, Rodney A., Assistant Professor of Geography at Pennsylvania State University, University Park. He earned his Ph.D. at the University of Washington in 1973, and has since done most of his research in the area of spatial dimensions of industrial linkages, income spread affects, industrial location, and urban and regional development strategies.

Fuguitt, Glenn, Professor of Rural Sociology at the University of Wisconsin, Madison. His major research interest is nonmetropolitan population redistribution. He has served as president of both the Rural Sociological Society and the International Rural Sociological Association.

Haren, Claude C., Economist with the Economics, Statistics, and Cooperatives Service, U.S. Department of Agriculture, Washington, D.C. Serving the USDA for 44 years, his research fields are land economics, geography, and economic growth and development.

Heaton, Tim, currently a Ph.D. candidate at the University of Wisconsin, Madison. Trends in population distribution in the United States and socioeconomic consequences of industrial change in nonmetropolitan areas are the subjects of his research.

Holling, Ronald W., Labor Economist with the Economics, Statistics, and Cooperatives Service, U.S. Department of Agriculture, Washington, D.C. His undergraduate and graduate work was in economics at Brigham Young University.

Kale, Steven, Economist at the Nebraska Department of Economic Development, Lincoln, where his major responsibilities are in industrial development research. He holds a Ph.D. in geography from the University of Nebraska.

Kinworthy, John C., Assistant Professor of Geography at Concordia College, Seward, Nebraska. His research interests are in economic geography. In addition to nonmetropolitan industrialization, he is presently engaged in analyses of the locational characteristics of medical facilities in urban areas.

Kuehn, John A., Economist with the Economics, Statistics, and Cooperatives Service, U.S. Department of Agriculture, Columbia, Missouri. He is also Assistant Professor of Agricultural Economics at the University of Missouri. Research emphases include rural community services, industrialization, and growth potential.

Leinbach, Thomas R., Associate Professor of Geography at the University of Kentucky, Lexington. He earned his Ph.D. at Pennsylvania State University in 1971, and has since done most of his research on the role of transportation improvements and information flows on regional development in Southeast Asia.

Lonsdale, Richard E., Professor of Geography at the University of Nebraska, Lincoln. His Ph.D. is from Syracuse University. His work has focused on industrial location and industrial decentralization, and he has done research in Australia and the Soviet Union as well as in the U.S. South and Great Plains.

Seyler, "Sy" H. L., Assistant Professor of Geography at Kansas State University, Manhattan. His Ph.D. is from the University of Indiana. His research has emphasized industrial and area development and social science methodology.

Shaffer, Ron E., Associate Professor of Agricultural Economics at the University of Wisconsin, Madison. His Ph.D. is from Oklahoma State University. His research has focused on economic impact analyses, especially in nonmetropolitan settings.

Snipp, C. Matthew, doctoral candidate in rural sociology at the University of Wisconsin, Madison. His primary interests are in the areas of social stratification, organizations, and social policy.

Summers, Gene F., Professor of Rural Sociology at the University of Wisconsin, Madison. For the past 10 years he has been examining the movement of industry into the nonmetropolitan areas of the U.S., and he is currently extending this research effort to other industrial nations. He was a Senior Fulbright Research Fellow to Norway in 1978 and is co-principal investigator in a U.S.-Spanish comparative analysis of industrial growth and population change in rural areas.

PREFACE

Nonmetropolitan industrialization is more than an interesting anomaly or temporary manifestation of the times. It is a widespread movement which has come to play a highly important role in the lives of the 63.8 million Americans (31.4% of nation's total population in 1970) living outside metropolitan areas. Almost six million nonmetropolitan jobs are in manufacturing, substantially more than in agriculture. Manufacturing's share of nonmetropolitan employment is almost on par with that in metropolitan areas. The social and economic changes wrought by this largely post-World War II development are having an effect on the welfare of the entire nation. The purpose of this book is to provide a survey and assessment of this remarkable phenomenon in the United States.

Opinions vary and emotions run high on the subject of nonmetropolitan manufacturing. Some view it as a kind of salvation for rural America that has provided jobs, given people an alternative to out-migration, and brought on a great economic and demographic turnaround. Others see it as a force undermining traditional rural values and institutions, exploiting rural labor, and encumbering small towns with a variety of obligations requiring increased local taxes. One can cite examples and statistics to support both of these polarized points of view. Hopefully, most will see in nonmetropolitan industrialization both the beneficial aspects and the problems associated with it. It is in this spirit that the book was written.

Some definitions are in order. Nonmetropolitan refers to areas outside Standard Metropolitan Statistical Areas (SMSAs). The latter embrace counties or groups of contiguous counties which contain at least one city of 50,000 population or more (or "twin cities" or other solidly built up areas with a total population of 50,000 or more). Contiguous counties are included in the SMSA if they are socially and economically integrated with the central city. "Industrialization" as used in this book refers to the establishment of new manufacturing plants (or enlargement of existing ones) to the extent that such industry becomes an important element in the local employment structure. The terms "industry" and "manufacturing" are used interchangeably, as has become customary in this country. Manufacturing includes the processing and fabrication of raw materials and/or semifinished goods into new products, but excludes construction, repair, and electric power generation.

It is hoped that the material presented in this book will be useful to the specialist and interested layperson alike in clarifying the issues involved in nonmetropolitan industrialization. In particular this includes community leaders, manufacturing officials, regional and community planners, geographers, economists, rural sociologists, and agricultural economists.

The papers were all commissioned and the book so organized as to provide a logical sequence of material and an integrated picture of nonmetropolitan manufacturing in the United States. Authors were drawn from several academic disciplines, and several papers (subsequently modified to comprise chapters) were presented at the New Orleans meeting of the Association of American Geographers in April 1978.

The book is divided into two parts. Part One treats the transformation of the nonmetropolitan industrial landscape, and is introduced in Chapter One, "Background and Issues." Part Two examines the impact of nonmetropolitan industrialization, and is introduced in Chapter Six, "Dimensions of Social and Economic Change."

PART I

TRANSFORMATION OF THE NONMETROPOLITAN INDUSTRIAL LANDSCAPE

Chapter 1

BACKGROUND AND ISSUES

Richard E. Lonsdale

Nonmetropolitan industrialization in the United States constitutes a whole new phase in the evolving economic geography of the nation. It represents a dramatic departure from the classic pattern of industrial concentration in or near metropolitan centers. The forces pulling industry to such centers are still strong, of course, and for many industries they will remain dominant, but the decentralizing forces have gained substantially in significance. The rate of increase in industrial employment in nonmetropolitan areas has recently been well ahead of the metropolitan pace, and since about 1960 nonmetropolitan areas have accounted for well over half of all new industrial jobs. Nonmetropolitan areas now have about 29% of the nation's manufacturing employees, not far behind their 31% share of the nation's population.

In examining this phenomenon, the broader issue of regional inequality or regional justice should be kept in mind. It is precisely because of this regional inequality (most specifically, the differential between metropolitan and nonmetropolitan areas) that nonmetropolitan industrialization has assumed such great significance. For years, many smaller communities have viewed "new industry" as their major hope, and now that industry has come to them on a major scale, it is being credited with helping to reverse the historic pattern of population net out-migration, promoting improved economic and social conditions, and bringing a renewed sense of confidence in the future of these areas. On the other hand, some warn that new industry is not a panacea for all communities; it may create serious problems, and the whole phenomenon of nonmetropolitan industrialization may be a temporary phase. Whatever the facts, and generalizations on these matters tend to be subjective, non-

3

metropolitan industrialization has clearly emerged as a major force to be reckoned with by government policy makers and others in assessing the nation's economic and social future.

The purpose of this chapter is to provide a setting for Part I of the book, which examines the record of nonmetropolitan industrialization in the U.S., factors encouraging and discouraging it, kinds of industries involved, and manufacturers' views of such locations. To put these presentations in clearer perspective, it seems appropriate to first review a number of background questions and issues. Specifically, is the U.S. experience unique on the world scene? What are the contemporary issues? Why is manufacturing seen as the key to redressing regional inequalities?

IS THE U.S. EXPERIENCE UNIQUE?

Nonmetropolitan industrialization may be the normal consequence of advanced industrial development, whatever the nation or the economic system. As production processes in a particular industry become more "routinized," there is a tendency for that industry to disperse from its original points of development and to "filter down" from larger urban places to smaller ones.[1] Williamson suggests that as a nation moves from underdevelopment to advanced industrial development, the nation passes through a cycle of regional inequality.[2] With industrialization regional inequality increases, but with industrial maturity there is a tendency for regional inequalities to diminish as a result of labor and capital migration, interregional linkages, and government policy.[3]

Summers et al. view nonmetropolitan industrialization as a general process within already industrialized societies and observe:[4]

> The industrial development of a rural area within a technologically and industrially advanced nation is a process unlike the historical emergence of industrialized Western societies. Industrialization is an evolutionary process of social change which had its origin in scientific discovery. Nonmetropolitan industrial development, on the other hand, is essentially a spatial redistribution of economic activity within a nation.

Concern with the spatial redistribution of manufacturing and the adoption of government programs to promote it certainly seem to be common to most advanced industrial societies.[5] The British have enacted a number of measures since the mid-1930s for the purpose of promoting manufacturing expansion in depressed industrial districts and in areas of rural depopulation.[6] In Sweden, an ambitious program to encourage industry and people to go to Norrland began in 1964. In Italy, the government has invested large sums to attract more industry to the south. In the U.S.S.R., the last three 5-year plans (i.e., since 1965) have called for more industry in small towns and restrictions on industrial expansion in the cities.[7] Many other examples could be cited. While the effectiveness of such government efforts on the whole has been poor,[8] the point is that nonmetropolitan industrialization is international in scope, and U.S. experiences should be viewed in that context.

There are, however, certain characteristics of the American scene which make its experience with nonmetropolitan industrialization reasonably unique. To begin with, regional wage differentials are substantially greater in the U.S. than in most advanced industrial societies. Directly related to this is the fact that labor unionization is largely a metropolitan phenomenon in the U.S., whereas in many nations it is national in scope. To appreciate the significance of these two points, one has only to imagine how many firms would have "moved" to the U.S. South if that area had had wage and unionization levels on par with the rest of the nation. In brief, the "pull" factors have been much more pronounced in the U.S. The same can probably be said of the "push" factors as well; in the opinion of many observers, the large cities of the U.S. have undergone much more social and environmental deterioration than have the large cities of most other industrial nations. Thus, with a minimum of formal federal policy on the matter, the U.S. has probably experienced more decentralization and, in effect, nonmetropolitan industrialization, than any major industrial nation, capitalist or socialist.

HISTORIC BACKGROUND OF PUBLIC CONCERN

The vast farmlands of the central U.S. had hardly been settled when the industrial revolution hit the nation with full force. With this revolution came the technological modernization of agriculture and the declining need for farm labor. With the development of major urban-industrial centers in the last quarter of the 19th century, rural–urban migration of people emerged as a natural consequence of geographic imbalances in the national labor market. There was set into motion the difficult process of rural transformation (common to all industrializing societies) which is still very active today.

As the migration of people from the farms accelerated, it became cause for national concern in the early part of the present century. One ramification of this was an early version of return-to-the-land thinking, the "country life movement" described by Bowers:[9]

> Ostensibly an effort to promote measures which could make the social, intellectual, and economic aspects of rural life equal to those of urban living, the movement was in reality a complex mixture of rural nostalgia, the desire to make agriculture more efficient and profitable, humanitarianism, and economic self-interest.

However sentimental and impractical, the widespread support the movement attracted reflected genuine public concern for the problems of rural/small-town areas in an era of urbanization.

Public interest was also asserted through the activities of land-grant colleges and churches and through the programs of state and federal departments of agriculture. Of special note was the 1914 Smith–Lever Act which established a unified national extension service, under federal funding, which attempted to go beyond concern with just production and marketing and encompass all aspects of rural life.[10]

For the nation as a whole, the farm population reached a peak of 32.5 million persons in 1916 (today it is less than 10 million), and rural–urban migration became a prominent issue with the 1920 census, which revealed that the nation had become more urban than rural.[11] The exodus continued full force through the 1920s, but paused during the depression years of the 1930s.

In the period of the New Deal, efforts of the federal government to cope with the problems of rural/small-town America attained new proportions. Of particular note were the creation of the Rural Electrification Administration (REA), the Tennessee Valley Authority (TVA), the Soil Conservation Service (SCS), and various agricultural price support programs. Of special interest was the Resettlement Administration which, among other things, attempted to formulate policy on rural–urban migration, new rural communities, and the distribution of population in general.[12]

These programs were shifted to a lower priority or phased out with the outbreak of war, and this deemphasis persisted through the Truman and Eisenhower years (through 1960). Perhaps preoccupied with absolute economic growth under conditions of the Cold War, national discussion of regional differentials in economic and social well-being remained relatively muted. Meanwhile, rural–urban migration resumed its pre-1930 intensity. In the 1950s, metropolitan areas increased their population by 26.5% while nonmetropolitan areas grew by just 5.1%.[13] The overall level of urbanization increased from 64.0% in 1950 to 69.9% in 1960 and 73.5% in 1970.

The contemporary era of heightened public and governmental concern with the problems of nonmetropolitan areas dates from about 1961, and seems to have been initiated by a number of interrelated national issues which hit the front pages of newspapers from the late 1950s on. These issues include civil rights, concern with poverty, environmental quality, urban congestion, the feeling that large cities have become too big, and school integration and the "white flight" to the suburbs. Perhaps the most critical catalyst of all were the big-city race riots of the mid-1960s. Now at last the whole nation saw the obvious link between the deterioration of urban environments and the problems of nonmetropolitan areas, most specifically the circumstances promoting the rural–urban migration of legions of poorly educated persons, black and white.

The improvement of nonmetropolitan economic and social conditions was widely perceived as the key to achieving a "more balanced" geography of population, i.e., avoiding the continued overloading of more highly urbanized areas. On this point there was a coalescing of interests on the part of rural and urban groups, blacks and whites, and conservatives and liberals alike. This situation permitted broadly supported political action, and a series of government programs were enacted.

Governments at the federal, state, and local levels began organizing and developing new programs to improve nonmetropolitan as well as metropolitan economic and social conditions. According to Hausler.[14]

> These programs were designed to 1) foster economic development of depressed areas or regions; 2) eradicate poverty and improve health, education, and welfare of our citizens; 3) attain better distribution of our population through better-balanced rural–urban growth; and 4) give citizens a bigger voice in decisions that affect their lives.

At the federal level there was the Area Redevelopment Act of 1961 which provided capital for problem areas through low-interest loans for industry and business, and loans and grants for problem communities to improve the infrastructural support for new industry.[15] This was followed in 1964 by the Economic Opportunity Act designed to attack poverty. In 1965 the Appalachian Regional Commission was established, the first large-scale effort employing an integrated approach to regional development since the TVA of the 1930s. The Economic Development Act of 1965 permitted the creation of additional regional commissions, and the Rural Development Act of 1972 provided further forms of assistance significant for smaller communities. A recurrent theme through most of these legislative efforts has been the need to enhance problem areas' ability to generate new employment opportunities, improve the quality of life, and reduce the need for out-migration.

CONTEMPORARY ISSUES

A number of issues dominate contemporary discussions of the problems of nonmetropolitan America. Some relate to matters beyond the scope of this book, e.g., crop and livestock prices, price-support levels, restrictions on the use of certain herbicides or pesticides, water and soil conservation, special problems of racial or ethnic minorities, land use planning restrictions, etc. Others, however, are more directly relevant to the subject of nonmetropolitan industrialization and the broader question of regional inequality. Any listing of contemporary issues is necessarily somewhat subjective, but with this reservation in mind, the following issues, all interrelated, are here noted:

Inadequate Employment Opportunities

With a declining need for farm labor, high rural fertility rates, and the economic stagnation of so many smaller communities, the employment opportunities in nonmetropolitan areas have traditionally fallen far short of the need. An alternative to farm or local service employment has generally been lacking, although more recently new industrial plants have helped to ease this problem.

For younger people, particularly those with some college education, the problem is particularly acute. Even if they were willing to accept a job with a modest starting wage, the prospects for promotion to higher wage levels are often bleak. Given the kinds of economic activities prevaling in non-metropolitan areas, upward job mobility is more restricted than in city environments.

Forced Out-Migration and Population Maldistribution

While out-migration, especially of younger people, is the product of several factors, the lack of suitable local employment has "forced" many to leave. The word "forced" is used, because residential preference surveys show that a great many nonmetropolitan residents prefer to remain in such places.[16] Between 1960 and 1970, there was a net out-migration from nonmetropolitan U.S. of 2.4 million persons, a tremendous loss of resources, especially since many of these migrants were well-educated and capable workers.[17]

After several generations of such out-migration, the public has come to view the nation's population as maldistributed and a serious national problem. They support governmental programs to discourage the further growth of large cities and strongly endorse efforts to encourage rural growth.[18]

Selectivity in Migration

Working to the general disadvantage of nonmetropolitan areas has been the selectivity in out-migration. Those who attained higher levels of education have been more likely to leave. Out-migrants also tend to be young (i.e., 17 to 29), often leaving after completing their schooling, and this has an obvious impact on the age structure of the remaining population in such areas. Persons from higher income families are more likely to migrate than those from poorer families. Given the above circumstances, it is not surprising that migration rates are higher among whites than blacks.[19]

Stagnation or Decline of Small Towns

It is a matter of common knowledge that large numbers of smaller towns have undergone economic and demographic stagnation, slow decline, or complete demise. In effect, with a decline in the farm population, they have experienced a dwindling economic base.[20] On the other hand, some non-metropolitan communities have grown impressively. Where growth occurred, it is often a case of that town emerging as the focal point within a particular region. All of this represents a natural adjustment to regional population decline and improved transportation and communication.

Whether growing slowly, stagnating, or declining, passions run high on the subject of a town's future. Not surprisingly, a recurrent theme is the creation of additional basic employment opportunities. It is easy to understand why new industrial plants, however small in employment and modest in wages, are generally viewed with favor by local community leaders.

Educational Standards and Health Care

The quality of public schooling and health care facilities is generally below national standards in nonmetropolitan areas by most objective indicators. Judging by educational attainment levels, number of medical specialists and dentists, hospital facilities, etc., nonmetropolitan Americans are disadvantaged.[21] Poorer schools and fewer years of schooling presumably take their toll in terms of the skill levels, trainability, and job aspirations of nonmetropolitan labor. Interestingly, educational and medical facilities are not necessarily perceived as subpar by local residents; a 1976 survey of small-town manufacturers in Nebraska found that educational and medical facilities were a major source of satisfaction with their location.[22]

Areas of Serious Poverty

Throughout much of this book, the subject of nonmetropolitan industrialization is discussed in a general way without very specific reference to individual states or areas. Of special significance, however, is the presence of several broad areas of widespread poverty and subpar per capita incomes which are largely nonmetropolitan in nature. The presence of such areas is partially responsible for the national concern with regional inequality, and it inevitably is one of the issues prominent in discussions of nonmetropolitan problems. These "distressed" areas include Appalachia, many sections of the South, the Ozarks, southern Texas, and the Indian reservations.[23]

Most of these areas possess large minority populations. They stand in sharp contrast with some other largely nonmetropolitan areas—the Great Plains, the Upper Great Lakes, and northern New England—which, while suffering out-migration and community stagnation, can be described as relatively prosperous.[24]

Other Issues

A number of other problems worthy of being described as "issues" could be noted. These include insufficient social services and cultural amenities, lack of confidence in the future, the increasing popularity of rural/small-town environments as preferred places to live, inequalities in the distribution of federal funds, housing, and the personal trauma of children moving long distances away from their parents. Still others could be noted. All of these issues are directly or indirectly related to the broader question of regional inequality or regional justice, and in most instances the creation of new job opportunities is seen by many as a key to their amelioration.

WHY MANUFACTURING?

Why is new industry—specifically manufacturing—seen as the key to easing the problems of nonmetropolitan areas? There are, after all, other forms of basic employment that a "lagging" region might acquire, e.g., recreation and tourism, expanded agricultural acreage through irrigation, new mining activities, government offices, military installations, etc. Unfortunately, only a few areas possess the scenic vistas, special resources, or other situational advantages necessary to attract such forms of activity.

Manufacturing is often cited as a "slow-growth" sector of the national economy, and for the nation as a whole this is basically true. In the 20-year period 1955-75, manufacturing employment increased only 8%, from 16.9 million to 18.3 million. In the same period overall employment rose 29%, from 65 million to 84 million. Manufacturing's share of total employment thus fell from 26% to 22%. However, by 1978 manufacturing employment increased to 19.9 million, or 23% of total employment.

While it might seem logical for nonmetropolitan areas to focus their efforts on the more rapidly growing sectors of the national economy (e.g., wholesale and retail trade, finance, insurance, real estate, professional and personal services, government, etc.), this is usually impractical. Most of these faster-growing sectors are "non-basic," i.e., community-serving rather than community forming, and in any event they have a pronounced preference for established and growing urban centers. Even when serving a largely nonmetropolitan area, they are likely to be concentrated in the largest city within that area.

The key to manufacturing's attractiveness is its locational mobility. Even though it may be a comparatively slow-growing sector of the national economy, many kinds of manufacturing activity have displayed a willingness to change their location. The whole post World War II phenomenon of large-scale industrialization of the U.S. South occurred in a period when national manufacturing employment was increasing only modestly. The same can be said about nonmetropolitan industrialization. For thousands of smaller communities manufacturing has been a growth sector. While older urban areas might be described as "post-industrial," nonmetro areas can be viewed as having been in the "take-off" phase of development. Heady states the case thusly:[25]

> Industrialization is one means by which rural communities can realize added economic activity to provide greater employment and family incomes. In many cases it provides growth to rural areas which more than offsets reductions in farm employment because of the ongoing mechanization and higher capitalization of agriculture in related service industries. In other cases rural industrialization may provide an opportunity to absorb labor released from farming and help keep economic activity of the community from rapid deterioration.

Manufacturing firms have a demonstrated record of willingness to locate in small towns, something that cannot be said for most other basic (community-forming) economic activities in many areas of nonmetropolitan America. In the 1960-70 period, nonmetropolitan manufacturing employment increased from 3.6 to 4.9 million, an impressive 34% increase, and it represented 46% of the total increased employment in nonmetropolitan areas.[26] Since most manufacturing is basic in nature, these new industrial jobs probably accounted for a very high share of new basic employment. It is, therefore, easy to understand and often quite rational that nonmetropolitan communities should look to manufacturing. Not all communities (especially the smaller ones) are going to be able to attract the amount and/or kind of industry they would like. That manufacturing is not appropriate for all communities is self-evident.

NOTES

[1] Rodney A. Erickson, "The Filtering-Down Process: Industrial Location in a Non-metropolitan Area," *The Professional Geographer,* Vol. 28 (1976), pp. 254-255.

[2] J. G. Williamson, "Regional Inequality and the Process of National Development: A Description of the Patterns," *Economic Development and Cultural Change,* Vol. 13 (1965), pp. 3-84.

[3] Ibid., pp. 8-9.

[4] Gene F. Summers et al., *Industrial Invasion of Nonmetropolitan America* (New York: Praeger Publishers, 1976) p. xv.

[5] *Rural Development: The Industrialized Free-Enterprise Nations,* U.S. Senate Committee on Agriculture and Forestry (Washington, D.C.: GPO, 1973).

[6] G. McCrone, *Regional Policy in Britain* (London: George Allen & Unwin, 1969).

[7] Richard E. Lonsdale, "Regional Inequity and Soviet Concern for Rural and Small-Town Industrialization," *Soviet Geography,* Vol. 18 (1977), pp. 590-602.

[8] Walter Stöhr and Franz Tödtling, "Spatial Equity – Some Anti-Theses to Current Regional Development Doctrine," *Papers of the Regional Science Association,* Vol. 38 (1977), p. 33.

[9] William L. Bowers, *The Country Life Movement in America 1900-1920* (Port Washington, N.Y.: Kennikat Press, 1974), p. 3.

[10] Ibid., pp. 89-90, 129.

[11] Calvin Beale, "Demographic Trends of the U.S. Rural Population," in George Brinkman, ed., *The Development of Rural America* (Lawrence: The University Press of Kansas, 1974), pp. 33-34.

[12] Paul K. Conkin, *Tomorrow a New World: The New Deal Community Program* (Ithaca: Cornell University Press, 1959), p. 153 ff.

[13] Beale, op. cit., note 11, p. 36.

[14] Richard Hausler, "The Emergence of Area Development," in George Brinkman, ed., *The Development of Rural America* (Lawrence: The University Press of Kansas, 1974), p. 17.

[15] Ibid.

[16] James J. Zuiches and Glenn V. Fuguitt, "Residential Preferences: Implications for Population Redistribution in Nonmetropolitan Areas," in Sara Mills Mazie, ed., *Population Distribution & Policy,* Vol. 5 of research reports (Washington, D.C.: U.S. Commission on Population Growth and the American Future, 1972), pp. 617-630.

[17] Luther Tweeten and George L. Brinkman, *Micropolitan Development* (Ames: Iowa State University Press, 1976), p. 13.

[18] James J. Zuiches and Glenn V. Fuguitt, "Public Attitudes on Population Distribution Policies," *Growth and Change,* Vol. 7 (1976), pp. 28-33.

[19] Daniel O. Price and Melanie M. Sikes, *Rural-Urban Migration Research in the United States* (Washington, D.C.: H.E.W. Center for Population Research, 1975), pp. 5–18.

[20] Gerald A. Doeksen, John Kuehn, and Joseph Schmidt, "Consequences of Decline and Community Economic Adjustment to It," in *Communities Left Behind* (Ames: Iowa State University Press, 1974), pp. 28–42.

[21] Tweeten and Brinkman, op. cit., note 17, pp. 14–15.

[22] Richard E. Lonsdale, John C. Kinworthy, and Thomas R. Doering, *Attitudes of Manufacturers in Small Cities and Towns of Nebraska* (Lincoln: Nebraska Dept. of Economic Development, 1976), pp. 14, 21.

[23] Niles M. Hansen, *Rural Poverty and the Urban Crisis* (Bloomington: Indiana University Press, 1970).

[24] Niles M. Hansen, "Factors Determining the Location of Industrial Activity," in *Rural Industrialization: Problems and Potentials* (Ames: Iowa State University Press, 1974), p. 43.

[25] Earl O. Heady, "Foreword," in *Rural Industrialization: Problems and Potentials* (Ames: Iowa State University Press, 1974), p. vii.

Chapter 2

INDUSTRIAL DEVELOPMENT IN NONMETROPOLITAN AMERICA: A Locational Perspective

Claude C. Haren and Ronald W. Holling

INTRODUCTION

The bright promise of rapid industrial decentralization of the 1960s has been increasingly overshadowed by the economic uncertainties of the 1970s. Rural and other nonmetropolitan areas added 1.8 million manufacturing jobs, or 56% of the U.S. increase between March 1962 and March 1978. But more than half of the gain occurred by March 1967, and practically all the remainder before March 1974.[1]

Until 1969-70, the industrial sector continued to furnish approximately 30% of the increase in nonfarm wage and salary employment in the smaller labor market areas.[2] By March 1978, the ratio had fallen to 26.4%, or still about 3.5 percentage points above manufacturing's contribution to employment in the larger job centers.

Despite the rise of the service industries and the ever-expanding role of government, the availability of close to 6 million manufacturing jobs in 1978 continued to exert a profound influence on family incomes and community well-being in hundreds of nonmetro counties. Although specific figures would be difficult to determine, there is little question that manufacturing jobs in nonmetro areas contribute at least a 25% share of nonfarm wage and salary earnings.

Factors Affecting Industrialization

Nonmetropolitan industrialization must be examined in the context of

13

trends and developments worldwide and in the national economy. Successive recessions in the 1970s, constant inflation or the threat of inflation, mounting conflict between economic growth and environmental protection, the energy crisis, and an unfavorable balance of trade have contributed to major alterations in production and technological processes, output per worker, management and control, marketing, and marketing demands.

Manufacturing and construction in the nonmetro areas proved every bit as recession-prone as in the metro centers during the 1974-75 economic downturn. In addition to swollen unemployment rolls locally, many smaller communities were forced to absorb numerous workers laid off from factory and other jobs in the larger cities. Typically, the economies of nonmetro areas rebound more promptly and vigorously from recessions than their metro counterparts. Once sluggish metro economies regain momentum, however, rapidly rising building material and other costs, and local labor shortages, often require postponement of construction activities in rural and other smaller communities.

Altered life styles, changing family composition, and the rapid enlargement of the number of households without children are beginning to exert greater and greater impacts on demands for goods. Slackening migration shifts and a progressive aging of the retirement population have already altered patterns of demand for housing and for the amount and kinds of home furnishings, food, and transportation. The rapid buildup of childless younger households in the old town sections of many cities and their nearby suburbs is modifying demographic relationships and consumption patterns, especially with reference to exurban or more outlying communities.

Recent acquisitions of existing industrial plants by large foreign as well as U.S. corporations, coupled with equally widespread mergers in the late 1960s, have contributed to a fairly sharp rise in the concentration of industrial capacity among fewer and fewer companies. Ordinarily, little if any productive capacity was added or new jobs created, and some acquisitions were liquidated simply to take advantage of existing tax write-offs. A relatively large number of U.S. corporations acquired extensive international operations, especially in the period since 1967. Initially, acquisitions were intended primarily to take advantage of pay scales several times lower then the prevailing U.S. minimum wage. More recently, certain ventures abroad were undertaken to avoid antipollution controls required in this country.

Inevitably, rapid industrialization of the developing nations, accompanied by further expansion in Japan, Germany, and other industrial countries, resulted in worldwide overcapacity in such industries as apparel, leather goods, textiles, steel, and shipbuilding. Contributing to the flood of imports and reduced exports in recent years was the relatively rapid recovery of the U.S economy from the 1973-75 recession, and the uncertainties of international monetary and trade relationships.

A high proportion of recent investment in manufacturing facilities was for pollution abatement and conservation of power and fuel. More and more attention also was given to computerization and application of other technological innovations designed to reduce employment, notably of production-line workers, through automation and promotion of cost-efficient inventory control, assembly, packaging, distribution, and related processes.

The competitive advantage of plastics over products manufactured from paper, metal, and galss has expanded dramatically in recent years. Yet, plastic feedstocks must be increasingly derived from imported oil, and production is highly costly. Future competitive ratios may well shift, as the oil-producing countries add petrochemical complexes. Also to be kept in mind is that plastics are not biodegradable.

From March 1977 to March 1978, manufacturing jobs nationally expanded by more than 600,000 workers, due mainly to 2 good years in succession for domestic auto production and homebuilding. Also instrumental was the massive retooling under way in the auto industry, together with the rapidly accelerating impact of energy conservation and development programs. Rural and other smaller communities benefitted chiefly from greatly expanded manufacturing activity through the ripple effects exerted on demands for auto components and accessories, building supplies, and household and office furniture, appliances, and other hard goods.

Increased imports of apparel and other soft goods reduce jobs available, particularly for women. Other imports drive up costs of materials for intermediate and almost entirely small-firm fabricators located in metro and nonmetro areas alike. Such firms suffer intense competition from new products constantly introduced, and are subject to equally keen competition for market outlets. They also are at a decided disadvantage in accumulating or borrowing capital required to enlarge capacity and increase employment.

GROWTH OF MANUFACTURING EMPLOYMENT SINCE 1962

Manufacturing employment in rural and other nonmetro areas grew from 3.9 million workers in March 1962 to 5.7 million in March 1978 (Table 1).[3] This represented a gain of 1.8 million jobs, against 1.4 million in metro areas. The addition was accompanied by a 6.7 million employment increase in service-performing and other nonmanufacturing industries. This meant that only about 20% of the nonmetro job gain during the 16-year period came in the industrial sector.

Nonmetro manufacturing's share of national nonfarm wage and salary employment dropped fractionally from 7.2 to 6.9%. However, its share of U.S. manufacturing employment rose from 23.5 to 28.8%, as jobs increased by nearly 50%, against only about 10% in metro areas. Within smaller communities, manufacturing's share of nonfarm wage and salary jobs fell from 29.7 to 26.4%, or by 3.3 percentage points.

March 1962–67 Additions

Over 900,000 manufacturing jobs, or 52% of the entire 1962–78 increase

Table 1. Nonfarm Wage and Salary Employment, United States, March 1962-78 Comparisons*

Area and industry group	Employment		Change		Share			
					Total		Industry group	
	1978 (thou.)	1962 (thou.)	N (thou.)	(%)	1978 (%)	1962 (%)	1978 (%)	1962 (%)
TOTAL	83,323	54,192	29,131	53.8	100.0	100.0	100.0	100.0
GOODS–PRODUCING	24,192	19,759	4,433	22.4	29.0	36.5	100.0	100.0
Manufacturing	19,870	16,622	3,248	19.5	23.8	30.7	100.0	100.0
Construction	3,644	2,495	1,149	46.1	4.4	4.6	100.0	100.0
Mining	678	642	36	5.6	0.8	1.2	100.0	100.0
SERVICE-PERFORMING	54,437	30,572	23,865	78.1	65.3	56.4	100.0	100.0
Private sector	38.492	21,572	16,920	78.4	46.2	39.8	100.0	100.0
Trade	18.547	11,215	7,332	65.4	22.3	20.7	100.0	100.0
Services	15,420	7,603	7,817	102.8	18.5	14.0	100.0	100.0
FIRE[a]	4,525	2.754	1,771	64.3	5.4	5.1	100.0	100.0
Government	15,945	9,000	6,945	77.2	19.1	16.6	100.0	100.0
TCU[b]	4,694	3,861	833	21.6	5.7	7.1	100.0	100.0
METRO[c]	61,628	41,030	20,598	50.2	73.9	75.7	74.0	75.7
GOODS–PRODUCING	16,955	14,823	2,132	14.4	20.3	27.4	70.1	75.0
Manufacturing	14,141	12,715	1,426	11.2	16.9	23.5	71.2	76.5
Construction	2,592	1,899	693	36.5	3.1	3.5	71.1	76.1
Mining	222	209	13	6.2	0.3	0.4	32.7	32.6
SERVICE-PERFORMING	41,039	23,191	17,848	77.0	49.2	42.8	75.4	75.9
Private sector	29,794	16,935	12,859	75.9	35.7	31.2	77.4	78.5
Trade	13,924	8,606	5,318	61.8	16.7	15.9	75.1	76.7
Services	12,090	5,990	6,100	101.8	14.5	11.0	78.4	78.8
FIRE[a]	3,780	2,339	1,441	61.6	4.5	4.3	83.5	84.9
Government	11,245	6,256	4,989	79.8	13.5	11.5	70.5	69.5
TCU[b]	3,634	3,016	618	20.5	4.4	5.5	77.4	78.1
NONMETRO	21,695	13,162	8,533	64.8	26.1	24.3	26.0	24.3
GOODS–PRODUCING	7,237	4,936	2,301	46.6	8.7	9.1	29.9	25.0
Manufacturing	5,729	3,907	1,822	46.6	6.9	7.2	28.8	23.5
Construction	1,052	596	456	76.5	1.3	1.1	28.9	23.9
Mining	456	433	23	5.3	0.5	0.8	67.3	67.4
SERVICE-PERFORMING	13,398	7,381	6,017	81.5	16.1	13.6	24.6	24.1
Private sector	8,698	4,637	4,061	87.6	10.5	8.6	22.6	21.5
Trade	4,623	2,609	2,014	77.2	5.6	4.8	24.9	23.3
Services	3,330	1,613	1,717	106.4	4.0	3.0	21.6	21.2
FIRE[a]	745	415	330	79.5	0.9	0.8	16.5	15.1
Government	4,700	2,744	1.956	71.3	5.6	5.1	29.5	30.5
TCU[b]	1,060	845	215	25.4	1.3	1.6	22.6	21.9

*Adapted from Bureau of Labor Statistics–Employment Security estimates for respective months and years.

[a]Finance, insurance, and real estate groups.

[b]Transportation, communications, and utilities groups.

[c]Includes 225 mostly larger of 278 SMSAs designated through December 31, 1977.

Note. 1978 estimates exclude miners involved in work stoppages.

of 1.8 million workers were added in smaller labor market areas between March 1962 and March 1967 (Tables 2 and 3). The larger employment centers gained almost twice as many manufacturing jobs—an expansion offering striking evidence of the vigorous growth of manufacturing and other jobs in metro as well as nonmetro areas of the South and West.

Prices and wages not only remained unusually stable throughout this period, but family income and buying power rose steadily. Imports remained relatively inconsequential. Home building activity continued at a rapid and virtually uninterrupted pace. Demands for food and clothing for growing households, and for bedroom and other furnishings, appliances, and housewares created constant and rapidly expanding markets for both hard and soft goods.

As demands for higher education began catching up with earlier stress on needs for new primary and secondary schools, construction programs on university and college campuses gained momentum. Progress on the Interstate System contributed to strong and persistent demands for reinforced concrete, bridge-building, and other materials. The NASA (National Aeronautics and Space Administration) program continued to stimulate demand for intricate electronic, communications, and control systems. The buildup in procurement of ordnance and other military hardware destined for Vietnam already had attained major proportions by 1967.

March 1967–70 Changes

Manufacturing employment in rural, small-town, and small-city communities increased by an unimpressive 260,000 workers, or by 5.4% between March 1967–70. Home building and related activities had reached saturation points at which sustained year-after-year employment levels of the March 1962-67 period were unlikely to be repeated. Rising prices reduced both consumer confidence as well as buying power.

Much capital went into underwriting widespread booms in downtown office building and suburban shopping mall construction. Investment in manufacturing in the developing nations accelerated. Within nonmetro areas, construction activity seriously lagged, minimg was at a standstill, and gains in the service-performing industries trailed metro expansions by comparatively wide margins.

March 1970–74 Gains

Employment in the industrial sector of the smaller labor market areas grew by more than a half-million workers, or by 10.8%, between March 1970 and March 1974. This compared with a loss of some 300,000 manufacturing jobs in the larger employment centers. Especially impressive gains were recorded in construction, trade, services, and FIRE industries (finance, insurance, and real estate).

Nonmetro areas benefited from greatly increased home building activities in

Table 2. Nonfarm Wage and Salary Employment, United States, March 1962-78 Comparisons*

Area and industry group	Mar. 1962 N (thou.)	Distribution (%)	Mar. 1967 N (thou.)	Distribution (%)	Mar. 1970 N (thou.)	Distribution (%)	Mar. 1974 N (thou.)	Distribution (%)	Mar. 1978 N (thou.)	Distribution (%)
TOTAL	54,192	100.0	64.701	100.0	70,369	100.0	77,509	100.0	83,323	100.0
GOODS–PRODUCING	19,759	36.5	22,893	35.4	23,545	33.5	24,424	31.5	24,192	29.0
Manufacturing	16,622	30.7	19,390	30.0	19,764	28.1	19,983	25.7	19,870	23.8
Construction	2,495	4.6	2,897	4.5	3,171	4.5	3,778	4.9	3,644	4.4
Mining	642	1.2	606	0.9	610	0.9	663	0.9	678	0.8
SERVICE–PERFORMING	30,572	56.4	37,606	58.1	42,377	60.2	48,425	62.5	54,437	65.3
Private sector	21,572	39.8	26,126	40.3	29,553	42.0	34,112	44.0	38,492	46.2
Trade	11,215	20.7	13,257	20.5	14,695	20.9	16,592	21.4	18,547	22.3
Services	7,603	14.0	9,735	15.0	11,264	16.0	13,373	17.3	15,420	18.5
FIRE[a]	2,754	5.1	3,134	4,8	3,594	5.1	4,147	5.3	4,525	5.4
Government	9,000	16.6	11,480	17.8	12,824	18.2	14,313	18.5	15,945	19.1
TCU[b]	3,861	7.1	4,202	6.5	4,447	6.3	4,660	6.0	4,694	5.7
METRO[c]	41,030	75.7	48,754	75.4	53,249	75.7	57,843	74.6	61,628	73.9
GOODS–PRODUCING	14,823	27.4	16,906	26.2	17,285	24.6	17,319	22.3	16,955	20.3
Manufacturing	12,715	23.5	14,541	22.5	14,654	20.8	14,320	18.4	14,141	16.9
Construction	1,899	3.5	2,160	3.4	2,422	3.5	2,776	3.6	2,592	3.1
Mining	209	0.4	205	0.3	209	0.3	223	0.3	222	0.3
SERVICE–PERFORMING	23,191	42.8	28.527	44.1	32,431	46.1	36,880	47.6	41,039	49.2
Private sector	16,935	31.2	20,526	31.7	23,393	33.3	26,736	34.5	29,794	35.7
Trade	8,606	15.9	10,205	15.8	11,372	16.2	12,641	16.3	13,924	16.7
Services	5,990	11.0	7,669	11.8	8,957	12.7	10,601	13.7	12,090	14.5
FIRE[a]	2,339	4.3	2,652	4.1	3,064	4.4	3,494	4.5	3,780	4.5
Government	6,256	11.6	8,001	12.4	9,038	12.8	10,144	13.1	11,245	13.5
TCU[b]	3,016	5.5	3,321	5.1	3,533	5.0	3,644	4.7	3,634	4.4
NONMETRO	13,162	24.3	15,947	24.6	17,120	24.3	19,666	25.4	21,695	26.1
GOODS–PRODUCING	4,936	9.1	5,987	9.2	6,260	8.9	7,105	9.2	7,237	8.7
Manufacturing	3,907	7.2	4,849	7.5	5,110	7.3	5,663	7.3	5,729	6.9
Construction	596	1.1	737	1.1	749	1.0	1,002	1.3	1,052	1.3
Mining	433	0.8	401	0.6	401	0.6	440	0.6	456	0.5
SERVICE–PERFORMING	7,381	13.6	9,079	14.0	9,946	14.1	11,545	14.9	13,398	16.1
Private sector	4,637	8.6	5,600	8.6	6,160	8.7	7,376	9.5	8,698	10.5
Trade	2,609	4.8	3,052	4.7	3,323	4.7	3,951	5.1	4,623	5.6
Services	1,613	3.0	2,066	3.2	2,307	3.3	2,772	3.6	3,330	4.0
FIRE[a]	415	0.8	482	0.7	530	0.7	653	0.8	745	0.9
Government	2,744	5.0	3,479	5.4	3,786	5.4	4,169	5.4	4,700	5.6
TCU[b]	845	1.6	881	1.4	914	1.3	1,016	1.3	1,060	1.3

*Adapted from Bureau of Labor Statistics–Employment Security estimates for respective months and years.
[a]Finance, insurance, and real estate groups.
[b]Transportation, communications, and utilities groups.
[c]Includes 225 mostly larger of 278 SMSAs designated through December 31, 1977.

Table 3. Changes in Nonfarm Wage and Salary Employment, United States, March 1962-78*

Area and industry group	1962-78 N (thou.)	1962-78 (%)	1962-67 N (thou.)	1962-67 (%)	1967-70 N (thou.)	1967-70 (%)	1970-74 N (thou.)	1970-74 (%)	1974-78 N (thou.)	1974-78 (%)
TOTAL	29,131	53.8	10,509	19.4	5,668	8.8	7,140	10.1	5,814	7.5
GOODS-PRODUCING	4,433	22.4	3,134	15.9	652	2.8	879	3.7	−232	−0.9
Manufacturing	3,248	19.5	2,768	16.7	374	1.9	219	1.1	−113	−0.6
Construction	1,149	46.1	402	16.1	274	9.5	607	19.1	−134	−3.5
Mining	36	5.6	−36	−5.6	4	0.7	53	8.7	15	2.3
SERVICE-PERFORMING	23,865	78.1	7,034	23.0	4,771	12.7	6,048	14.3	6,012	12.4
Private sector	16,920	78.4	4,554	21.1	3,427	13.1	4,559	15.4	4,380	12.8
Trade	7,332	65.4	2,042	18.2	1,438	10.8	1,897	12.9	1,955	10.0
Services	7,817	102.8	2,132	28.0	1,529	15.7	2,109	18.7	2,047	15.3
FIRE[a]	1,771	64.3	380	13.8	460	14.7	553	15.4	378	9.1
Government	6,945	77.2	2,480	27.6	1,344	11.7	1,489	11.6	1,632	11.4
TCU[b]	833	21.6	341	8.8	245	5.8	213	4.8	34	0.7
METRO[c]	20,598	50.2	7,724	18.8	4,495	9.2	4,594	8.6	3,785	6.5
GOODS-PRODUCING	2,132	14.4	2,083	14.1	379	2.2	34	0.2	−364	−2.1
Manufacturing	1,426	11.2	1,826	14.4	113	0.8	−334	−2.3	−179	−1.3
Construction	693	36.5	261	13.8	262	12.1	354	14.6	−184	−6.6
Mining	13	6.2	−4	−1.9	4	2.0	14	6.7	−1	−0.4
SERVICE-PERFORMING	17,848	77.0	5,336	23.0	3,904	13.7	4,449	13.7	4,159	11.3
Private sector	12,859	75.9	3,591	21.2	2,867	14.0	3,343	14.3	3,058	11.4
Trade	5,318	61.8	1,599	18.6	1,167	11.4	1,269	11.2	1,283	10.1
Services	6,100	101.8	1,679	28.0	1,288	16.8	1,644	18.4	1,489	14.0
FIRE[a]	1,441	61.6	313	13.4	412	15.5	430	14.0	286	8.2
Government	4,989	79.7	1,745	27.9	1,037	13.0	1,106	12.2	1,101	10.9
TCU[b]	618	20.5	305	10.1	212	6.4	111	3.1	−10	−0.3
NONMETRO	8,533	64.8	2,785	21.2	1,173	7.4	2,546	14.9	2,029	10.3
GOODS-PRODUCING	2,301	46.6	1,051	21.3	273	4.6	845	13.5	132	1.9
Manufacturing	1,822	46.6	942	24.1	261	5.4	553	10.8	66	1.2
Construction	456	76.5	141	23.7	12	1.6	253	33.8	50	5.0
Mining	23	5.3	−32	−7.4	–	–	39	9.7	16	3.6
SERVICE-PERFORMING	6.017	81.5	1,698	23.0	867	9.6	1,599	16.1	1,853	16.1
Private sector	4,061	87.6	963	20.8	560	10.0	1,216	19.7	1,322	17.9
Trade	2,014	77.2	443	17.0	271	8.9	628	18.9	672	17.0
Services	1,717	106.4	453	28.1	241	16.7	465	20.2	558	20.1
FIRE[a]	330	79.5	67	16.2	48	10.0	123	23.2	92	14.1
Government	1,956	71.3	735	26.8	307	8.8	383	10.1	531	12.7
TCU[b]	215	25.4	36	4.3	33	3.7	102	11.2	44	4.3

*Adapted from Bureau of Labor Statistics–Employment Security estimates for respective months and years.
[a]Finance, insurance, and real estate groups.
[b]Transportation, communications, and utilities groups.
[c]Includes 225 mostly larger of 278 SMSAs designated through December 31, 1977.

19

1972-73 and by a good year for domestically produced autos in 1973. However, toward the end of 1973 local construction activities were increasingly affected by severe shortages of materials and labor, triggered by the 1972-73 building boom in luxury condominiums, resort-recreation complexes, shopping malls, and downtown office and convention centers. Imports continued to rise, including such items as apparel, textiles, and leather goods, strongly competitive with products typically manufactured in smaller communities.

March 1974-78 Transitions

The sharp decline in manufacturing employment in 1974-75 in the larger job centers was partially offset by the resurgence of 1977-78. Nevertheless, employment in metro manufacturing declined by nearly 200,000 workers between 1974 and 1978. Manufacturing jobs in rural and other smaller labor market areas expanded between March 1974 and March 1978, but the increase was less than 70,000. More so than in 1970-74, nonmetro employment gains between 1977-78 in the industrial sector were affected by increased imports, as well as by rapidly rising material, labor, and related costs.

Relative job gains in the service-performing industries held even with 1970-74 additions, as expansions in government employment offset reduced percentage increases in the private sector. Construction employment also held up well, especially in comparison with the sizeable losses sustained in the larger job centers.

RESPONSES TO CYCLICAL INFLUENCES

An economic decline such as the slowdown of 1967 may be of too short duration to meet criteria for designation as a recession, yet the year 1967 comprised a turning point in U.S. manufacturing employment—metro and nonmetro alike—far too distinctive and meaningful to be disregarded.

The 1954 and 1970 recessions were triggered primarily by sharp cutbacks in military procurement. In 1954, many long-obsolete industrial facilities, lacking procurement contracts of any sort, were marked for complete closure. In 1970, reductions in manufacturing jobs resulted even more than in 1954 from drastic cutbacks, if not complete termination, of primary and secondary procurement contracts. This time, however, it was chiefly listless demand that kept much new capacity, added to nondefense industries in the late 1960s, partly idle or on standby condition.

The 1960-62 recession was succeeded by a long and relatively trouble-free period, extending through the 1967 slowdown and 1970 minirecession to the 1973 peak in economic activity. In contrast, most of the steep drop in employment during the 1973-75 recession occurred in fourth quarter 1974 and first quarter 1975. Subsequently, recovery fluctuated before economic momentum was regained.

The 1970-71 Economic Decline

The combination of sharp rollbacks in defense and space procurement with a poor year for domestic auto production in 1970 was reflected in a decline of more than a million manufacturing jobs between March 1970 and March 1971 in the larger employment centers (Tables 4 and 5). Similar cutbacks in the smaller labor market areas stemmed mainly from job reductions at several geographically dispersed ordnance and other military-related facilities. Non-metro job losses in nondefense industries and in construction were minimal. Meanwhile, sizeable gains in the private sector of the service-performing industries evidenced the catalytic role increasingly performed by rising household incomes on demands for better health, education, banking, credit, and related services and facilities.

The 1971-74 Economic Upturn

The smaller labor market areas added three-quarters of a million manufacturing jobs between March 1971 and March 1974, together with 1.7 million more employment opportunities in service-performing and other nonmanufacturing industries. The rapid upsurge in home building activity in 1972-73, coupled with the runaway boom in office building, condominium, and shopping center construction in 1973, created many additional jobs in building materials industries and in the manufacture of household and office furnishings and equipment.

Increasing shares of the production of pleasure boats, farm and garden equipment and supplies, camping and recreational vehicles, electrical equipment and supplies, and light-weight fabricated metals were being located in smaller communities. A truly remarkable expansion continued to take place in the manufacture of the many small items, ranging from kitchen utensils to waste containers, in daily use in households and offices.

In addition to coping with previously unmet housing, health, sanitation, and related needs, nonmetro gains in construction employment reflected growing demands for new eating places, food stores, and retail shops, especially in the South and West. Also rapidly expanding were additions of resort and recreation centers and lodging places serving the traveling and vacationing public.

The 1974-75 Economic Decline

Practically all of the 1971-74 increase in manufacturing employment in the smaller labor market areas was erased during the March 1974-75 downturn in the economy. As in the larger employment centers, fairly severe reductions took place in construction employment accompanied by considerable decline in the TCU industries (transportation, communication, and utilities). Local layoffs were widespread, especially in various building materials, textile, apparel, and construction industries. Complicating the unemployment situation

Table 4. Nonfarm Wage and Salary Employment, United States, March 1970-78 Comparisions*

Area and industry group	Mar. 1970 N (thou.)	Mar. 1970 Distribution (%)	Mar. 1971 N (thou.)	Mar. 1971 Distribution (%)	Mar. 1974 N (thou.)	Mar. 1974 Distribution (%)	Mar. 1975 N (thou.)	Mar. 1975 Distribution (%)	Mar. 1978 N (thou.)	Mar. 1978 Distribution (%)
TOTAL	70,369	100.0	69,664	100.0	77,509	100.0	75,995	100.0	83,323	100.0
GOODS–PRODUCING	23,545	33.5	22,092	31.7	24,424	31.5	21,990	28.9	24,192	29.0
Manufacturing	19,764	28.1	18,399	26.4	19,983	25.7	18,029	23.7	19,870	23.8
Construction	3,171	4.5	3,085	4.4	3,778	4.9	3,245	4.3	3,644	4.4
Mining	610	0.9	608	0.9	663	0.9	716	0.9	678	0.8
SERVICE–PERFORMING	42,377	60.2	43,151	62.0	48,425	62.5	49,494	65.1	54,437	65.3
Private sector	29,553	42.0	29,941	43.0	34,112	44.0	34,532	45.4	38,492	46.2
Trade	14,695	20.9	14,784	21.2	16,592	21.4	16,644	21.9	18,547	22.3
Services	11,264	16.0	11,500	16.5	13,373	17.3	13,728	18.0	15,420	18.5
FIRE[a]	3,594	5.1	3,657	5.3	4,147	5.3	4,160	5.5	4,525	5.4
Government	12,824	18.2	13,210	19.0	14,313	18.5	14,962	19.7	15,945	19.1
TCU[b]	4,447	6.3	4,421	6.3	4,660	6.0	4,511	6.0	4,694	5.7
METRO[c]	53,249	75.7	52,489	75.3	57,843	74.6	56,710	74.7	61,628	73.9
GOODS–PRODUCING	17,285	24.6	16,044	23.0	17,319	22.3	15,662	20.6	16,955	20.3
Manufacturing	14,654	20.8	13,498	19.4	14,320	18.4	13,077	17.2	14,141	16.9
Construction	2,422	3.5	2,341	3.3	2,776	3.6	2,349	3.1	2,592	3.1
Mining	209	0.3	205	0.3	223	0.3	236	0.3	222	0.3
SERVICE–PERFORMING	32,431	46.1	32,947	47.3	36,880	47.6	37,525	49.4	41,039	49.2
Private sector	23,393	33.3	23,604	33.9	26,736	34.5	26,918	35.4	29,794	35.7
Trade	11,372	16.2	11,388	16.3	12,641	16.3	12,618	16.6	13,924	16.7
Services	8,957	12.7	9,102	13.1	10,601	13.7	10,808	14.2	12,090	14.5
FIRE[a]	3,064	4.4	3,114	4.5	3,494	4.5	3,492	4.6	3,780	4.5
Government	9,038	12.8	9,343	13.4	10,144	13.1	10,607	14.0	11,245	13.5
TCU[b]	3,533	5.0	3,498	5.0	3,644	4.7	3,523	4.7	3,634	4.4
NONMETRO	17,120	24.3	17,175	24.7	19,666	25.4	19,285	25.3	21,695	26.1
GOODS–PRODUCING	6,260	8.9	6,048	8.7	7,105	9.2	6,328	8.3	7,237	8.7
Manufacturing	5,110	7.3	4,901	7.0	5,663	7.3	4,952	6.5	5,729	6.9
Construction	749	1.0	744	1.1	1,002	1.3	896	1.2	1,052	1.3
Mining	401	0.6	403	0.6	440	0.6	480	0.6	456	0.5
SERVICE–PERFORMING	9,946	14.1	10,204	14.7	11,545	14.9	11,969	15.7	13,398	16.1
Private sector	6,160	8.7	6,337	9.1	7,376	9.5	7,614	10.0	8,698	10.5
Trade	3,323	4.7	3,396	4.9	3,951	5.1	4,026	5.3	4,623	5.6
Services	2,307	3.3	2,398	3.4	2,772	3.6	2,920	3.8	3,330	4.0
FIRE[a]	530	0.7	543	0.8	653	0.8	668	0.9	745	0.9
Government	3,786	5.4	3,867	5.6	4,169	5.4	4,355	5.7	4,700	5.6
TCU[b]	914	1.3	923	1.3	1,016	1.3	988	1.3	1,060	1.3

*Adapted from Bureau of Labor Statistics–Employment Security estimates for respective months and years.
[a]Finance, insurance, and real estate groups.
[b]Transportation, communications, and utilities groups.
[c]Includes 225 mostly larger of 278 SMSAs designated through December 31, 1977.

Table 5. Changes in Nonfarm Wage and Salary Employment, United States, March 1970-78*

Area and industry group	Overall 1970-78 N (thou.)	Overall 1970-78 (%)	Decline 1970-71 N (thou.)	Decline 1970-71 (%)	Upturn 1971-74 N (thou.)	Upturn 1971-74 (%)	Decline 1974-75 N (thou.)	Decline 1974-75 (%)	Upturn 1975-78 N (thou.)	Upturn 1975-78 (%)
TOTAL	12,954	18.4	−705	−1.0	7,845	11.3	−1,514	−2.0	7,328	9.6
GOODS-PRODUCING	647	2.7	−1,453	−6.2	2,332	10.6	−2,434	−10.0	2,202	10.0
Manufacturing	106	0.5	−1,365	−6.9	1,584	8.6	−1,954	−9.8	1,841	10.2
Construction	473	14.9	−86	−2.7	693	22.5	−533	−14.1	399	12.3
Mining	68	11.1	−2	−0.3	55	9.1	53	8.0	−38	−5.3
SERVICE-PERFORMING	12,060	28.5	774	1.8	5,274	12.2	1,069	2.2	4,943	10.0
Private sector	8,939	30.2	388	1.3	4,171	13.9	420	1.2	3,960	11.5
Trade	3,852	26.2	89	0.6	1,808	12.2	52	0.3	1,903	11.4
Services	4,156	36.9	236	2.1	1,873	16.3	355	2.7	1,692	12.3
FIRE[a]	931	25.9	63	1.8	490	13.4	13	0.3	365	8.8
Government	3,121	24.3	386	3.0	1,103	8.4	649	4.5	983	6.6
TCU[b]	247	5.6	−26	−0.6	239	5.4	−149	−3.2	183	4.1
METRO[c]	8,379	15.7	−760	−1.4	5,354	10.2	−1,133	−2.0	4,918	8.7
GOODS-PRODUCING	−330	−1.9	−1,241	−7.2	1,275	8.0	−1,657	−9.6	1,293	8.3
Manufacturing	−513	−3.5	−1,156	−7.9	822	6.1	−1,243	−8.7	1,064	8.1
Construction	170	7.0	−81	−3.4	435	18.6	−427	−15.4	243	10.3
Mining	13	6.2	−4	−1.9	18	8.8	13	5.8	−14	−5.9
SERVICE-PERFORMING	8,608	26.5	516	1.6	3,933	11.9	645	1.8	3,514	9.4
Private sector	6,401	27.4	211	0.9	3,132	13.3	182	0.7	2,876	10.7
Trade	2,552	22.4	16	0.1	1,253	11.0	−23	−0.2	1,306	10.4
Services	3,133	35.0	145	1.6	1,499	16.5	207	2.0	1,282	11.9
FIRE[a]	716	23.4	50	1.6	380	12.2	−2	−0.1	288	8.3
Government	2,207	24.4	305	3.4	801	8.6	463	4.6	638	6.0
TCU[b]	101	2.9	−35	−1.0	146	4.2	−121	−3.3	111	3.2
NONMETRO	4,575	26.7	55	0.3	2,491	14.5	−381	−1.9	2,410	12.5
GOODS-PRODUCING	977	15.6	−212	−3.4	1,057	17.5	−777	−10.9	909	14.4
Manufacturing	619	12.1	−209	−4.1	762	15.6	−711	−12.6	777	15.7
Construction	303	40.5	−5	−0.7	258	34.7	−106	−10.6	156	17.4
Mining	55	13.7	2	0.5	37	9.2	40	9.1	−24	−5.0
SERVICE-PERFORMING	3,452	34.7	258	2.6	1,341	13.2	424	3.7	1,429	11.9
Private sector	2,538	41.0	177	2.9	1,039	16.4	238	3.2	1,084	14.2
Trade	1,300	39.1	73	2.2	555	16.4	75	1.9	597	14.8
Services	1,023	44.3	91	4.0	374	15.6	148	5.3	410	14.0
FIRE[a]	215	40.6	13	2.5	110	20.3	15	2.3	77	11.5
Government	914	24.1	81	2.1	302	7.8	186	4.5	345	7.9
TCU[b]	146	16.0	9	1.0	93	10.1	−28	−2.8	72	7.3

*Adapted from Bureau of Labor Statistics—Employment Security estimates for respective months and years.
[a]Finance, insurance, and real estate groups.
[b]Transportation, communications, and utilities groups.
[c]Includes 225 mostly larger of 278 SMSAs designated through December 31, 1977.

23

in parts of Appalachia, upper Michigan, and other localities were influxes of laid-off factory, construction, and retail trade workers from Detroit and other metro centers.

The 1975-78 Economic Upturn

An upsurge in the economy contributed to the addition of more than three-quarters of a million jobs in the industrial sector of rural and other smaller communities between March 1975 and March 1978. Although impressive, the 3-year gain left March 1978 manufacturing employment somewhat short of the peak attained in 1973, and for that matter only about 900,000 workers above the March 1967 level. The resurgence of metro factory, construction, and related jobs was again attracting large numbers of workers residing in smaller nearby communities. Increased competition from imports of paper products and copper, zinc, aluminum, and other nonfuel minerals was restricting expansions of U.S. capacity, if not forcing frequent shutdowns or outright closure of existing facilities.

Comparative March 1977-78 Gains in Manufacturing Jobs

Rural and other smaller communities added 200,000 manufacturing jobs, for an increase of 3.7%, between March 1977 and March 1978 (Table 6). For larger communities, the comparative gains were 435,000 workers—more than twice as many—and 3.2%.

In decided contrast, the smaller labor market areas gained some 400,000 manufacturing workers between March 1970-77, against a loss of nearly a million industrial jobs in the larger employment centers. As for overall nonfarm wage and salary employment, nonmetro areas—with about a fourth of total jobs—gained 29% of 1977-78 additions, compared with 37% of the 1970-77 increase.

In reality, the future of U.S. manufacturing may well hinge, in part, on the revitalization of the long-stagnant and declining economies of areas like Youngstown and the Mahoning Valley—places typical of the old industrial heartlands of the Northeast and the Great Lakes Industrial Belt. The same innovativeness and technological leadership would be required that already have been shown in retooling the domestic auto industry, and in the increasing stress on energy conservation and development, and pollution abatement.

This and similar undertakings are especially challenging because of (1) the imperative need for a full partnership between industry, business, labor, and government; (2) the sheer magnitude of the air and water pollution problems to be overcome; and (3) the necessity for rehabilitating the entire infrastructure, not simply an individual industrial plant or plants. Solutions will not require the abandonment of free trade in favor of protectionism, but rather a satisfactory balance between imports and exports, coupled with the normalization of monetary as well as trade relationships with both developing nations and the industrial countries.

Table 6. Nonfarm Wage and Salary Employment, United States, March 1970-77 and 1977-78 Comparisons*

Area and industry group	1978 (thou.)	1977 (thou.)	Change N (thou.)	Change (%)	1977 (thou.)	1970 (thou.)	Change N (thou.)	Change (%)
TOTAL	83,323	80,637	2,686	3.3	80,637	70,369	10,268	14.6
GOODS-PRODUCING	24,192	23,467	725	3.1	23,467	23,545	−78	−0.3
Manufacturing	19,870	19,233	637	3.3	19,233	19,764	−531	−2.7
Construction	3,644	3,434	210	6.1	3,434	3,171	263	8.3
Mining	678	800	−122	−15.3	800	610	190	31.1
SERVICE-PERFORMING	54,437	52,590	1,847	3.5	52,590	42,377	10,213	24.1
Private sector	38,492	37,118	1,374	3.7	37,118	29,553	7,565	25.6
Trade	18,547	17,923	624	3.5	17,923	14,695	3,228	22.0
Services	15,420	14,819	601	4.1	14,819	11,264	3,555	31.6
FIRE[a]	4,525	4,376	149	3.4	4,376	3,594	782	21.8
Government	15,945	15,472	473	3.1	15,472	12,824	2,648	20.6
TCU[b]	4,694	4,580	114	2.5	4,580	4,447	133	3.0
METRO[c]	61,628	59,733	1,895	3.2	59,733	53,249	6,484	12.2
GOODS-PRODUCING	16,955	16,395	560	3.4	16,395	17,285	−890	−5.1
Manufacturing	14,141	13,706	435	3.2	13,706	14,654	−948	−6.5
Construction	2,592	2,436	156	6.4	2,436	2,422	14	0.6
Mining	222	253	−31	−12.2	253	209	44	21.0
SERVICE-PERFORMING	41,039	39,784	1,255	3.2	39,784	32,431	7,353	22.7
Private sector	29,794	28,856	938	3.2	28,856	23,393	5,463	23.4
Trade	13,924	13,499	425	3.1	13,499	11,372	2,127	18.7
Services	12,090	11,695	395	3.4	11,695	8,957	2,738	30.6
FIRE[a]	3,780	3,662	118	3.2	3,662	3,064	598	19.5
Government	11,245	10,928	317	2.9	10,928	9,038	1,890	20.9
TCU[b]	3,634	3,554	80	2.2	3,554	3,533	21	0.6
NONMETRO	21,695	20,904	791	3.8	20,904	17,120	3,784	22.1
GOODS-PRODUCING	7,237	7,072	165	2.3	7,072	6,260	812	13.0
Manufacturing	5,729	5,527	202	3.6	5,527	5,110	417	8.2
Construction	1,052	998	54	5.4	998	749	249	33.2
Mining	456	547	−91	−16.6	547	401	146	36.4
SERVICE-PRODUCING	13,398	12,806	592	4.6	12,806	9,946	2,860	28.8
Private sector	8,698	8,262	436	5.3	8,262	6,160	2,102	34.1
Trade	4,623	4,424	199	4.5	4,424	3,323	1,101	33.1
Services	3,330	3,124	206	6.6	3,124	2,307	817	35.4
FIRE[a]	745	714	31	4.3	714	530	184	34.7
Government	4,700	4,544	156	3.4	4,544	3,786	758	20.0
TCU[b]	1,060	1,026	34	3.3	1,026	914	112	12.2

*Adapted from Bureau of Labor Statistics—Employment Security estimates for respective months and years.

[a]Finance, insurance, and real estate groups.

[b]Transportation, communications, and utilities groups.

[c]Includes 225 mostly larger of 278 SMSAs designated through December 31, 1977.

REGIONAL DIFFERENTIALS

There were pronounced regional differences, metro and nonmetro alike, in the expansion of industrial employment between March 1962-78. These differences are summarized by the 4 major geographic divisions of the U.S. Bureau of the Census (Tables 7 and 8).[4] The South had the greater share—more than half—of the increase in nonmetro manufacturing, while the North Central region was a strong second with about 30%. Manufacturing activity in the long-industrialized Northeast and the more recently industrializing West remained overwhelmingly metro in character, especially in comparison with the relatively modest nonmetro employment located in their nonmetro communities.

Both the 1969 distribution and 1959-69 changes in manufacturing employment in rural and other nonmetro counties were concentrated in the eastern part of the nation, particularly in the more densely populated localities (Figures 1 and 2). Also reflected were differences due to variations in climatic conditions, accessibility, and the traditional strength of agricultural, grazing, forestry, recreation, and wilderness uses in the Great Plain State and the West, including Alaska and Hawaii.

Much of the decentralization of U.S. industry to rural and other smaller communities occurred before 1970—meaning that the 1969 pattern of distribution would not be greatly altered, provided 1976 and especially 1978 data were fully available. As determined from a preliminary analysis of 1969-76 changes, the chief exceptions would be those counties, metro as well as nonmetro, experiencing sizeable job gains or losses in the 1970s, due either to the increased demand for plastic, furniture, and related items or to plant closings. Figures 3 and 4, prepared at Kansas State University, represent an effort to bring SMSA and non-SMSA coverage by counties somewhat more up to date.

Northeast

Nonmetro areas gained about 100,000 manufacturing employees between 1962 and 1978, a modest 13%. In that period, the Northeast's share of U.S. nonmetro factory employees fell from 20% to 15%. Only 18% of Northeast manufacturing was outside metro areas in 1978. New York, Philadelphia, and other metro areas lost nearly 600,000 manufacturing jobs between March 1962-78, leaving the Northeast with about a half million fewer manufacturing jobs in 1978 than 16 years earlier. Employment additions of about 50% in the service-performing industries of the metro areas lagged considerably behind both the U.S. gain and increases in the other three regions. In contrast, an expansion by 80% in the nonmetro areas not only matched the U.S. addition but trailed the percentage increase only in the West.

The 1977-78 turnaround in manufacturing activity was reflected in an increase of about 100,000 jobs in the industrial sector of the Northeast's larger employment centers, accompanied by an equally nominal gain in the region's rural and other smaller communities. It reduced, but failed to fully overcome, job cutbacks sustained during the 1974–75 economic downslide, let alone compensate for reductions earlier in the 1970s.

North Central

The 1962–78 period saw a gain of 564,000 nonmetro factory jobs, a 48% increase. The region's share of total U.S. nonmetro industrial employment held steady at about 30%. In 1978, 28% of its industry remained outside metro areas. Detroit, Cleveland, Chicago, and other metro jobs centers of the North Central region gained about 400,000 manufacturing jobs in the 1962–78 period, about 160,000 fewer than in nonmetro areas. In the service-performing sectors, employment increases of about 70% in both metro and nonmetro areas were appreciably under the U.S. expansion pace of 78%.

March 1969–76, losses in manufacturing employment comparable to those taking place in the metro concentrations of the Great Lakes Industrial Belt were sustained by many interspersed nonmetro counties whose economies were oriented around lesser urban centers (e.g., Newark and Zanesville in Ohio). Otherwise, fairly substantial gains in manufacturing jobs continued to occur in the 1970s, mainly in nonmetro counties located within and especially on the northern and western margins of the Great Lakes Industrial Belt.

Gains in manufacturing jobs between 1969–76 in many nonmetro as well as fringe or outlying metro counties extended over a broad spectrum of both industrial and consumer products. Included were plastics, farm feeds, poultry products, lumber and millwork, fabricated metals, household appliances, farm machinery, trucks, and instruments. Yet, often in nearby counties, output and jobs were reduced in meat packing, feed processing, ordnance, and radio–TV and other electronic facilities.

Much the same as in the Northeast, the 1977–78 turnaround in manufacturing activity contributed to a modest job increase in the industrial sector of the region's larger employment centers, and an equivalent gain in its smaller labor market areas. Again, however, the additions reduced but failed to fully offset setbacks during the 1974–75 and 1970–71 declines in the economy.

South

The South's rural and other smaller labor market areas added almost a million manufacturing jobs in the 1962–78 period, for an increase of 57%. This gain represented 53% of the nonmetro gain nationally—an expansion raising the South's share from 43.4 to 46%. Atlanta, Dallas–Fort Worth, and other larger employment centers added somewhat over a million manufacturing jobs in the 16-year period. Contrasted with the fairly balanced metro–nonmetro growth exhibited in manufacturing, metro gains in service activities outpaced nonmetro additions by a margin of 102 to 81%.

Contributing to recent job increases in manufacturing in the metro South was the extraordinary buildup in Houston's refining, petrochemical, and related industries, together with the continued strength of shipbuilding.

Table 7. Nonfarm Wage and Salary Employment, United States and by Regions, March 1962-78 Comparisons*

Area and industry group	Overall 1978 (thou.)	Overall 1962 (thou.)	Northeast 1978 (thou.)	Northeast 1962 (thou.)	North Central 1978 (thou.)	North Central 1962 (thou.)	South 1978 (thou.)	South 1962 (thou.)	West 1978 (thou.)	West 1962 (thou.)
TOTAL	83,323	54,192	19,197	15,430	22,695	15,557	25,991	14,676	15,440	8,529
GOODS–PRODUCING	24,192	19,759	5,599	6,111	7,249	6,052	7,688	5,006	3,656	2,590
Manufacturing	19,870	16,622	5,001	5,475	6,319	5,350	5,813	3,818	2,737	1,979
Construction	3,644	2,495	564	576	838	587	1,489	837	753	495
Mining	678	642	34	60	92	115	386	351	116	431
SERVICE-PERFORMING	54,437	30,572	12,514	8,246	14,209	8,399	16,818	8,619	10,896	5,308
Private sector	38,492	21,572	9,179	6,176	10,227	6,047	11,500	5,795	7,586	3,554
Trade	18,547	11,215	4,029	2,964	5,126	3,264	5,802	3,144	3,590	1,843
Services	15,420	7,603	3,921	2,288	3,993	2,059	4,394	1,965	3,112	1,291
FIRE[a]	4,525	2,754	1,229	924	1,108	724	1,304	686	844	420
Government	15,945	9,000	3,335	2,070	3,982	2,352	5,318	2,824	3,310	1,754
TCU[b]	4,694	3,861	1,084	1,073	1,237	1,106	1,485	1,051	888	631
METRO[c]	61,628	41,030	16,188	13,399	16,033	11,289	17,055	9,363	12,352	6,979
GOODS–PRODUCING	16,955	14,823	4,587	5,227	5,158	4,603	4,287	2,825	2,923	2,168
Manufacturing	14,141	12,715	4,122	4,700	4,574	4,169	3,150	2,121	2,295	1,725
Construction	2,592	1,899	458	502	568	413	996	579	570	405
Mining	222	209	7	25	16	21	141	125	58	38
SERVICE-PERFORMING	41,039	23,191	10,656	7,220	9,969	5,875	11,697	5,791	8,717	4,305
Private sector	29,794	16,935	7,927	5,518	7,418	4,415	8,204	4,011	6,245	2,991
Trade	13,924	8,606	3,433	2,625	3,579	2,309	4,010	2,145	2,902	1,527
Services	12,090	5,990	3,365	2,029	2,966	1,526	3,179	1,344	2,580	1,091
FIRE[a]	3,780	2,339	1,129	864	873	580	1,015	522	763	373
Government	11,245	6,256	2,729	1,702	2,551	1,460	3,493	1,780	2,472	1,314
TCU[b]	3,634	3,016	945	952	906	811	1,071	747	712	506
NONMETRO	21,695	13,162	3,009	2,031	6,662	4,268	8,936	5,313	3,088	1,550
GOODS–PRODUCING	7,237	4,936	1,012	884	2,091	1,449	3,401	2,181	733	422
Manufacturing	5,729	3,907	879	775	1,745	1,181	2,663	1,697	442	254
Construction	1,052	596	106	74	270	174	493	258	183	90
Mining	456	433	27	35	76	94	245	226	108	78
SERVICE-PERFORMING	13,398	7,381	1,858	1,026	4,240	2,524	5,121	2,828	2,179	1,003
Private sector	8,698	4,637	1,252	658	2,809	1,632	3,296	1,784	1,841	563
Trade	4,623	2,609	596	339	1,547	955	1,792	999	688	316
Services	3,330	1,613	556	259	1,027	533	1,215	621	532	200
FIRE[a]	745	415	100	60	235	144	289	164	121	47
Government	4,700	2,744	606	368	1,431	892	1,825	1,044	838	440
TCU[b]	1,060	845	139	121	331	295	414	304	176	125

*Adapted from Bureau of Labor Statistics–Employment Security estimates for respective months and years.
[a]Finance, insurance, and real estate groups.
[b]Transportation, communications, and utilities groups.
[c]Includes 225 mostly larger of 278 SMSAs designated through December 31, 1977.
Note. Regions coincide with four geographic divisions of U.S. Bureau of Census.

Table 8. Changes in Nonfarm Wage and Salary Employment, United States and by Regions, March 1962-78 Comparisons*

Area and industry group	Overall N (thou.)	Overall (%)	Northeast N (thou.)	Northeast (%)	North Central N (thou.)	North Central (%)	South N (thou.)	South (%)	West N (thou.)	West (%)
TOTAL	29,131	53.8	3,767	24.4	7,138	45.9	11,315	77.1	6,911	81.0
GOODS-PRODUCING	4,433	22.4	−512	−8.4	1,197	19.8	2,682	53.6	1,066	41.2
Manufacturing	3,248	19.5	−474	−8.7	969	18.1	1,995	52.3	758	38.3
Construction	1,149	46.1	−12	−2.1	251	42.8	652	77.9	258	52.1
Mining	36	5.6	−26	−43.3	−23	−20.0	35	10.0	50	43.1
SERVICE-PERFORMING	23,865	78.1	4,268	51.8	5,810	69.2	8,199	95.1	5,588	105.3
Private sector	16,920	78.4	3,003	48.6	4,180	69.1	5,705	98.4	4,032	113.4
Trade	7,332	65.4	1,065	35.9	1,862	57.0	2,658	84.5	1,747	94.8
Services	7,817	102.8	1,633	71.4	1,934	93.9	2,429	123.6	1,821	141.1
FIRE[a]	1,771	64.3	305	33.0	384	53.0	618	90.1	464	110.5
Government	6,945	77.2	1,265	61.1	1,630	69.3	2,494	88.3	1,556	88.7
TCU[b]	833	21.6	11	1.0	131	11.8	434	41.3	257	40.7
METRO[c]	20,598	50.2	2,789	20.8	4,744	42.0	7,692	82.2	5,373	77.0
GOODS-PRODUCING	2,132	14.4	−640	−12.2	555	12.1	1,462	51.8	755	34.8
Manufacturing	1,426	11.2	−578	−12.3	405	9.7	1,029	48.5	570	33.0
Construction	693	36.5	−44	−8.8	155	37.5	417	72.0	165	40.7
Mining	13	6.2	−18	−72.0	−5	−23.8	16	12.8	20	52.6
SERVICE-PERFORMING	17,848	77.0	3,436	47.6	4,094	69.7	5,906	102.0	4,412	102.5
Private sector	12,859	75.9	2,409	43.7	3,003	68.0	4,193	104.5	3,254	108.8
Trade	5,318	61.8	808	30.8	1,270	55.0	1,865	86.9	1,375	90.0
Services	6,100	101.8	1,336	65.8	1,440	94.4	1,835	136.5	1,489	136.5
FIRE[a]	1,441	61.6	265	30.7	293	50.5	493	94.4	390	104.6
Government	4,989	79.7	1,027	60.3	1,091	74.7	1,713	96.2	1,158	88.1
TCU[b]	618	20.5	−7	−0.7	95	11.7	324	43.4	206	40.7
NONMETRO	8,533	64.8	978	48.2	2,394	56.1	3,623	68.2	1,538	99.2
GOODS-PRODUCING	2,301	46.6	128	14.5	642	44.3	1,220	55.9	311	73.7
Manufacturing	1,822	46.6	104	13.4	564	47.8	966	56.9	188	74.0
Construction	456	76.5	32	43.2	96	55.2	235	91.1	93	103.3
Mining	23	5.3	−8	−22.9	−18	−19.1	19	8.4	30	38.5
SERVICE-PERFORMING	6,017	81.5	832	81.1	1,716	68.0	2,293	81.1	1,176	117.2
Private sector	4,061	87.6	594	90.3	1,177	72.1	1,512	84.8	778	138.2
Trade	2,014	77.2	257	75.8	592	62.0	793	79.4	372	117.7
Services	1,717	106.4	297	114.7	494	92.7	594	95.7	332	166.0
FIRE[a]	330	79.5	40	66.7	91	63.2	125	76.2	74	157.4
Government	1,956	71.3	238	64.7	539	60.4	781	74.8	398	90.5
TCU[b]	215	25.4	18	14.9	36	12.2	110	36.2	51	40.8

*Adapted from Bureau of Labor Statistics—Employment Security estimates for respective months and years.

[a]Finance, insurance, and real estate groups.

[b]Transportation, communications, and utilities groups.

[c]Includes 225 mostly larger of 278 SMSAs designated through December 31, 1977.

Note. Regions coincide with four geographic divisions of U.S. Bureau of Census.

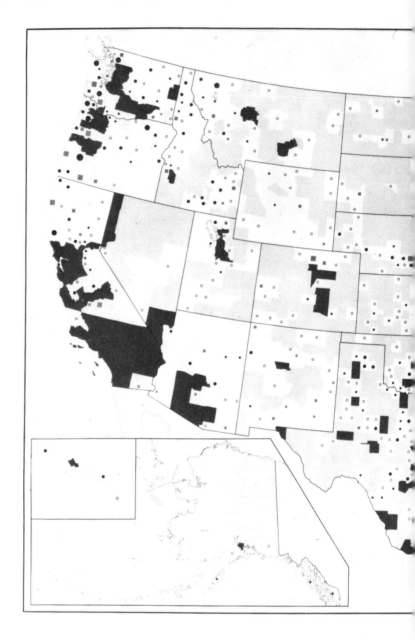

Fig. 1. Manufacturing employment in nonmetropolitan counties, 1969.

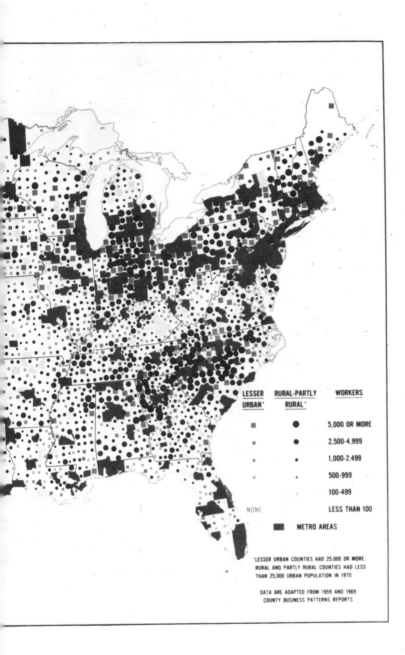

LESSER URBAN*	RURAL-PARTLY RURAL*	WORKERS
■	●	5,000 OR MORE
■	●	2,500-4,999
▪	•	1,000-2,499
▫	·	500-999
	◦	100-499
NONE		LESS THAN 100
■ METRO AREAS		

*LESSER URBAN COUNTIES HAD 25,000 OR MORE.
RURAL AND PARTLY RURAL COUNTIES HAD LESS
THAN 25,000 URBAN POPULATION IN 1970

DATA ARE ADAPTED FROM 1959 AND 1969
COUNTY BUSINESS PATTERNS REPORTS

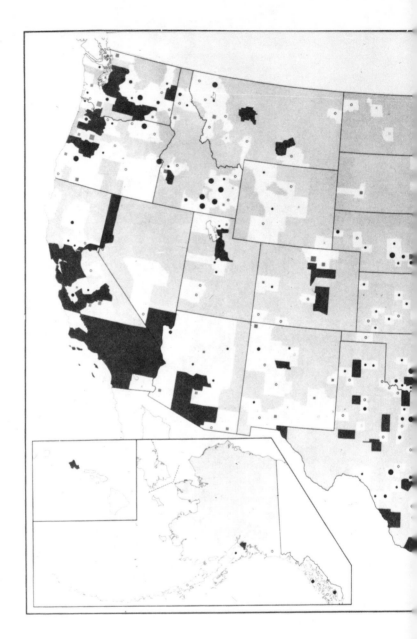

Fig. 2. Growth of manufacturing employment in nonmetropolitan counties, 1959–69.

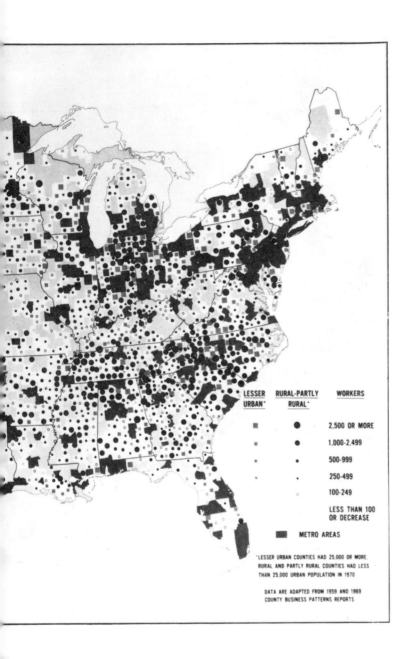

LESSER URBAN*	RURAL-PARTLY RURAL*	WORKERS
▪	●	2,500 OR MORE
▪	●	1,000-2,499
▪	•	500-999
▪	•	250-499
	○	100-249
		LESS THAN 100 OR DECREASE
▬	METRO AREAS	

*LESSER URBAN COUNTIES HAD 25,000 OR MORE. RURAL AND PARTLY RURAL COUNTIES HAD LESS THAN 25,000 URBAN POPULATION IN 1970

DATA ARE ADAPTED FROM 1959 AND 1969 COUNTY BUSINESS PATTERNS REPORTS

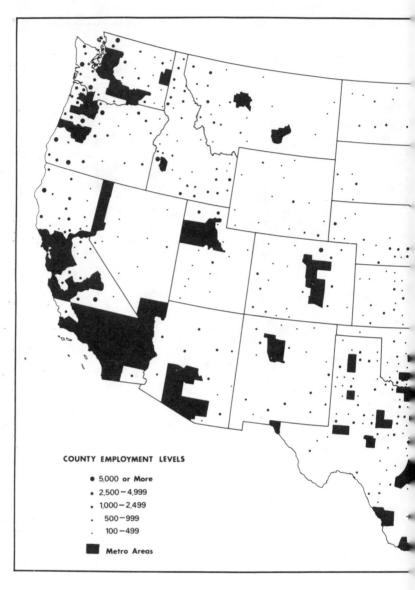

Fig. 3. Manufacturing employment in nonmetropolitan counties, 1974.

COUNTY EMPLOYMENT LEVELS

- 5,000 or More
- 2,500 – 4,999
- 1,000 – 2,499
- 500 – 999
- 100 – 499

■ Metro Areas

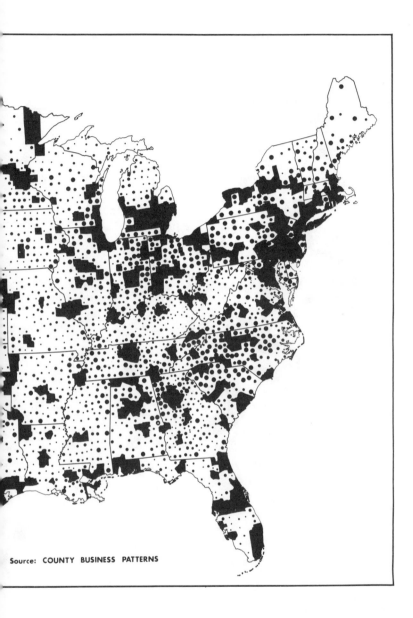

Source: COUNTY BUSINESS PATTERNS

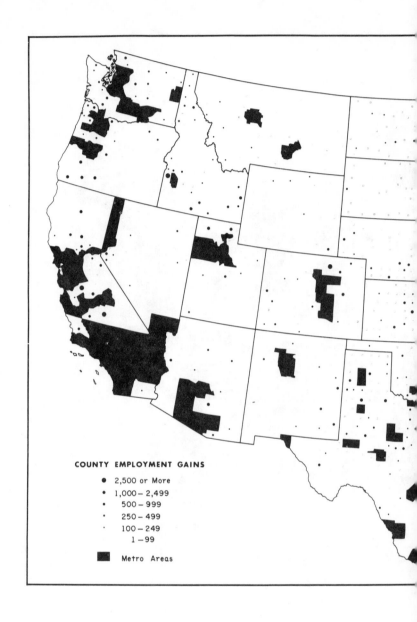

Fig. 4. Growth of manufacturing employment in nonmetropolitan counties, 1969-74.

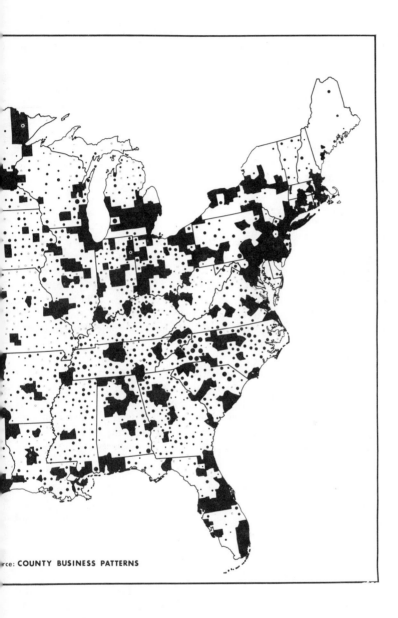

rce: COUNTY BUSINESS PATTERNS

Elsewhere, job cutbacks resulting from the 1974-75 economic downturn were fairly severe and not reversed by March 1976 or possibly later, except mainly in various fringe and outlying metro centers and their nonmetro counterparts.

A preliminary look at 1969-76 county data shows strong survivorship abilities on the part of a great many of the highly seasonal, low-profit margin, and other often short-lived manufacturing ventures traditionally gravitating to small and very small labor market areas of the South. This is particularly true in the Deep South and parts of central and southern Appalachia. As in the North Central region, there is a need for a thorough study identifying differences, inherent either within individual firms or in local work climates, setting these communities apart from neighboring units in which similar ventures have seriously faltered if not ended in failure.

West

The Western region, with a combination of major urban centers and vast expanses of lightly populated areas, added 190,000 nonmetro manufacturing jobs in the 1962-78 period. This constituted a 74% gain for the region, but the absolute gain was a small part (10%) of the U.S. nonmetro increase. The West's share of national nonmetro manufacturing employment increased from 6.5 to 7.7%, but in 1978 it represented only 16% of all manufacturing jobs in the West. Given the physical environment and the geographic distribution of the population, Western industrialization is likely to remain heavily metro in character.

As in other sections of the Sun Belt, the ever-increasing population in the Southwest was accentuated by a rapid aging of the large retiree population and a resulting impact on the nature of demands for both hard and soft goods. Denver and Salt Lake City were emerging as future energy capitals. Increased mining of uranium, coal, and various nonfuel minerals and prospecting for oil and gas were generating new construction projects and supportive forms of manufacturing.

The conflict between economic development and environmental protection is nowhere more evident than in the West. Water is required for irrigation, the generation of hydroelectric power, and for household, commercial, and industrial uses, but supplies have become increasingly inadequate. Protracted drought in 1976-77 led to widespread brownouts, curtailed crop yields, reduced industrial output, water rationing, and damaging forest and brush fires. The rapid expansion of strip-mining of coal has been accompanied by extensive reclamation. Yet, both coal and lignite deposits not only are comparatively limited, but control of particulate emissions in the generation of electricity remains largely unresolved. Stepped-up logging could only temporarily alleviate shortages of marketable sawtimber.

INDUSTRY AND SUBINDUSTRY SHIFTS

Earlier efforts to identify the industries and subindustries locating or expanding in rural and other smaller communities between March 1962-67 relied mainly on individual case studies, *County Business Patterns,* and listings of million-dollar plants in the *Industrial Development* journal. Sources added later included official newsletters, annual summaries, and estimates for smaller labor market areas published by various State Employment Security agencies.

In updating estimates to March 1978, chief reliance was on current State Employment Security newsletters in determining location and nature of geographic shifts in manufacturing and other nonfarm wage and salary employment in the aftermath of the 1974–75 economic decline. Confirmation came mostly from ucrrent issues of *Industrial Development* and appropriate tables (B-2 and B-3) of *Employment and Earnings.* Although data are current only to 1976, equally valuable leads on directions of change came from 1969–76 *County Business Patterns* reports.

Metro-Centered Industries and Subindustries

Processing of steel and most other primary metals (33) remained concentrated in the larger employment centers (Table 9).[5] Much decentralization of printing and publishing occurred in the 1960s and 1970s, especially to the South and West and from larger metro complexes to smaller metro centers.

The 1977–78 resurgence in manufacturing output and employment in the old industrial districts of the Northeast and North Central Region involved essentially the same industries and subindustries as in the 1970–71 and 1974–75 economic downturns. They included heavy industrial, construction, and mining machinery (351,3); machine tools, dies, and other metal working machinery (354); office and computer machines (357); electrical industrial apparatus (362); and communication equipment (366). The same applied to the 1977–78 upsurge in production of motor vehicles and parts (371), the strength of shipbuilding (373) through 1977, and the tremendous expansion under way in aircraft and parts (372) as domestic commercial airlines began replacing their present jet fleets.

Expansion since 1967 to meet increased demands for gasoline, residual fuel oil, plastic feedstocks, etc., raised employment in the highly metro-centered petroleum refining subindustry (291) by about 10%, or to approximately the 1962 level. Over the same 11-year period, jobs grew by 50% in the much more widely dispersed paving and roofing materials subindustry (295).

Employment in chemicals, including such strongly metro-oriented subgroups as industrial or commodity chemcials (281), plastic materials (2821), synthetic fibers (2823,4), drugs (283), soaps (284), and paints (285), as well as agricultural chemicals (287), has increased very little, if at all, in the 1970s. Constant technological advances, intense competition for both domestic and worldwide markets, and a major shift of facilities to the developing nations added to the lack of job growth, especially when contrasted with the 1960s.

Nonmetro-Oriented Industries and Subindustries

Lumber and wood products (24), paper and allied products (26), agricultural chemicals (287), farm machinery (352), and stone, clay, and glass

Table 9. Manufacturing Employment: Fluctuations by Industry Groups in Response to Cyclical Swings in Economic Activity, United States, February 1960-March 1978*

Industry group	Feb. 1960 Peak (thou.)	Feb. 1961 Trough (thou.)	Jan. 1967 Peak (thou.)	Jul. 1967 Trough (thou.)	Sep. 1969 Peak (thou.)	Nov. 1970 Trough (thou.)	Dec. 1973 Peak (thou.)	Apr. 1975 Trough (thou.)	Mar. 1978 Current (thou.)
ALL MANUFACTURING	17,153	16,076	19,606	19,335	20,265	18,462	20,359	18,183	20,146
30−RubPlastics	387	359	530	482	599	566	687	573	702
38−Instruments	360	342	447	451	477	444	512	487	544
29−PetroCoal	216	204	182	182	188	190	198	194	217
25−FurniFix	390	359	463	448	485	453	537	436	540
35−NonelecMach	1,512	1,411	1,983	1,971	2,052	1,866	2,176	2,100	2,293
24−LumberWood	653	574	604	593	602	562	651	537	670
34−FabMetals	1,172	1,060	1,376	1,362	1,448	1,303	1,533	1,332	1,512
27−PrintPub	906	914	1,039	1,049	1,102	1,089	1,110	1,083	1,131
28−Chemicals	826	820	992	1,000	1,061	1,031	1,044	1,005	1,073
32−StoneCG	618	567	636	624	658	629	707	610	680
26−PaperAllied	601	596	676	682	714	694	705	631	713
22−Textiles	942	883	966	947	1,001	957	1,026	866	994
36−ElecEquipSup	1,490	1,447	1,989	1,935	2,056	1,798	2,083	1,748	2,038
39−Misc.	393	375	436	426	439	415	456	397	428
20−FoodKindred	1,793	1,777	1,791	1,790	1,796	1,768	1,734	1,664	1,733
37−TransptEquip	1,642	1,410	1,955	1,951	2,076	1,496	1,902	1,634	1,885
23−Apparel	1,244	1,200	1,425	1,390	1,404	1,339	1,395	1,195	1,289
33−PrimMetals	1,332	1,088	1,373	1,302	1,387	1,254	1,357	1,194	1,214
21−Tobacco	96	92	90	87	86	83	81	76	70
31−Leather	366	359	359	345	333	309	287	246	262
19−Ordnance	214	239	294	318	301	216	178	175	158

Index: January 1967 = 100%

Industry group	Feb. 1960 Peak (%)	Feb. 1961 Trough (%)	Jan. 1967 Peak (%)	Jul. 1967 Trough (%)	Sep. 1969 Peak (%)	Nov. 1970 Trough (%)	Dec. 1973 Peak (%)	Apr. 1975 Trough (%)	Mar. 1978 Current (%)
ALL MANUFACTURING	87	82	100	99	103	94	104	93	103
30−RubPlastics	73	68	100	91	113	107	129	108	132
38−Instruments	81	77	100	101	107	99	115	109	122
29−PetroCoal	119	112	100	100	103	104	109	107	119
25−FurniFix	84	78	100	97	105	98	116	94	117
35−NonelecMach	76	71	100	99	103	94	110	106	116
24−LumberWood	108	95	100	98	100	93	108	89	111
34−FabMetals	85	77	100	99	105	95	111	97	110
27−PrintPub	87	88	100	101	106	105	107	104	109
28−Chemicals	83	83	100	101	107	104	105	101	108
32−StoneCG	97	89	100	98	103	99	111	96	107
26−PaperAllied	89	88	100	101	106	103	104	93	105
22−Textiles	98	91	100	98	104	99	106	90	103
36−ElecEquipSup	75	73	100	97	103	90	105	88	102
39−Misc.	90	86	100	98	101	95	105	91	98
20−FoodKindred	100	99	100	100	100	99	97	93	97
37−TransptEquip	84	72	100	100	106	77	97	84	96
23−Apparel	87	84	100	98	99	94	98	84	90
33−PrimMetals	97	79	100	95	101	91	99	87	88
21−Tobacco	107	102	100	97	96	92	90	84	78
31−Leather	102	100	100	96	93	86	80	69	73
19−Ordnance	73	81	100	108	102	73	61	60	54

*Adapted from seasonally adjusted series, summarized in *Employment and Earnings, United States, 1909–75*, Bul. 1312-10, and updated in December 1976 and April 1978 issues of *Employment and Earnings*. Individual months and years represent high and low points in manufacturing employment, associated with 1960–61 recession, 1967 slowdown, and 1969–70 and 1973–75 recessions.

(32) remain the major industry groups or subgroups in which production and unemployment continue to be most strongly nonmetropolitan. Until the 1970s, food and kindred products (20) were heavily represented in rural and other small communities, but more recently this geographic pattern has been altered by (1) volume purchasing by major supermarket chains, (2) the expansion of air freight and direct-to-market highway transport of fresh fruits and vegetables, and (3) widespread adoption of automation and cost-efficient processes.

Miscellaneous plastics (307), instruments (38), and furniture and fixtures (25) stand out conspicuously as growth industries in both metro and nonmetro areas. Much the same can be said for fabricated metals (34) and stone, clay, glass, and concrete (32).

Serious reservations, however, can be raised about other industries in nonmetro areas. Employment prospects for lumber and wood products (24) and paper and allied products (26) are questionable because of the increasing severity of shortages of marketable sawtimber, mounting competition from greatly enlarged worldwide paper supplies, and rapid escalation of paperboard costs. The main exceptions were the production of millwork and related items (243), mobile homes (2451), and insulating and similar materials (264). Smaller communities have been affected as much or more so than their larger counterparts by the flood of imports of apparel, textiles, leather goods, radio-TV receivers, and other low-technology items, as well as by pronounced changes in domestic merket outlets and marketing practices. But aside from the export of agricultural products, nonmetro areas were affected very lightly by either exports or imports of semiconductors and other high-technology items, or a low-technology product such as steel.

Miscellaneous plastics. Combined employment in this subindustry (307), well-represented in nonmetro communities, grew by 130,000 workers, or well over 50%, in the 1967-78 period. Tile flooring, carpeting, roofing, and similar plastic products played more important roles in new housing construction and remodeling and refurnishing existing homes in 1977-78 than in 1972-73. Recent efforts to reduce domestic auto weight in the interests of gasoline conservation were showing up by 1977-78 in increased employment in nonmetro areas in the production of plastic components and accessories. Meanwhile, the sustained strength of consumer buying power was reflected in rapidly expanding markets for the dozens of plastic items in regular household and office use.

Furniture and Fixtures. Fluctuations in employment in the furniture and fixtures industry (25) in the 1970s were closely identified with periodic ups-and-downs in home building. Jobs declined only moderately during the 1970-71 economic downturn. After a strong recovery in 1972-73, employment plummeted to about the 1967 level in 1974-75. Since then, 2 good years in succession in home building activity restored jobs to approximately the 1973 level. With minor variations, employment changes in the production of office furniture (252) paralleled shifts in the household subgroup (251). Gains between 1967-78 in the manufacture of wooden furniture (2511)—the more rural-oriented segment of the household furnishings subindustry—were appreciably lower, due at least in part to increasingly scarce supplies of walnut, wild cherry, maple, and other desirable hardwoods.

Fabricated metals. Beginning in 1962 or earlier, the buildup in employment in the smaller labor market areas in the manufacture of an infinite number and variety of light-weight fabricated metal products has continued more or less interruptedly in the 1970s. Contributing to reductions in susceptibility to cyclical influences was the fairly constant demand not only for adding or replacing hardware and related items, but for materials for maintenance and improvement as well as construction of housing, and public, commercial, farm, and industrial buildings. Subindustries recording especially impressive employment gains since 1967 included cutlery, hand tools, and hardware (342), and fabricated structural metal products (344).

Stone, clay, and glass. Such prime sources of building materials as stone, clay, and glass products (32) closely resemble fabricated metals in growth characteristics, and are a comparatively good insulation against cyclical influences and competition from imports. Nevertheless, individual subgroups vary greatly in responsiveness to various economic stimuli. Glass and glassware (322) have exceptionally favorable growth records, due to the subgroup's transcending importance as a source material for the production of fiberglass, demanded both by the auto industry and for insulation purposes. Concrete, gypsum, and plaster (327) and cut stone and related products (328,9) have exhibited steady and remarkably even growth throughout both the 1960s and 1970s. Employment has at best held its own in the flat glass (321), structural clay (325), and pottery (326) subgroups as a result of competition from plastic and other substitute materials.

Farm and garden machinery. Employment in the production of farm and garden machinery, equipment, and supplies (352) declined sharply from the 1967 level through the 1970–71 downturn. Then, after again rising during the 1974–75 economic downturn to approximately the 1967 level, jobs fell off by about 20,000, or more than 10%, in the 1975–78 period. In other words, recent employment changes in the subindustry were more closely related to fluctuations in farm income levels than ups-and-downs in the overall economy.

Household appliances and related subindustries. Employment since March 1970 has remained relatively steady and unchanging from year-to-year in 3 fairly nonmetro-oriented growth subindustries of the 1960s—household appliances (363), electric lighting and wiring equipment (364), and radio and TV receiving equipment (365). Competition from imports has appreciably affected domestic output only of radio and TV receivers. Otherwise, the principal impediments to job growth again were automation coupled with the fact domestic outlets were not expanding nearly as rapidly as in the 1960s.

Special transportation equipment. Steps currently under way to redesign passenger cars to conserve energy have already shown up in increased employment in nonmetro as well as metro areas in the production of engines, transmissions, grills, panels, and other light-weight metal and plastic components and parts. Meanwhile, employment in the manufacture of pleasure boats, auto homes, campers, and recreation vehicles showed few signs of revival until 1978 from the sharp declines experienced in 1974-75.

Textiles. A sizeable number of textile mills located in smaller communities produce synthetic carptes, upholstery, tire cord, and other fabrics (227,8,9) in strong demand in present-day domestic markets. Although somewhat sus- ceptible to cyclical and other influences, employment in the 1970s in knitting mills (225), including many new plants in smaller as well as larger job centers, expanded by a modest 10% or so. In contrast, employment in weaving mills (221,2,3,4), including many older facilities particularly in metro areas, de- clined by 15-20%. Whether located in smaller or larger labor market areas, weaving plants generally are in a poor position to compete in markets chronically affected by worldwide overcapacity.

Apparel. Employment in the manfuacture of curtains, draperies, and other housefurnishings, shipping and commercial bags, canvas, auto trim, uniforms, and related products (239) continues to show the brightest, if not the only realistic, promise for the future for the trouble-plagued domestic apparel industry. But regardless of location, employment since 1970 fluctuated widely and was down 10% by March 1978. Competitive advantages of new and modernized apparel factories, located in large numbers in the South's rural and other smaller communities in the 1960s, have been retained as production processes have been further improved. Also contributing to survival was the introduction of rigid inventory controls and accommodation of sales to today's speciality and high-volume market outlets.

CONCLUSIONS

The addition of nearly 2 million manufacturing jobs in rural and other smaller communities between 1962 and 1978 raised manufacturing employ- ment from 3.9 to 5.7 million workers, for an increase of almost 50%. The share of the nation's manufacturing found in nonmetro areas increased from 23.5 to 28.8%. Nearly a million of the new manufacturing jobs, or more than half, were located in the South's smaller labor market areas. More than a half million, or about 30%, came in the North Central region. The smaller communities of the Northeast and West shared the remaining 300,000 additions.

The catalytic effect of the addition of new plants and expansion of existing facilities in hundreds of rural and other smaller communities was expressed in a gain of nearly 7 million nonmanufacturing jobs between 1962-78, 4 million of which were created in the private sector of the service-performing industries. Greatly increased household incomes and buying power were progressively translated into long-lacking and much-needed improvements in rural housing, health care, schools, public water and waste disposal systems, banking, credit and related facilities, etc. Though the eventual result was to reduce the industrial sector's share of nonfarm wage and salary employment, manufacturing continues to furnish a quarter of the jobs and an equivalent share of earnings from establishment employment. Yet, serious concern arises over whether manufacturing employment in nonmetro areas hasn't already reached a peak, possibly as early as 1973.

Practically all nonmetro employment gains since 1973 came in non-manufacturing employment. The rise of childless householders, young and old alike, already is rapidly altering consumer demands for shelter, food, transportation, medical care, and leisure-time activities. Restoration of reciprocity in international trade relationships would benefit rural and other smaller communities chiefly by expanding farm exports. Much of recent and antici-pated increases in manufacturing output in the larger job centers has and will undoubtedly continue to exert minor ripple effects on nonmetro areas.

A great many rural-oriented industries and subindustries have lost employ-ment or barely held their own, dating back in some instances to 1970 or as early as 1967. Competition from imports has particularly hurt domestic output and jobs in textiles, apparel, leather goods, radio–TV receivers, paper and allied products, and watches and clocks. But other forces have also contributed. For example, such industries as lumber and wood products, agricultural chemicals, farm machinery, and food and kindred products have sustained job losses for a variety of reasons bearing little relationship to competition from imports.

As with smaller firms everywhere, those situated in rural and other smaller communities are confronted with intense competition, both for domestic market outlets and from new products constantly being introduced on U.S. and worldwide markets. In addition to contending with mounting material, labor, and other costs, such firms also experience profound difficulties in adopting labor-saving and other cost-cutting practices and accumulating or borrowing capital required to add capacity, improve productivity, and hire more workers.[6]

NOTES

[1] Statistics mainly adapted from Bureau of Labor Statistics–Employment Security estimates for respective months and years.

[2] This and similar expressions, frequently substituted for metropolitan and nonmetro-politan, originated in research in the Department of Agriculture in the 1920s and early 1930s. Such present usage is highly fitting, inasmuch as the employment data necessarily relied on do not coincide fully with current SMSA–non-SMSA delineations.

[3] The 225 larger SMSAs (Standard Metropolitan Statistical Areas) and LMAs (Labor Market Areas) from which metro data were derived exclude an estimated 2 million nonfarm wage and salary jobs in SMSA designations through December 31, 1977, but include 4 million or more workers in secondary or fringe counties.

[4] Northeast region: PA, NJ, NY, CT, RI, MA, VT, NH, ME; North Central region: OH, MI, IN, IL, WI, MN, IA, MO, KS, NB, SD, ND; South region: MD, DE, VA, WV, NC, SC, GA, FL, AL, MS, TN, KY, AR, LA, TX, OK; West region: MT, WY, CO, NM, AZ, UT, NV, ID, WA, OR, CA, AK, HI.

[5]These and other numbers in parentheses conform to the SIC codes listed in *1972 Standard Industrial Classification Manual.*

General References

[6]Philip H. Abelson, "Learning about Energy the Hard Way," *Science,* Vol. 195 (Feb. 25, 1977), p. 733.

[7]Tom Alexander, "A Promising Try at Environmental Detente for Coal," *Fortune,* Vol. 97 (Feb. 1978), pp. 95-96, 100-102.

[8]Ronald Alsop, "Moving In–Beneficial Ripples of 1977 Housing Boom Are Expected to Last Well into New Year," *Wall Street Journal,* Vol. 191 (Jan. 31, 1978), p. 48.

[9]C. Fred Bergsten et al., *American Multinationals and American Interests* (Washington, D.C.: Brookings Institute, 1978).

[10]William M. Bulkeley, "Raising the Roof–Baby Boom of 1947-57 a Key Economic Force, *Wall Street Journal,* Vol. 192 (July 27, 1978. pp. 1, 21.

[11]Gene Bylinsky, "New Companies that Beat the Odds," *Fortune,* Vol. 96 (Dec. 1977), pp. 76-84.

[12]Victor R. Fuchs, *The Service Economy* (New York: National Bureau of Economic Research, 1968).

[13]Gloria P. Green et al., "Employment and Unemployment Trends during 1977," *Monthly Labor Review,* Vol. 101 (Feb. 1978), pp. 12-23.

[14]Allen L. Hammond et al., "An Interim Look at Energy," *Science,* Vol. 199 (Feb. 10, 1978), pp. 607-664.

[15]Claude C. Haren, "A Changing Rural and Urban America," paper presented at annual meeting of the American Association for the Advancement of Science, Washington, D.C., Dec. 26-31, 1966.

[16]Claude C. Haren, "Current Spatial Organization of Industrial Production and Distribution Activity," paper presented at Conference on Problems and Potentials of Rural Industrialization, Purdue University, July 11-13, 1972.

[17]Pamela G. Hollie, "Overcapacity and Poor Demand Dog Fiber Industry," *New York Times,* Vol. 127 (Feb. 13, 1978), pp. D1, 2.

[18]Richard F. Janssen, "Trade Tussle–Surge in Protectionism Worries and Perplexes Leaders of Many Lands," *Wall Street Journal,* Vol. 191 (Apr. 14, 1978), pp. 1, 20.

[19]N. R. Kleinfield, "Technology–Gingerly Steps to Computer-Run Plants," *New York Times,* Vol. 127 (Oct. 12, 1978), pp. 55, 67.

[20]Robert Z. Lawrence, *An Analysis of the 1977 U.S. Trade Deficit* (Washington, D.C.: Brookings Institute, 1978), pp. 159-189.

[21]"Petrochemicals: The Prodigious Costs of Facing the Future," *Business Week* (July 18, 1977), pp. 44-54.

[22]Sanford Rose, "Why the Multinational Tide is Ebbing," *Fortune,* Vol. 96 (Aug. 1977), pp. 111-120.

[23]Lee Smith, "Hard Times Come to Steeltown," *Fortune,* Vol. 96 (Dec. 1977), pp. 87-93.

[24]"Standard Metropolitan Statistical Classification: Proposed Changes in SMSA and SCSA Criteria for the 1980 Census," *Statistical Reporter,* Vol. 78 (May 1978), pp. 265-273.

[25]John E. Tilton, *The Future of Nonfuel Minerals* (Washington, D.C.: Brookings Institution, 1978).

[26]Ralph E. Winter, "On the Prowl–Conservative Firms Bent on Profit Join the Merger Chase," *Wall Street Journal,* Vol. 191 (Feb. 11, 1978), p. 1, 35.

[27]Deborah Sue Yaeger, "Change in Style–Apparel Makers Face Consolidation as Stores Stiffen Delivery Terms," *Wall Street Journal,* Vol. 191 (Feb. 6, 1978), pp. 1, 18.

FACTORS ENCOURAGING AND DISCOURAGING PLANT LOCATION IN NONMETROPOLITAN AREAS

Steven R. Kale and Richard E. Lonsdale

Many factors influence the selection of a new manufacturing plant location.[1] Most writers discussing these factors, however, do not distinguish between metropolitan and nonmetropolitan influences. Therefore, in this chapter, selected factors influencing the recent and continued desirability of nonmetropolitan areas for new manufacturing plants are reviewed.

Although numerous factors may enter into the selection of a new location for a nonmetropolitan manufacturing plant, only 11 are considered here. The selection of these factors is based upon previous studies in which non-metropolitan manufacturing has been examined, and upon the personal observations of professional industrial development personnel. What appear to be the more important regional factors are presented first, followed by a discussion of local or community influences. Additionally, because there are important geographic variations in the degree to which each regional or local factor is an encouraging or discouraging force, the factors will be examined from a rather broad locational perspective.

REGIONAL FACTORS

Labor Availability

The availability of low-cost labor has probably been the most important attraction influencing industry to locate in nonmetropolitan America.[2] The importance of labor availability has arisen, in part, because of high labor costs

47

in metropolitan areas, and these increased costs have contributed to industrial decentralization.

There has been a growing concern, however, that nonmetropolitan areas will be unable to meet future industrial demands for labor. Many nonmetropolitan areas have a rather small base of labor available at any given time, and it is becoming imperative to identify the potential sources of labor supply with as much accuracy as possible.

Prospective workers for new manufacturing plants are generally attracted from the ranks of the unemployed, underemployed, currently fully employed, labor force nonparticipants, inmigrants, and/or high school and post-secondary school leavers.[3] Where data permit, an evaluation of the number of persons in these sectors for a given community is made at the state level by Departments of Labor, Employment Security Divisions, or Departments of Economic Development. At the local level, the enumeration of potential workers is obtained through labor surveys. Interviews with local community leaders and employers also provide an important indication of labor supplies.

In general, it appears that many of the workers for new manufacturing plants will be obtained from the existing work force. Where the existing work force is underemployed, i.e., working involuntarily at part-time jobs or employed at occupations which do not make full use of the person's educational training, a prospective manufacturer may discover a sizeable labor reserve. Unfortunately, estimates of underemployment are difficult to derive, and a prospective employer must rely on an assessment of other factors to arrive at an indication of underemployment. The most commonly used indicator is the wage rate. If wages are low, workers may be underemployed. Even if the workers are not underemployed, low wage rates among a substantial portion of the work force may indicate a sizeable labor supply.

In some areas, labor force nonparticipants may comprise an important component of the labor supply. Labor force nonparticipants are persons of working age who are neither employed nor officially registered as unemployed. Housewives who are not employed outside the home fall into the category of labor force nonparticipants and have been a significant component of the work force at a number of recently located nonmetropolitan manufacturing plants.

The importance of unemployment as a labor supply source varies substantially from region to region. For example, in the Plains states, unemployment rates in nonmetropolitan areas are generally low; thus few of the employees at new manufacturing plants have been obtained from this sector. On the other hand, unemployment rates are higher in the South, and the significance of this sector is somewhat greater.

The inmigration of workers in response to job opportunities in nonmetropolitan areas also varies substantially from region to region. Inmigrants are likely to comprise a large proportion of the new industrial work force in nonmetropolitan "boom towns," such as those occurring in response to the development of energy resources in the sparsely populated areas of the Northern Great Plains. Conversely, the contribution of inmigrants to a new plant's work force will probably be small where wages are low and there is a sizeable number of unemployed or underemployed persons in the area.

The number of high school and post-secondary students who will decide to accept a job at a nonmetropolitan manufacturing plant is a difficult factor to assess. There has long been a desire among many youths to remain in nonmetropolitan areas, and the presence of manufacturing jobs has enabled them to stay. Nevertheless, nonmetropolitan manufacturers paying low wages will probably not obtain many youths, especially those with college or vocational school training, for their work force. On the other hand, an employer paying relatively high wages (at least for a nonmetropolitan area) will likely attract a sizeable number of school leavers for his work force.

In summary, labor availability will undoubtedly remain an important locational attraction for nonmetropolitan areas. It will, however, become increasingly critical to understand the characteristics of the labor supply as well as the continuing adjustments being made in the area from which it is obtained.

Labor Skills

Manufacturing plants locating in nonmetropolitan areas are typically oriented to low-skilled or medium-skilled labor. Several writers have suggested that this orientation occurs as a result of the "routinization" of production processes.[4] This routinization enables the "filtering down" of industries from metropolitan to nonmetropolitan areas. Despite the primary orientation to low- or medium-skilled workers, some plants may require a certain number of more highly skilled workers such as machinists, engineers, or electricians. In the past, such workers may have been transferred to the area from elsewhere; however, there has been an increasing tendency for these needs to be fulfilled by local or regional vocational training programs. Indeed, it appears that nonmetropolitan areas of the South have especially benefitted from training programs provided at low or no cost to either employees or employers. It is likely that nonmetropolitan areas which offer comprehensive and well-supported training programs will continue to enjoy a locational advantage over areas which have not established such programs or which have not effectively coordinated course offerings with employer needs.

Labor Productivity and Unionization

Many nonmetropolitan manufacturers believe that their employees provide a greater level of output per unit cost than employees in large urban areas. The extent to which this higher level of productivity in nonmetropolitan areas actually occurs is difficult to assess. Moreover, the productivity of nonmetropolitan employees undoubtedly varies regionally as well as among industry types.

It appears that some manufacturers believe that productivity is associated with labor turnover and absenteeism. These manufacturers feel that nonmetropolitan employees possess a stronger "work ethic" than their counterparts in metropolitan areas and are thus more dependable.

The absence of labor unions is also considered a contributing factor to productivity by many nonmetropolitan employers. The possibility of avoiding labor unions remains a highly attractive consideration to these employers, and unionization of manufacturing employees has not yet occurred in many nonmetropolitan communities. Indeed, much of the recent manufacturing growth in nonmetropolitan areas has occurred in "right-to-work" states, and despite organized labor's attempts to convince the federal government to eliminate or modify "right-to-work" laws, several state legislatures have recently considered their establishment.[5] Moreover, it appears that employers are realizing that if their pay-scale and fringe benefits are sufficiently attractive, employees are less likely to unionize. In the long run, organized labor will undoubtedly continue its efforts to establish itself in nonmetropolitan areas, while many manufacturers will continue to seek areas which are nonunionized.

Transportation

The construction of a network of interstate highways has been a major contributing force to nonmetropolitan industrialization. With the construction of these highways, manufacturers have been able to locate at greater distances from metropolitan areas but, at the same time, have maintained the ability to ship their products quickly and economically to markets in these areas.

Rail service is also an important consideration for many manufacturers, and many nonmetropolitan communities have benefitted from their location on a rail line. There is, nevertheless, growing alarm among many small towns over the increasing occurrence of branch-line abandonment. Local officials and businesses are concerned not only about increased transportation costs brought by rail abandonment to existing businesses, but also about the effect abandonment will have on the town's ability to attract new businesses, especially manufacturing, in the future.[6] These concerns are undoubtedly legitimate; nevertheless, there appears to have been a tendency for railroad companies to let many of the lines they wish to abandon deteriorate to such a condition that existing rail-using businesses switch to truck transportation, despite the higher cost. The trend appears to be in the direction of an increasing number of rail abandonments, especially among financially troubled railroads, and rail service as a locational attraction will decrease for many small nonmetropolitan communities.[7]

Increased costs for gasoline may also reduce the locational attractiveness of nonmetropolitan communities. These increased costs could lead to an end of the advantages brought about by interstate highways. In classical Weberian terms, if the transport cost penalties resulting from high gasoline prices become so great that they are not offset by labor and other advantages in nonmetropolitan areas, the locational attractiveness of these areas will undoubtedly decline. Moreover, increased gasoline prices may restrict the ability of nonmetropolitan employees to commute long distances to work. The extent to which these higher prices will discourage commuting should be an important topic of concern to persons investigating nonmetropolitan industrialization, but, to date, this topic has received little attention.

A third transportation factor is airline service. The absence of scheduled airline service (passenger and freight) may limit the ability of nonmetropolitan areas to attract new industries. Some companies may refuse to consider a location beyond a reasonable distance from an airport with regularly scheduled service or one which can accommodate small, business-type jets. For many firms, however, regularly scheduled airline service is only a minor consideration, and nonmetropolitan communities with airports which can accommodate smaller aircraft are in a relatively favorable position.

Markets

The absence of a sizeable internal market has historically been a constraining factor to nonmetropolitan industrialization. In the absence of this market, most manufacturing industries locating in nonmetropolitan areas have been export-oriented. The extent to which the market constraint will continue to be a discouraging factor to nonmetropolitan industrialization is open to question. On the one hand, many nonmetropolitan areas have experienced a reversal of the population declines occurring in the first half of the 20th century. During the 1960s and especially the 1970s, population increases and net inmigration have been widely documented for nonmetropolitan America.[8] These population gains could lead to the development of a sizeable internal market. On the other hand, by definition, once a nonmetropolitan community exceeds 50,000 population, it is no longer nonmetropolitan. Thus, while internal markets may become large in and around these communities, if the place exceeds 50,000, neither it or the county in which it is located will be nonmetropolitan.

Environmental Considerations

Nonmetropolitan America has generally been relatively free of the serious water and air pollutionn problems which have plagued many large urbanized areas. Nevertheless, a number of industries which discharge large quantities of air or water effluents, or which accumulate solid waste materials through processing, are located in nonmetropolitan areas where basic raw materials occur.

The continued attractiveness of nonmetropolitan areas for resource-oriented and other industries will be influenced by water and air quality standards established by the U.S. Congress. Industries are no longer able to discharge large quantities of effluents into the nation's air and streams, and both metropolitan and nonmetropolitan industries have been encouraged and, in some instances, forced to reduce the amount of pollutants discharged.

The establishment of effluent guidelines may tend to enhance the attractiveness of nonmetropolitan areas for industry. For example, 1977 amendments to the national Clean Air Act specify that states designate air quality control regions.[9] These regions can be divided into various nonattainment, attainment, or unclassified portions. Portions designated in the nonattainment category are those which do not meet national ambient air quality standards. If the national standards are not met, procedures must be developed to insure compliance at a specified future date. Additionally, the amendments to the Clean Air Act specify that, except under certain predetermined conditions, no major new construction will be allowed in a nonattainment area if the new facility emits pollutants for which a national ambient air quality standard is exceeded in the area. Since metropolitan areas are more likely to be classified as nonattainment areas than are nonmetropolitan ones,[10] there may be additional incentives for industry to locate in nonmetropolitan areas. Nonetheless, while the designation of air quality attainment areas may contribute to the movement of industries to nonmetropolitan areas, the recency of the 1977 amendments to the Clean Air Act precludes the measurement of any industrial migration which may have occurred in response to the amended law.

Energy

The rate structure for electric power and natural gas is very complex, varying both through time and from place to place. While utility rates are significant considerations for many industries and critical ones for some, the actual availability of energy supplies has become an increasingly important location factor. Unfortunately, very little research comparing the relative vulnerability of nonmetropolitan areas to metropolitan ones with reference to energy availability and costs has been undertaken.

Although the locational response of industries to variations in energy supplies and costs from metropolitan to nonmetropolitan areas has received little documentation, it is clear that much of America's current and future energy resources occur in nonmetropolitan areas. Oil and gas have long been extracted in nonmetropolitan America, and coal is mined chiefly in rural areas of Appalachia, the Midwest, and the Northern Great Plains. Mining has been the primary economic activity in many of these areas, and the attempt to reduce the nation's dependence upon foreign energy sources will probably contribute to further nonmetropolitan growth in mining regions, especially those in the western states. Additionally, because of space requirements, much of the future development in large-scale solar and wind energy complexes may occur in nonmetropolitan areas.

LOCAL COMMUNITY INFLUENCES

Housing

The absence of suitable housing for employees can be a discouraging factor to nonmetropolitan industrialization. The lack of suitable middle-income housing, either rental or for sale, is a problem in many small communities, and can be particularly critical when key personnel must be transferred from company plants elsewhere.

Where existing housing is available in nonmetropolitan areas, costs are generally lower than in many large cities. Construction costs for new housing, however, are frequently similar to those in metropolitan areas. Moreover, because wages are typically lower in nonmetropolitan areas, the ability of employees to purchase $40,000 to $50,000 new homes is restricted. To a certain extent, this difficulty has been reduced by the availability of low-interest loans from governmental agencies such as the Farmer's Home Administration and by low-cost mobile homes and modular housing. On balance, a shortage of housing will probably continue to restrict the locational attractiveness of nonmetropolitan communities.

Developed Sites and Parks

The presence of developed industrial sites or parks will probably become an increasingly important consideration for many industries seeking a non-metropolitan location.[11] In general, a developed site or park is one where legal questions concerning the industrial use of the property have been resolved, necessary grading or leveling completed, arrangements for water, sewerage, and utility connections made, and road access provided. Specific sites or lots within industrial parks are often made available at reasonable cost, and they can enable an industry to begin operations more quickly. Because many communities offer developed sites, towns without one or more developed industrial sites may find themselves automatically excluded from consideration by prospective industries. The desirability of industrial parks is somewhat more questionable inasmuch as some companies may object to the regulations imposed at such parks. Moreover, industrial parks are expensive to establish, and only the larger nonmetropolitan communities can typically afford them.

Available Buildings

The availability of an existing building has frequently been promoted as a locational asset in nonmetropolitan areas. As with sites, existing buildings can enable an industry to begin operations more quickly, and the costs of purchasing an existing building may be less than those of erecting a new one. Some communities have attempted to capitalize on this locational incentive and have constructed "speculative" buildings. The communities then offer the buildings for sale or lease to new industries. To date, very little systematic investigation of the effectiveness of speculative buildings as a locational attraction for nonmetropolitan communities has been undertaken; however, the available evidence suggests that such incentives have generally been successful, especially in the larger nonmetropolitan communities.[12] Existing studies nevertheless indicate that speculative buildings will not be sufficient to attract new industry to communities lacking the basic locational resources, such as a favorable labor supply, adequate transportation facilities, etc.

Community Livability and Leadership

Community livability is undoubtedly an important factor contributing to the movement of manufacturing to some nonmetropolitan areas. The desire to avoid real and perceived problems in large urban areas has led a number of companies to seek locations where these problems can be avoided, and nonmetropolitan America is perceived to offer favorable living situations.[13]

Nonmetropolitan communities, however, are not similarly endowed in terms of the advantages they offer new industry. Community attitudes and attributes tend to vary from one place to another. Some communities are extremely anxious to attract new industry, while others have very little desire to do so. Moreover, some communities are more favorably endowed with regard to external ecologic attributes, such as nearness to SMSAs, natural resources, and transportation routes, as well as to internal attributes, such as available housing, adequate water supply and sewerage facilities, industrial sites and buildings, etc.

Many observers feel that the development of these internal attributes will continue to be a critical factor in determining which nonmetropolitan communities experience manufacturing growth.[14] The development of these attributes requires dedicated leaders who are willing to spend both time and money in the pursuit of community objectives. Unfortunately, a willingness by local leaders to improve community attributes is not always sufficient. Expanded water systems, new housing, and other improvements are beyond the limited fiscal capabilities of many communities, and outside funds must be sought, usually from the federal government. Obtaining these funds requires the submission of applications (with no assurance of success), many of which are long, tedious, and difficult for community leaders to comprehend and complete. To ease these difficulties, federal, state, and regional organizations offer training seminars and "how-to" programs to local community leaders. Additionally, some nonmetropolitan communities, especially the larger ones, have hired full-time personnel to assist in handling the complex responsibilities associated with local improvement.

Communities possessing the required leadership have frequently been successful in obtaining federal grants, improving community livability, and attracting new industries. On the other hand, many nonmetropolitan communities have not been able to satisfactorily meet the challenge. For these communities, local leadership becomes an even more critical factor influencing the location of new industry.

SUMMARY

The influences encouraging and discouraging nonmetropolitan industrialization have been many and diverse. In this chapter, some of the more important regional and community influences have been discussed. Labor, transportation, market, environmental, and energy considerations have been significant influences at the regional level, while housing, industrial sites and parks, available buildings, and community livability and leadership are noteworthy at the local level.

Each of the factors will probably continue to influence the nature and extent of nonmetropolitan industrialization in the future. The availability of low-cost labor, for example, will serve as a primary locational attraction for many nonmetropolitan areas. Nevertheless, because many nonmetropolitan areas are rather sparsely populated, it will become increasingly important to obtain reliable information about the various sources of labor supply. Regarding labor skills, nonmetropolitan areas which offer comprehensive and well-supported training programs should continue to enjoy an advantage over areas which do not have such programs. The presence of nonunionized labor will also be an important consideration for many prospective manufacturers. Proximity to an interstate highway has been a major contributing force to industrialization in many nonmetropolitan communities and undoubtedly will continue to be in the future. On the other hand, the abandonment of railroad branch-lines may restrict nonmetropolitan industrialization in some areas. Increased costs of gasoline may also reduce the locational attractiveness of nonmetropolitan communities. The absence of a sizeable internal market has historically been a constraining factor to nonmetropolitan industrialization. Recent population gains in nonmetropolitan America could, however, lead to the development of a sizeable internal market. The establishment of air and water quality guidelines may contribute to the movement of industries to nonmetropolitan areas, but the extent to which this migration will occur is uncertain. The attempt to reduce the nation's dependence upon foreign energy sources should lead to some industrialization in nonmetropolitan regions rich in energy resources.

At the local level, the absence of suitable housing will probably continue to restrict the locational attractiveness of nonmetropolitan communities. Conversely, the presence of developed industrial sites, speculative buildings, and overall community livability should contribute to the attractiveness of many communities. Finally, community leadership will remain an important variable influencing the location of nonmetropolitan manufacturing.

NOTES

[1] An extensive listing of locational considerations is provided in H. M. Conway and Linda Liston, eds., *Industrial Facilities Planning* (Atlanta: Conway Publications, 1976), pp. 303-309. Also, see David Smith, *Industrial Location* (New York: John Wiley & Sons, 1971), pp. 23-94; Henry Hunker, *Industrial Development* (Lexington, Massachusetts: D. C. Heath, 1974), pp. 83-188; and "Rapid Geo-Economic Changes Pose Elusive Targets for Facility Planners," *Site Selection Handbook*, Vol. 23 (1978), pp. 80-83.

[2] Richard Lonsdale, "Rural Labor as an Attraction for Industry," *AIDC Journal*, Vol. 4 (1969), pp. 11-17; A. Wade Martin, "Problems and Advantages of Rural Labor for Industrial Operations," in *Rural Development Problems and Advantages of Rural*

Locations for Industrial Plants (Raleigh: Agricultural Policy Institute, North Carolina State University, 1970), pp. 49–57; and Rodney Erickson, "The Filtering-Down Process: Industrial Location in a Nonmetropolitan Area," *Professional Geographer*, Vol. 28 (1976), pp. 259–260.

[3] Potential sources of labor supplies are more thoroughly discussed in Steven Kale, "Labor Supplies for Rural Manufacturing Plants," unpublished Ph.D. dissertation, University of Nebraska, 1978.

[4] Erickson, op. cit., note 3, p. 254; and Wilbur Thompson, "The Economic Base of Urban Problems," in Neil Chamberlain, ed., *Contemporary Economic Issues* (Homewood, Illinois: Richard Irving, 1969), pp. 1–47.

[5] As of January 1, 1978, 20 states had right-to-work laws. Most of these states are in the South and the Great Plains. See "The Fifty Legislative Climates," *Industrial Development*, Vol. 147 (1978), p. 4.

[6] William Black and James Runke, *The States and Rural Rail Preservation* (Lexington: Council of State Governments, 1975), pp. 46–53.

[7] As of July 1977, approximately 20,000 miles (10%) of the Nation's rail mileage was identified for pending or prospective abandonment. Much of this mileage is in nonmetropolitan areas. See *Rail Systems Diagram* (Washington, D.C.: Interstate Commerce Commission, September 1977), p. 10.

[8] U.S. Department of Agriculture, Economic Research Service, *The Revival of Population Growth in Nonmetropolitan America*, by Calvin Beale, ERS-605 (1975); and Peter Morrison and Judith Wheeler, "Rural Renaissance in America? The Revival of Population Growth in Remote Areas," *Population Bulletin*, Vol. 31 (1976).

[9] U.S. Congress, Senate, Committee on Environment and Public Works, *The Clean Air Act as Amended August 1977*, 95th Cong., 1st Session, November 1977, pp. 10–12.

[10] U.S. Environmental Protection Agency, "National Ambient Air Quality Standards, States Attainment Status," *Federal Register*, Vol. 43 (March 3, 1978), pp. 8962–9057.

[11] An evaluation of the factors contributing to the "success" of industrial parks in nonmetropolitan Ohio is provided in Fred Hitzhusen and Tom Gray, "Factors Related to 'Success' of Industrial Parks in Nonmetropolitan Communities," *AIDC Journal*, Vol. 12 (1977), pp. 15–31.

[12] Robert Cleaves, "The Role of Speculative Buildings in the Industrial Development Effort of Small Communities," unpublished thesis, Industrial Development Institute, University of Oklahoma, 1971; and Sharon Elliott, *Speculative Shell Buildings: An Incentive for New Industry* (Jefferson City: Missouri Division of Commerce and Industrial Development, July 1976), pp. 7–8.

[13] Recent population increases in nonmetropolitan areas (see note 8) support the notion that favorable living environments are perceived to occur in nonmetropolitan America. Also, see Don Dillman and Russell Dobash, *Preferences for Community Living and Their Implications for Population Redistribution*, Bulletin 764 (Pullman: Agricultural Experiment Station, Washington State University, 1972); James Zuiches and Glenn Fuguitt, "Residential Preferences: Implications for Population Distribution in Nonmetropolitan Areas," Chapter 2 in S. M. Mazie, ed., *Research Reports, Volume V, Population Distribution and Policy* (Washington, D.C.: Commission on Population Growth and the American Future, 1973), pp. 620–630; and Larry Blackwood and Edwin Carpenter, "The Importance of Anti-Urbanism in Determining Residential Preferences and Migration Patterns," *Rural Sociology*, Vol. 43 (1978), pp. 31–47.

[14] The relative importance of ecologic factors and of internal factors over which community leaders may exercise some control is examined in James Williams, Andrew Sofranko, and Brenda Root, "Change Agents and Industrial Development in Small Towns," *Journal of the Community Development Society*, Vol. 8 (1977), pp. 19–29.

Chapter 4

CHARACTERISTICS OF BRANCH PLANTS ATTRACTED TO NONMETROPOLITAN AREAS

Rodney A. Erickson and Thomas R. Leinbach

Any examination of the nonmetropolitan industrialization of the United States must inevitably focus on the kind of manufacturing plants attracted to these areas. This chapter analyzes the characteristics of branch plants established in four states in the 1967–1976 period. The analysis focuses on the "filter-down" phenomenon, based on the proposition that industries filter down through the system of urban places from cities of greater to lesser industrial sophistication.[1] However, there continues to be a paucity of empirical information regarding the characteristics and contribution of filtering-down establishments in nonmetropolitan areas.[2] This is surprising in view of the "micropolitan turnaround" credited by many to nonmetropolitan industrialization.[3]

In this chapter, several elements of the filtering-down process are expanded.[4] These include the locational pattern of corporate headquarters and main plants in relation to branch plants established in nonmetropolitan areas, the characteristics of branch plants with respect to products and production processes, the locational pattern of branch plants in nonmetropolitan areas and the associated characteristics of communities selected for operation, and the importance of branch plants' contribution relative to the expansion of area manufacturing employment in general.[5]

Data regarding branch plant localizations in nonmetropolitan areas of four states are analyzed on an aggregate as well as a comparative basis. The results suggest considerable pattern similarity in the filtering-down process across geographic regions. Recent evidence indicates that branch plants of metropolitan manufacturing corporations have been more significant in contributing to employment growth and stability in nonmetropolitan areas than previously reported.

THE FILTERING–DOWN PROCESS

Manufacturing activity, like most other economic sectors in the national economy, has become increasingly dominated by corporate enterprises over the past several decades.[6] Corporate organizations engaged in manufacturing have tended to grow functionally more complex, as well as larger in size. A growing literature in managerial economics suggests that increasing organizational size has become a more prominent goal of management than profit maximization.[7]

Coupled with management's prevailing organizational goals, fluctuations in demand (in part, a reflection of a rapid rate of technological change and obsolescence) have fostered increased organizational size and functional diversity.[8] In advanced economies, many products are increasingly short-lived, competing with a large number of similar products.

Many products and services proceed through a staggered life cycle. Hirsch has noted that these changes in the rates of growth of product industries "occur in a fairly systematic fashion, and are therefore predictable."[9] He has used the concept of the "product cycle" in examining the expansion paths of product industries. A typical product life cycle may be divided arbitrarily into three phases—early, growth, and mature.[10]

The "early" phase of the product cycle is typically characterized by low capital intensity in relatively short production runs with rapidly changing technology. Producers prefer to keep down their investment in fixed assets. Dependence on external economies and large-scale subcontracting are evidenced among a limited number of firms in a sellers' market. Scientific and engineering skills represent the critical human inputs.

In the "growth" phase, individual producers face increasing price elasticity of demand. Methods of mass production are gradually introduced, thereby increasing the capital–labor ratio in production. This phase is characterized by a growing number of firms as product information spreads. Intra-industry competition reduces prices, which leads to many business casualties and a growth in mergers and vertical integration. Management skills represent the critical human inputs in the growth phase.

In the "mature" phase, production technology tends to be stable, characterized by long-runs and few innovations of importance. Capital intensity remains relatively high due to the large amounts of specialized equipment. The buyer's market leads to a declining number of firms, and large capital requirements for entry into the product market. Unskilled and semi-skilled labor become the critical human inputs in the mature product phase.

The relative importance of individual production factors therefore changes in each phase of the product cycle (Fig. 1). The filtering-down process is based on the notion that corporate organizations respond to changing critical

PRODUCTION FACTORS	PRODUCT CYCLE PHASE		
	early	growth	mature
MANAGEMENT	2	1	3
SCIENTIFIC – ENGINEERING KNOWHOW	1	2	3
UNSKILLED LABOR	3	2	1
EXTERNAL ECONOMIES	1	2	3
CAPITAL	3	1ᵃ	1ᵃ

1ᵃconsidered to be of equal importance.

Fig. 1. The relative importance of various production factors in different phases of the product cycle (in rank order of importance).

input requirements by altering the geographic location of production to minimize costs and thereby insure competitiveness in a tightening market.

Thompson has reasoned that when a business organization begins production of a new product, the site of production is likely to be the metropolitan area where its main plants and principal management functions are located.[11] Within the metropolitan area, the critical external economies and skilled labor are widely available. However, if and when the product can be manufactured using routinized processes, increasing competition may force the original production unit to be replaced by larger-scale branch plants in smaller cities where labor or other cost savings are available.[12] Thus, manufacturing activity filters down to locations in the "urban field" of the metropolitan area wherein the organizational headquarters are located, or into distant urban fields or even interstitial nonmetropolitan areas at some distance from metropolitan population concentrations.[13] Increasingly, corporations manufacture multiple products in multiple branch plants in multiple locations.

There is thought to be a pattern underlying the spatial distribution of functions and products amongst plants, and the interactions between plants.[14] Those branch plants closest to the main factory or corporate headquarters appear to be the smallest and least independent, requiring constant managerial attention and often maintaining direct flows of materials with the main plant.[15] They tend to be feasible only within a relatively short radius of the main plant.[16] More distant are the intermediate, semi-independent branches, which have some management and other services on the spot, and usually perform parts of processes. Most distant are the larger, self-contained, and virtually independent branches which may duplicate all or part of the parent factory's product range or perhaps become the firm's sole manufacturing unit for certain products.[17]

The most distant plants may also be situated to supply regional markets.[18] These larger, distant plants tend to have standardized products whose specifications and technology have reached a stage in which they need little change.[19] Similarly, the range of managerial functions represented in these plants is narrow, often being limited to little more than production engineering. Marketing, purchasing, and research and development in particular are likely to be handled centrally at corporate headquarters and main plants located in metropolitan areas.

DATA SOURCES

The analysis of the filtering-down process is based upon information regarding branch plant localizations in four states during the 1967–1976 period. Data were gathered for nonmetropolitan counties of Kentucky, New Mexico, Vermont, and Wisconsin. While data availability influenced the selection of these particular areas, these data provide the basis for a comparative analysis of the filtering-down phenomenon in parts of four different regions with substantial nonmetropolitan populations—the South/ Appalachia, Southwest, New England, and the Upper Midwest.

Data on individual branch plant localizations were obtained from state government agencies, including industrial development and business research departments. Such agencies typically collect and disseminate information on both new plants and plant expansions in their respective states. New branch plants are generally identified using sources such as unemployment compensation records, annual reports of corporations filed with state agencies, tax records, inspection reports for occupational safety and other governmental regulations, and field reports from agency representatives and local Chambers of Commerce or other business associations. These data tend to be very reliable in nonmetropolitan areas, where the addition of a new plant is not only noted, but frequently much-heralded, especially in the case of larger plants.

In addition to the identification and location of new branch plants, information on the plant's principal product(s) and the original level of employment was provided. The identification of the branch plant's parent corporation and its location was made using state agency records and, in some cases, industrial directories. Data on the current (1976) level of employment in individual plants were obtained from industrial directories, state agency records, or direct correspondence with management at the branch plants or parent corporations.

In the following analysis, the term "branch plant" refers only to those plants with corporate headquarters/main plants located in metropolitan areas. Inasmuch as the analysis is focused on the filtering-down process, branch operations of nonmetropolitan firms are excluded. The analysis is restricted to those plants which had five or more employees when established during the 1967-1976 period.[20] In addition, the analysis includes only those plants which were still operating in 1976. The difficulty of obtaining information on (or from) defunct plants precluded their inclusion in the analysis. Thus, the level of employment associated with branch plants operating in 1976 underestimates the total number of jobs created during the study period.[21]

EMPIRICAL ANALYSIS

During the 1967-1976 period, a total of 264 branch plants was established in the four nonmetropolitan study areas. Differences among areas regarding the number of plants were considerable: Wisconsin and Kentucky accounted for 80% of the branch plants which were identified (107 and 106 plants, respectively), while the remainder established operations in New Mexico (32 plants) and Vermont (19 plants). These plants ranged in size from 5 to 1,300 employees, and were established in both rural and urban places ranging in size from less than 100 to nearly 50,000 population. The following analysis attempts to extract some elements of order from the complex patterns of locational relationships and plant functions characterizing the filtering-down process.

Corporate Headquarters and Branch Plant Locational Relationships

Corporate headquarters of manufacturing firms are widely distributed geographically, with some headquarters representation in all metropolitan areas. Some metropolitan areas, however, have far greater concentrations of corporate headquarters, and consequently have a higher probability of spawning branch plants. If corporate enterprises in these metropolitan areas are indeed establishing branch plants, a significant degree of filtering-down activity should be evidenced on the nonmetropolitan periphery of such metropolitan agglomerations.

In the United States, the region of greatest corporate activity in the manufacturing sector has traditionally been the Manufacturing Belt, where the concentration of manufacturing employment has been the highest in the nation. This area, as initially delimited by de Geer and later modified by Pred, covers the Northeast quadrant of the United States stretching from St. Louis and Minneapolis on the western edge to Baltimore and Boston on the eastern edge.[22] This region has traditionally been the location for an overwhelming majority of the headquarters of the larger manufacturing corporations.[23] While the evidence suggests that corporate headquarters functions are increasingly decentralizing to new metropolitan areas of the South and West, a major proportion of manufacturing corporate activity continues to be concentrated in the Manufacturing Belt.[24] Thus, nonmetropolitan areas on the periphery of the Manufacturing Belt are likely to be attractive sites into which branch plants may be filtered down.

Empirical analysis indicates that the vast majority of the branch plants localized in the four nonmetropolitan study areas have corporate headquarters located within the Manufacturing Belt (Figs. 2-5). Of the 255 branch plants with corporate headquarters located in metropolitan areas of the U.S. (nine are foreign corporations), 211 branch plants were spawned from metropolitan headquarters located in the American Manufacturing Belt (Table 1). This figure is not particularly surprising given the focus on Kentucky, Wisconsin, and Vermont nonmetropolitan areas; however, this predominance holds even in the case of New Mexico, where 19 of 31 domestically-owned branch plants have corporate headquarters located in the Manufacturing Belt—a considerable distance from the nonmetropolitan area (Table 1).[25] Thus it would not be surprising to find among the branch plants of other distant regions numerous representatives of corporations headquartered in Chicago, New York, Cleveland, Detroit, and Pittsburgh as well as other metropolitan areas of the Manufacturing Belt.

Given the role of major metropolitan areas of the Manufacturing Belt in spawning branch plants, the disproportionate share of plants located in nonmetropolitan Kentucky and Wisconsin is better explained. Both areas are relatively large areas immediately adjacent to (and partially within) the Manufacturing Belt. These areas are likely to be particularly attractive locations for branch plants, permitting management to control many of the plant's activities and permitting a reasonable transport time for intrafirm integration of production processes.

Only about 14% of all branch plants in the study filtered down to locations in the urban field, a much smaller proportion than would be expected based on Thompson's previously stated notions of the filtering-down process (Table 2).[26] Less than 40% of the branch plants filtered down to nonmetropolitan locations within 250 miles, and approximately 60% were located within 500 miles of the corporate headquarters and main plants (Table 2).

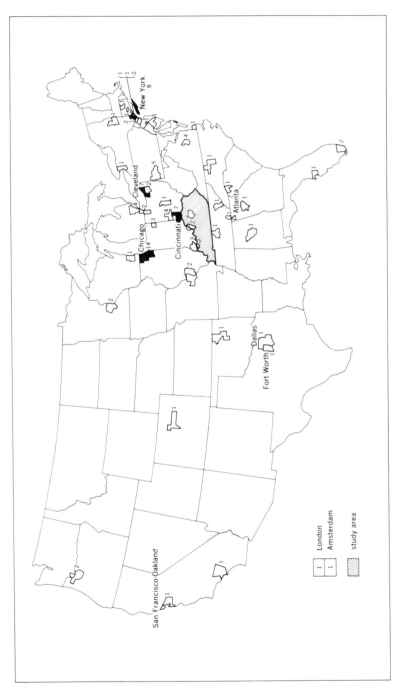

Fig. 2. Metropolitan location of corporate headquarters of branch plants established in nonmetropolitan Kentucky, 1967–1976.

63

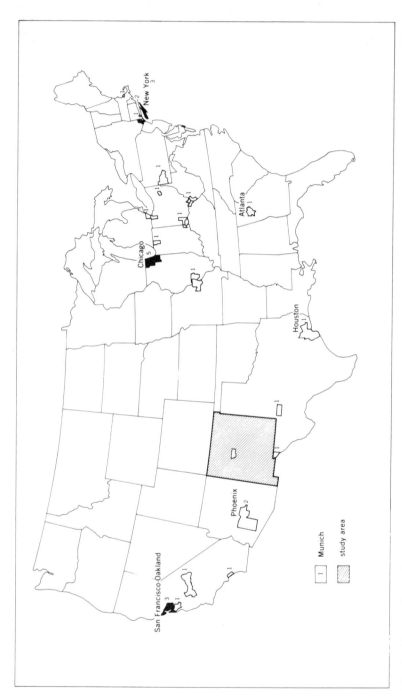

Fig. 3. Metropolitan location of corporate headquarters of branch plants established in nonmetropolitan New Mexico, 1967–1976.

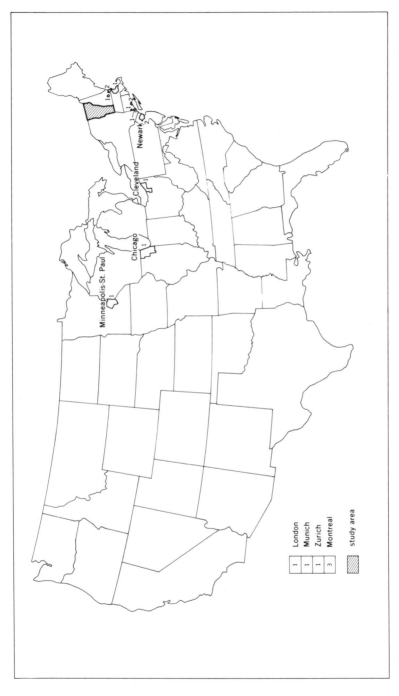

Fig. 4. Metropolitan location of corporate headquarters of branch plants established in Vermont, 1967–1976.

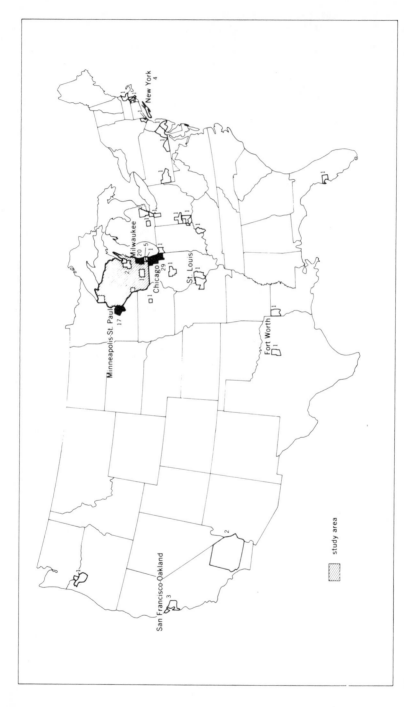

Fig. 5. Metropolitan location of corporate headquarters of branch plants established in nonmetropolitan Wisconsin, 1967-1976.

Table 1. Major Manufacturing Belt Metropolitan Locations of Corporate Headquarters for Branch Plants Located in Nonmetropolitan Study Areas, 1967–1976

Headquarters location	Number of plants in nonmetropolitan areas				
	Kentucky	New Mexico	Vermont	Wisconsin	Total
Chicago	14	5	1	28	48
Milwaukee	1	0	0	20	21
Minneapolis-St. Paul	2	0	1	17	20
New York	8	3	0	4	15
Cincinnati	7	1	0	1	9
Cleveland	7	0	1	0	8
Detroit	4	0	0	3	7
Pittsburgh	5	1	0	1	7
St. Louis	2	1	0	1	4
Toledo	2	1	0	1	4
Subtotal	52	12	3	76	143
Other Manufacturing Belt metropolitan areas	29	7	10	22	68
Non-Manufacturing Belt metropolitan areas (domestic)	23	12	0	9	44
Foreign	2	1	6	0	9
Total	106	32	19	107	264

Table 2. Distance of Branch Plants from Corporate Headquarters in Nonmetropolitan Study Areas

Distance from corporate headquarters (in miles)	Number of branch plants				
	Kentucky	New Mexico	Vermont	Wisconsin	Total
0–100	7	1	2	26	36
101–250	14	1	7	38	60
251–500	39	0	4	22	65
501–	46	30	6	21	103
Total	106	32	19	107	264

There are, however, some notable differences which distinguish the filtering distances among the four nonmetropolitan areas. Wisconsin's nonmetropolitan area is situated between the large urban consolidation on the western shore of Lake Michigan stretching from Chicago to Green Bay, and the Twin Cities (Minneapolis-St. Paul) metropolitan area to the west. Thus, there is evidence of plant localization at shorter distances, and a strong role played by corporations headquartered on the immediate periphery of the area. Kentucky is also strongly influenced by corporate headquarters located in the Manufacturing Belt stretching along its northern border, with less influence from corporations in southern metropolitan areas than might be expected. However, most plants have been located at distances greater than those usually considered in the context of urban fields. Vermont presents an interesting example of a filtering-down pattern confined primarily to New England and Quebec (Montreal) manufacturing corporations. Again, its location outside of the urban fields of major metropolitan areas precludes extensive filtering-down at short distances. New Mexico, on the other hand, is primarily influenced by corporate headquarters in the Manufacturing Belt and in California metropolitan areas, with a minimal level of plants headquartered in the newer and smaller metropolitan areas which surround it; consequently, virtually all of its branch plants are located at rather long distances from their metropolitan headquarters and main plants.

There is also evidence of a relationship between the employment size of branch plants and the distance from the branch plant to the corporate headquarters and main plants (Table 3). When the three largest branch plants (significant outlying values in the distribution) are excluded, the mean employment size of the branch plants increases from 70 employees for those plants which are operated within the urban fields of the corporate headquarters to 117 employees for those plants which are located more than 500

Table 3. Branch Plant Employment and Distance from Corporate Headquarters

Distance from corporate headquarters (in miles)	Mean employment of branch plants
100 or less	70
101–250	95[a]
251–500	112[b]
more than 500	117

[a]One branch plant (1,300 employees) excluded from the distribution.
[b]Two branch plants (1,050 and 1,263 employees) excluded from the distribution.

miles from the corporate headquarters/main plants. This size progression helps to explain why Wisconsin, characterized by rather short headquarters to branch plant distances, exhibits the smallest average plant size (85 employees) and why New Mexico and Kentucky, characterized by relatively longer distances, exhibit larger average plant sizes (99 employees and 162 employees, respectively).

Sectoral Distribution of Branch Plants

The localization of branch plants has been described previously as a process in which metropolitan corporations seek out nonmetropolitan sites for establishing branch plants so as to secure relative reductions in the costs of production when methods become routinized. The major items where cost savings can be achieved are labor and fixed costs of operation (land, facilities, taxes, etc.). The typical nonmetropolitan branch plant is far less likely to be either dependent upon or influenced by the area's physical resource base (except in the case of some branch plants serving regional or national markets in the food and wood products sectors) than the area's existing set of establishments. Thus, it is not to be expected that the sectoral distribution of branch plants would mirror the pattern of existing manufacturing activity in nonmetropolitan areas.[27]

Indeed, the sectoral distribution of branch plants is far different from the existing sectoral distribution of manufacturing establishments in the nonmetropolitan study areas (Table 4). This divergence exists for the aggregate nonmetropolitan manufacturing distribution as well as for each of the four nonmetropolitan areas individually.

Likelihood ratio tests were used to compare the statistical significance of the apparent differences in the sectoral distributions.[28] The aggregate distribution, as well as that for each nonmetropolitan area, exhibits a statistically significant difference in the structural pattern.[29] This nonparametric statistical test also identifies those sectors providing the greatest contribution to the observed differences in structure.

There is considerable uniformity across areas in the types of branch plants overrepresented and underrepresented in comparison to the existing industrial structure. In nonmetropolitan Kentucky, paper products, chemicals, rubber and plastics, fabricated metals, and electrical equipment are overrepresented, while the traditional resource-based sectors—food products and wood products—are greatly underrepresented among the plants. In nonmetropolitan New Mexico, apparel and chemicals are significantly overrepresented. In Vermont, textiles and electrical equipment are overrepresented. In nonmetropolitan Wisconsin, the most overrepresented sector is electrical equipment, followed by fabricated metals, apparel, and printing. The traditionally dominant manufacturing sectors—food products and wood products—are disproportionately absent among the sectors represented by these branch plants.

Thus, branch plants are typically producing products in the industry sectors characterized by substantial labor requirements. Textiles, apparel, fabricated

Table 4. Sectoral Distribution of Branch Plants and the Existing (1967) Industrial Structures of Nonmetropolitan Study Areas

Sector	Kentucky		New Mexico		Vermont		Wisconsin	
	Branch plants	Existing	Branch plants	Existing	Branch plants	Existing	Branch plants	Existing
20 Food products	1	270	3	101	1	111	10	1,024
21 Tobacco products	0	17	0	0	0	0	0	2
22 Textiles	2	18	0	1	2	14	2	26
23 Apparel	11	95	8	6	2	30	8	61
24 Wood products	6	532	3	84	3	284	5	719
25 Furniture	0	45	0	10	1	26	5	69
26 Paper & allied products	5	6	0	0	2	24	3	65
27 Printing	7	192	0	82	1	100	2	360
28 Chemicals	12	40	6	15	0	17	0	68
29 Petroleum products	2	11	1	5	0	1	0	9
30 Rubber & plastics	6	14	0	4	0	12	5	56
31 Leather products	4	15	0	4	0	7	2	59
32 Stone, clay & glass	4	146	2	56	0	118	1	201
33 Primary metals	2	17	1	4	0	13	1	53
34 Fabricated metals	12	74	2	10	0	35	20	188
35 Nonelectrical equipment	15	84	3	49	2	70	14	340
36 Electrical equipment	8	31	1	12	4	10	19	63
37 Transportation equipment	5	31	2	4	0	11	5	72
38 Instruments	2	5	0	1	0	5	2	21
39 Miscellaneous	2	29	0	19	1	28	3	107
Total	106	1,672	32	467	19	916	107	3,563

metals, and electrical equipment (electronics) are typical. Chemicals is a notable exception from this pattern, and may reflect corporate decisions to decentralize plants from densely populated metropolitan areas, difficulties in meeting metropolitan environmental regulations, or simply to serve better more distant regional markets.[30]

An interesting pattern also emerges when the relationship between the products of the branch plants and the location of the plant with respect to the corporate headquarters and main plant(s) is examined. Relatively few types of manufacturing activities dominate those plants which filtered down within the urban fields of their metropolitan main plants. Eleven of the 36 plants manufacture wearing apparel (clothing and shoes/accessories). Eight of the 10 plants filtering down to urban field locations in Kentucky, New Mexico, and Vermont manufacture wearing apparel or apparel accessories. Nine of the 36 plants manufacture or assemble electronic components, electronic instrumentation, or parts of other electrical equipment. Most of the remaining plants manufacture metal fabrications/machined parts or plastic extrusions. Nearly all of the products of these branch plants are closely tied to the production processes or products of the main plants.

The product distribution of plants shifts perceptibly with distance from the main plant(s) and corporate headquarters. While parts fabrication and assembly still retain a sizeable role at distances up to 250 miles from headquarters, the mix of products includes far more plants producing products directly for intermediate or final markets, e.g., paper products, machinery, mobile homes, and printing. Beyond the 500-mile radius from headquarters, products produced by the branch plants are characterized by a very high proportion of "finished" products such as food and animal feeds, chemicals, machinery, building and construction products, and complete items of electrical equipment.

The Distribution of Plants in Rural and Urban Places

For the past two decades, many geographers, economists, and regional development planners have argued for policy strategies that would channel public investment into the largest nonmetropolitan urban places. These arguments were based on the premise that only the largest nonmetropolitan urban places could take advantage of the scale economies in the provision of community infrastructure and the agglomeration economies necessary to attract industry and generate sustained economic growth. The branch plants of metropolitan corporations would presumably be attracted by such locational attributes. However, the data from this study do not support these conclusions in general.

It is clear that, in general, the large nonmetropolitan urban places do not account for the majority of branch plant localizations or the employment associated with them (Table 5). In Wisconsin, Kentucky, and Vermont, 70 to 95% of the employment is associated with locations in urban and rural places with less than 20,000 population. New Mexico is the only exception, where

Table 5. Branch Plants and Employment by Place Population Size Class[a]

Population size class	Kentucky			New Mexico			Vermont			Wisconsin		
	Number of plants	Employment	Percentage of total	Number of plants	Employment	Percentage of total	Number of plants	Employment	Percentage of total	Number of plants	Employment	Percentage of total
Rural places	30	3,401	19.9	3	141	4.4	11	673	37.8	47	3,330	36.8
Urban places:												
2,500–4,999	30	2,923	17.1	1	100	3.2	3	235	13.2	21	2,481	27.4
5,000–19,999	37	8,119	47.4	6	532	16.8	3	325	18.3	32	2,791	30.8
20,000–49,999	9	2,678	15.6	22	2,393	75.6	2	546	30.7	7	454	5.0
Total	106	17,121	100.0	32	3,166	100.0	19	1,779	100.0	107	9,056	100.0

[a]Employment is for 1976: population of places is taken from the *Census of Population* (1970).

over three-fourths of its branch plant employment is associated with locations in urban places with more than 20,000 population.

A previous survey-based study has shown that branch plants choose locations to avoid competition for an available labor force.[31] In addition, accessibility to the main plants and corporate headquarters, and accessibility to an expanded market area, were also cited. The pattern of the distribution of plants seems to conform to these locational factors.

For Vermont and Wisconsin, in which filtering-down of plants is accomplished over rather short distances, the relatively smaller sizes of plants involved requires a smaller labor supply area, especially given the relatively high nonmetropolitan population densities and the possibility of drawing upon extensive commuting fields. For Kentucky, in which the filtering-down process is accomplished over longer distances with average plant size nearly double that of Wisconsin, the need to maintain an adequate labor supply probably has the effect of encouraging branch plants to locate in intermediate-sized urban places. Alternatively, New Mexico, with relatively large plants filtered down over extensive distances, can probably assure an adequate labor supply only in the larger urban places of the area, given the extremely low population densities of the region (less than 10 persons per square mile in much of the nonmetropolitan area of the state).

Accessibility factors also appear to have impinged on the location decisions regarding branch plants (Fig. 6). In general, the distribution of plants in Kentucky follows closely the pattern of the Interstate Highway System, the

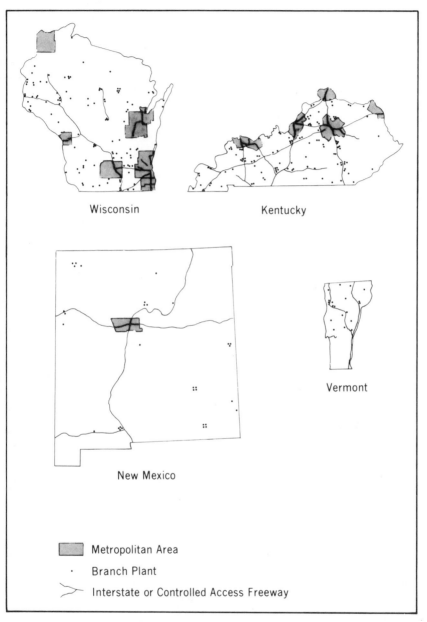

Wisconsin

Kentucky

New Mexico

Vermont

Metropolitan Area
· Branch Plant
Interstate or Controlled Access Freeway

Fig. 6. Location of branch plants in nonmetropolitan areas.

extensive Kentucky Parkway System, and the U.S. highways which feed into those systems. Similarly, Wisconsin and Vermont plants have located either along or with relatively short access distances to the Interstate or feeder highway systems. While New Mexico has relatively fewer firms located directly on the Interstate Highway System, all other plants have been located in places either along or at junctions of major U.S. highways. Most plant locations in the four regions thus have relatively easy access to either airfields or commercial air passenger service in cities along the major highway thorough-fares. While a majority of plants are located in places which are served by railway freight service, previous studies indicate that only a few plants are dependent upon it.[32]

The Contribution of Branch Plants to Manufacturing Employment Growth

The contribution of branch plants to nonmetropolitan manufacturing employment growth has been a topic of considerable debate in recent years. Previous research has found, for a limited set of nonmetropolitan com-munities, that expansions of existing plants and the creation of new in-digenous establishments were more important in employment increase than the addition of new branch plants.[33] Given the rather short duration of many products in advanced economies, other researchers have argued that many branch plants in nonmetropolitan areas will have a limited life-span, as corporations are likely to exploit the tax benefits or other incentives used to attract them and then leave after a few years with their facilities fully depreciated.[34] Other research has questioned the positive economic welfare (income) implications of the attraction of plants which hire predominantly unskilled and semiskilled workers at low wage levels.[35]

The data available within the context of this study can provide only limited additional information on some of these important topics. The data indicate that at least four branch plants closed in nonmetropolitan New Mexico and at least 12 plants closed in nonmetropolitan Wisconsin during the study period. While most closings were smaller branch plants, a few were relatively large and likely had a significant impact on their communities and surrounding areas. The only pattern evident in the timing of plant closings is that 1975 was a particularly bad year for nonmetropolitan manufacturing. Similarly, the rather steady number of new branch plants opened in each of the study years was noticeably interrupted only in 1975.

Overall, the filtering-down process was extremely important in contributing to manufacturing employment growth in each of the four nonmetropolitan study areas (Table 6). The employment contributions to individual com-munities (and their surrounding commuting areas) were frequently substantial, given the rather large contributions of these plants to aggregate manufacturing employment growth in each of the nonmetropolitan areas. Without the infusion of employment from branch plants, both Vermont and Wisconsin would have shown larger or substantial absolute manufacturing employment

Table 6. Total Manufacturing Employment Change (1967–1975) and Branch Plants' Employment (1976) in Nonmetropolitan Study Areas

Nonmetropolitan area	Total manufacturing employment				Employment in filtering-down plants
	1967	1975	Absolute change	Percentage change	
Kentucky	102,746	138,865	34,119	33	17,121
New Mexico	9,883	13,873	3,990	40	3,166
Vermont	44,280	39,579	–4,701	–11	1,779
Wisconsin	173,137	176,891	3,754	2	9,056

Source: Total manufacturing employment and employment change has been derived from data provided by the Bureau of Economic Analysis, U.S. Department of Commerce.

declines.[36] Thus, arguments that branch plants contribute little to aggregate nonmetropolitan manufacturing employment growth are not substantiated by this evidence.

CONCLUSIONS

Analysis of branch plant localization in the four study areas indicates that there are several important common pattern elements that characterize the filtering-down process as it affects nonmetropolitan regions. In addition, there are some notable differences in the pattern elements which also emerge, based largely on the location of the nonmetropolitan areas in relation to the focal areas of metropolitan corporate manufacturing concentration and the particular settlement features of the nonmetropolitan region itself.

Among the common elements is the overwhelming role which manufacturing corporate headquarters in the Manufacturing Belt play in the filtering-down process. Nearly 83% of all domestically owned branch plants established in the study regions were spawned from corporations headquartered in the Manufacturing Belt. Each of the four nonmetropolitan areas was differentiated by its ties to particular metropolitan centers or clusters of corporate manufacturing activity—to some extent, a function of distance and the area's regional orientation.

There is evidence that a pattern also exists with regard to distance from headquarters and plant size. Plants established within the urban fields or at shorter distances from the main plants and corporate headquarters are typically smaller and oriented to assembly, parts and accessories fabrication, or a portion of the production process which is closely tied to that of the main plant(s). Plants established at greater distances (several hundred miles or more) from the main plants/corporate headquarters are typically larger production units producing goods duplicating those produced in other plants of the organization and in "finished" products for both intermediate users and final consumers. Thus, there are differences in the average size of plant and the character of production in each of the four nonmetropolitan study areas.

The types (sectors) of industrial activity attracted to nonmetropolitan areas were remarkably similar in each of the study regions. Textiles, apparel, metal fabrication, and electrical equipment (electronics)—all industries with substantial labor inputs—dominated the filtering-down process irrespective of the region considered.

The analysis reveals that the localization of branch plants from metropolitan areas has made a significant contribution to nonmetropolitan area manufacturing employment growth. Except in New Mexico, the vast majority of plants has been located in and around those nonmetropolitan urban and rural places with less than 20,000 population, the particular size of community apparently depending upon the labor requirements of the plant and its ability to secure a sufficient labor supply in the community and its surrounding commuting field. Location in relatively accessible places (particularly with regard to the Interstate Highway System or its feeder highways) has been a dominant feature of branch plant establishment in each of the nonmetropolitan locations studied.[37]

NOTES

[1] Wilbur R. Thompson, "The Economic Base of Urban Problems," in Neil W. Chamberlain, ed., *Contemporary Economic Issues* (Homewood: Richard D. Irwin, 1969).

[2] Related research on branch plants may be found in the following articles: John R. Borchert and Frank E. Horton, "Geography and Urban Public Policy," in *Geographic Perspectives and Urban Problems* (Washington, D.C.: National Academy of Sciences, 1973), pp. 1–24; Rodney A. Erickson, "The Filtering-Down Process: Industrial Location in a Nonmetropolitan Area," *Professional Geographer,* Vol. 28 (1976), pp. 254–60; Rodney A. Erickson, "Nonmetropolitan Industrial Expansion: Emerging Implications for Regional Development," *Review of Regional Studies,* Vol. 6 (1977), pp. 35–48; and Thomas R. Leinbach, "Locational Trends in Nonmetropolitan Industrial Growth: Some Evidence from Vermont," *Professional Geographer,* Vol. 30 (1978), pp. 30–36.

[3] Niles M. Hansen, *The Future of Nonmetropolitan America* (Lexington: D.C. Heath, 1973); and Luther Tweeten and George L. Brinkman, *Micropolitan Development* (Ames: Iowa State University Press, 1976).

[4] Erickson, op. cit., note 2.

[5] Indigenous enterprises are those which are created locally within the nonmetropolitan area.

[6] Allan R. Pred, *Major Job-Providing Organizations and Systems of Cities,* Commission on College Geography Resource Paper No. 27 (Washington, D.C.: Association of American Geographers, 1974).

[7] Robin Marris, *The Economic Theory of Managerial Capitalism* (New York: Free Press, 1964).

[8] Pred, op. cit., note 6, pp. 6–7.

[9] Seev Hirsch, *Location of Industry and International Competitiveness* (Oxford: Clarendon Press, 1967), p. 16; and Seev Hirsch, "The United States Electronics Industry in International Trade," *National Institute Economic Review*, No. 34 (1965), pp. 92–97.

[10] Various elements of Hirsch's model are supported in the following research: Raymond A. Vernon, "International Investment and International Trade in the Product Cycle," *Quarterly Journal of Economics*, Vol. 80 (1966), pp. 190–207; and Louis T. Wells, Jr., "Test of a Product Cycle Model of International Trade: U.S. Exports of Consumer Durables," *Quarterly Journal of Economics*, Vol. 83 (1969), pp. 152–62.

[11] Wilbur R. Thompson, *A Preface to Urban Economics* (Baltimore: Johns Hopkins Press, 1965).

[12] Pred, op. cit., note 6, p. 7.

[13] John R. Friedmann and John Miller, "The Urban Field," *Journal of the American Institute of Planners*, Vol. 31 (1965), pp. 312–19.

[14] Gunter Krumme, "Notes on Locational Adjustment Patterns in Industrial Geography," *Geografiska Annaler*, Vol. 51B (1969), pp. 15–19; and Guy P. F. Steed, "Forms of Corporate Environmental Adaptation," *Tijdschrift voor Economische en Sociale Geografie*, Vol. 62 (1971), pp. 90–94.

[15] The term "subsidiary branch plant" has been coined for this group of branches in the following research: W. F. Luttrell, *Factory Location and Industrial Movement*, Vol. 1 (London: National Institute for Economic and Social Research, 1962).

[16] David J. North, "The Process of Locational Change in Different Manufacturing Organizations," in F. E. Ian Hamilton, ed., *Spatial Perspectives on Industrial Organization and Decision-Making* (London: John Wiley & Sons, Ltd., 1974), pp. 213–44.

[17] Luttrell, op. cit., note 15.

[18] David E. Keeble, "Industrial Decentralization and the Metropolis: The North-West London Case," *Transactions of the Institute of British Geographers*, Vol. 44 (1968), pp. 1–54; and David Law, "Industrial Movement and Locational Advantage," *Manchester School of Economic and Social Studies*, Vol. 32 (1964), pp. 131–54.

[19] Vernon, op. cit., note 10.

[20] Plants with fewer than five employees were virtually nonexistent among the corporations establishing branch plants in the nonmetropolitan areas. The period 1967–1976 was chosen for analysis in order to coincide with the beginnings of notable nonmetropolitan turnaround. In addition, manufacturing employment data used in assessing the contribution of branch plants are not available prior to 1967.

[21] Given the openings, closings, expansions, and contractions of plants over time, data should ideally be collected for person-years of employment; unfortunately, such information is virtually impossible to collect.

[22] The Manufacturing Belt was originally delimited by Sten de Geer in the following article: "The American Manufacturing Belt," *Geografiska Annaler*, Vol. 9 (1927), pp. 233–359. A later update was by Allan Pred: "The Concentration of High-Value-Added Manufacturing," *Economic Geography*, Vol. 41 (1965), pp. 108–32. As Pred points out, the Manufacturing Belt is an amorphous and continually evolving area. The Manufacturing Belt concept used in this analysis is basically the same as Pred's, with the addition of the Minneapolis–St. Paul metropolitan area.

[23] According to *Fortune*'s 1960 listing of corporations, over 70% of the 500 largest manufacturing corporations were headquartered in U.S. Manufacturing Belt metropolitan areas.

[24] By 1970, the proportion of the 500 largest manufacturing corporations headquartered in the Manufacturing Belt had fallen to 65%.

[25] Half of the remaining New Mexico branch plants are headquartered in California, concentrated mainly in the San Francisco area.

[26] See note 11.

[27] In addition, sectoral growth trends selectively affect certain manufacturing activities, increasing the probability of filtering in the more rapidly growing sectors (particularly durable goods).

[28] The likelihood ratio test is described in the following text: Alexander M. Mood and Franklin A. Graybill, *Introduction to the Theory of Statistics* (New York: McGraw–Hill, 1963), pp. 300–01. A more complete treatment may be found in the following article: S. S. Wilks, "The Likelihood Test of Independence in Contingency Tables," *Annals of Mathematical Statistics*, Vol. 6 (1935), pp. 190–96. The likelihood ratio (λ) approximates the chi-square distribution in the form $-2 \log_e \lambda$ for large samples.

[29] The differences in each of the pairs of sectoral structures for the nonmetropolitan study areas were statistically significant at the .01 level.

[30] National and state standards have served to eliminate an advantage of nonmetropolitan operation to avoid environmental regulations. However, in many highly industrialized areas, state and local environmental standards are set above the prevailing state and national levels for surrounding areas.

[31] Erickson (1976), op. cit., note 4.

[32] Erickson (1977), op. cit., note 4.

[33] Erickson (1977), op. cit., note 4. The author analyzed data for 163 communities in 52 northern and western Wisconsin counties for the period 1970–1974. The evidence indicated that smaller places (particularly rural) not covered in the reporting communities were experiencing significant manufacturing employment declines. Plant expansions were clearly a dominant growth factor in 1973 and 1974.

[34] Pred, op. cit., note 6, p. 63; and Guy P. F. Steed, "Changing Processes of Corporate Environment Relations," *Area*, Vol. 3 (1971), pp. 207–11.

[35] Erickson (1977), op. cit., note 4; and H. L. Seyler, "Industrialization and Household Income Levels in Nonmetropolitan Areas," Chapter 10 in this volume.

[36] The use of 1975 as the terminal year in calculating manufacturing employment change in the nonmetropolitan areas probably overstates slightly the contribution of branch plants. Data for 1976, when it becomes available, will probably show that the rate of manufacturing employment growth has rebounded from declines experienced in many nonmetropolitan areas in 1975.

[37] The authors wish to acknowledge the assistance of the following individuals who provided data for this research: Ann Peel (Kentucky Department of Commerce); Fred Newhall (Vermont Agency of Development and Community Affairs); Richard Kotenbeutel (Wisconsin Department of Business Development); John Temple (Bureau of Business and Economic Research, University of New Mexico); and Paul Levitt (Bureau of Economic Analysis, U.S. Department of Commerce).

Chapter 5

THE COMMUNITY SATISFACTIONS OF NONMETROPOLITAN MANUFACTURERS

Thomas R. Doering and John C. Kinworthy

Traditional studies of industrial location have focused on why manufacturing plants are in certain areas and what operational factors act to reinforce those locations. These studies have typically viewed markets, raw materials, labor, transportation, and other economic considerations as the major determinants of an industrial location.[1] Increasingly, however, it is recognized that such studies represent a somewhat limited focus. Specifically, they do not examine the feelings of existing manufacturers toward their community locations—whether or not they are satisfied with them and to what extent these satisfactions are influenced by the manufacturers' personal and social relationships with their communities vis-a-vis the traditional operational factors. These feelings, while largely subjective, are believed to have important implications for nonmetropolitan industrialization, and their analysis can provide new insights for community development planners and other local decision-makers.

NONMETROPOLITAN AMERICA'S IMPROVED IMAGE

In investigating the community satisfactions of manufacturers, an important consideration is the general corporate image of nonmetropolitan America. Until recent years, this vast region was essentially thought of as a backwater for industrial growth, "trading dying industries for mature, low-skill, low-wage industries."[2] This situation was especially pronounced in the rural South and Great Plains, where prospective manufacturers saw the advantages of abundant, cheap, and/or nonunion labor but maybe little else. Certainly, most manufacturers from metropolitan America perceived few personal benefits in living in the nonmetropolitan areas. To be sure, many envisioned a lower cost of living and perhaps a better natural setting, but such assets were likely viewed as more than offset by limited local services, both for themselves and their firms, and a presumably inferior social and cultural environment. Even "home-grown" nonmetropolitan manufacturers probably recognized these disadvantages to the extent they could empathize with their metropolitan counterparts. In short, nonmetropolitan America presented an image of stagnation to many manufacturers.

During the past decade, however, this situation has changed dramatically. Since 1970, the nonmetropolitan counties of the United States have grown faster than the metropolitan counties—the first period in this century for such an occurrence.[3] To some extent, these changes may be interpreted as adjustments to perceived metropolitan-nonmetropolitan differences in quality of life. Metropolitan settings, increasingly characterized by congestion, pollution, crime, unemployment, and public financing difficulties, are perceived to be less desirable places to live and work. Rural and small town settings, by contrast, have acquired much of the material prosperity once associated principally with metropolitan America without inheriting many of the latter's maladies. The result has been a slight shift of population and economic activity back to the nonmetropolitan areas.

As this shift proceeds, manufacturers are taking a less restrictive view of industrial locations in nonmetropolitan America. Instead of focusing on a limited number of operational considerations such as labor factors, their interest is expanding to give greater attention to amenities for themselves and their employees. Many of these manufacturers now seem to regard nonmetropolitan areas as safer, healthier, and offering more relaxed life-styles than highly urbanized centers. Yet they may be less certain about the capacity of small towns and rural areas to provide adequate housing, educational opportunities, medical services, recreation, and other personal and social wants and needs. These factors might therefore by hypothesized to be important determinants of whether or not manufacturers will locate in nonmetropolitan communities and, if they do, whether or not they will be satisfied with those communities.

COMMUNITY SATISFACTION

Research on the community satisfactions of manufacturers may be viewed as a subset of research on the community satisfactions of all residents, which in turn may be viewed as a subset of research on the quality of life of those residents. The interest in community satisfaction and quality of life is largely an outgrowth of the so-called "social indicators movement."[4] This movement, which has greatly accelerated since its inception in the mid-1960s, has the general objective of developing a set of measures and data that will evaluate and summarize the state of society relative to national goals. Its impetus comes primarily from the realization that economic indicators, such as Gross National Product or the Consumer Price Index, are alone not enough to gauge the general well-being. In the words of some of the leading researchers on American quality of life, "the bright promise of economic prosperity has proved illusory, and the naive faith that national affluence would produce national well-being has been severely shaken."[5]

When applied to the community level, the social indicators movement suggests that the well-being of a place should not be gauged solely by measures such as median family income or per capita retail sales. Rather, its assessment should be based on a broad range of quality of life indicators, including economic, social, psychological, and environmental criteria. Many of these indicators are conducive to measurement by Census figures or other objective data and may thus be termed objective indicators. The remaining indicators are best measured by some form of attitude survey and may thus be termed subjective indicators. Because community satisfaction is essentially a subjective component of quality of life, its measurement is logically tied more to subjective than objective indicators. This is an important distinction, since subjective indicators have lately shown satisfaction to be relatively high in areas where objective indicators show the overall quality of life to be low.[6]

Community Satisfactions of General Residents

Although of comparatively recent origin, studies of community satisfaction have already uncovered some interesting and, in some cases, surprising relationships. Durand and Eckart, for example, found no support for the common belief that individuals who inhabit socially homogeneous areas are more satisfied with their communities than those living in socially dissimilar areas.[7] Satisfaction may thus be greatest in an area that is intermediate socially between very homogeneous and very heterogeneous. Durand and Eckart also found little support for the hypothesis that community satisfaction increases with length of residence, even after testing it under varying conditions of social stability and homogeneity.

A further clarification of the relationship between community satisfaction and quality of life has been supplied by Marans and Rodgers.[8] They produced a simple conceptual model whose purpose was to outline "the manner in which objective attributes of the environment are linked to subjective experiences of people in that environment."[9] In testing this model, they found the attitudes of residents toward a number of public services and facilities to be strongly related to community satisfaction. At a more local (or macro-neighborhood) level, they further found that people's assessments of their neighbors and of housing conditions were important satisfaction determinants. On the other hand, they found only a modest relationship between community satisfaction and personal characteristics, such as race, income, age, education, job status, and length of residence in the community. This substantiates the belief that perceived environmental characteristics are better indicators of community satisfaction than the more familiar demographic variables.

Marans and Rodgers also examined the relationship between satisfaction and town population. They found no direct causal relationship between community size and satisfaction but did note a tendency for satisfaction levels to be higher in small towns and rural areas than in the central cities of SMSAs, large cities, and suburbs. This finding is consistent with several studies of residential preferences as well as with a series of Gallup polls running from the mid-1960s through 1977.[10] It is tempered somewhat, however, by the research of Jesser, who found that at least among professionals in rural areas (clergymen, teachers, lawyers, doctors, and dentists), community satisfaction did not decrease, but increased with town size.[11] This is in line with a much earlier finding of Davies, who found a positive relationship between population and the satisfactions of high school and college students from rural communities.[12]

Recent studies by Johnson and Knop and Rojek et al. have tended to discount the satisfaction-town size relationship.[13] Johnson and Knop noted that urban residents were more satisfied than rural residents with various services and opportunities available to them (shopping, medical, entertainment, and employment), but that no distinction could be drawn on the basis of such intangibles as cooperation, progressiveness, leadership, and local pride. Rojek et al. took this a step further, being unable to even confirm the relationship between satisfaction with community services and town size, at least among residents in communities of less than 10,000 population. Both studies further established the multidimensional nature of community satisfaction. Using factor analysis, Johnson and Knop extracted seven dimensions of community satisfaction (civic cooperation, shopping facilities, medical facilities, teacher ability, employment opportunities, salary scale, and relative location), while Rojek et al. extracted four dimensions of satisfaction with community services (medical, public, educational, and commercial). The existence of so many dimensions can of course hinder the construction of indices that attempt to provide an aggregate measure of community satisfaction. However, as in the case of quality of life, the increased interest in community satisfaction as a generic concept seems to dictate that it receive greater definitional precision and measurement specification, and that attempts to construct such indices continue to be encouraged.

Community Satisfactions of Manufacturers

As research on community satisfaction advances, it is likely to follow a more disaggregated approach, focusing on specific groups of community residents. Manufacturers constitute one of the more important of these groups for investigation, because their decisions can play a prominent role in determining overall community development. It is possible for a single small town manufacturer, for example, to make decisions that will significantly increase or decrease population growth, alter the tax base or local infrastructure, and even to a large extent define the short-term social and economic viability of a community. Many of these decisions are undoubtedly the result of desires on the part of the manufacturer to minimize costs and/or maximize profits. In this respect, the manufacturer may be thought to conform more closely than most other community residents to the traditional model of "rational economic man." However, as mentioned previously, any such distinction is becoming more blurred as manufacturers increasingly emphasize amenity factors in their locational decision-making.

A recent spatial model of manufacturing decision-making identifies an industrial location as a product of "the goals and objectives of the enterprise and the personal space preferences of the individual decision-makers."[14] Such a model is illustrative of the behavioral or firm-oriented approach that has modified classical industrial location theory during the past decade. This behavioral approach has facilitated the consideration of a wide range of noneconomic factors, including the personal or "psychic income" factors first stressed by Greenhut.[15] Relying heavily on the subjective responses to attitude and opinion surveys, this approach also represents a sufficiently broad perspective with which to consider a manufacturer's community satisfaction.

Perhaps because of the comparative infancy of the behavioral approach in industrial location research, few attempts have been made to examine the quality of life and community satisfactions of manufacturers. An exception is a study by Foster of manufacturers in Canada and the United States.[16] Based on the responses of 2,877 manufacturers, he analyzed the relative importance they attached to economic and quality of life considerations. He found that the chief economic considerations were labor factors, especially worker dependability/productivity, wage rates, and availability. Among the quality of life considerations, he discovered that crime, the cleanliness of the environment, educational facilities, and medical services were most important. Although Foster made no attempt to combine these factors into an overall satisfaction measure, he did ask the manufacturers to indicate the degree to which they would be willing to trade-off various economic factors for a "substantially improved quality of life."[17] The manufacturers were somewhat flexible in their willingness to trade-off market and raw materials factors, but they were less inclined to jeopardize their present positions regarding labor. These results suggest that among the operational considerations contributing to a manufacturer's community satisfaction, labor factors may be the most important.

Unfortunately, Foster did not distinguish between metropolitan and non-metropolitan manufacturers in his study. Nevertheless, his research and the literature on community satisfaction previously reviewed illustrate a number of investigatory possibilities in the realm of nonmetropolitan industrialization. For example, what is the general make-up of the community satisfactions of nonmetropolitan manufacturers? The literature indicates that manufacturers share desires similar to those of other community residents for medical, educational, and other personal and social services, but that they are also strongly influenced by labor and other locational factors associated with their plant operations. There is, therefore, a need for some prioritization of these factors according to their subjective importance to nonmetropolitan manufacturers.

Similarly, some interesting research possibilities lie in discovering the relationships between, on the one hand, the community satisfactions of nonmetropolitan manufacturers and, on the other, selected community and firm characteristics. For example, what is the relationship for nonmetropolitan manufacturers between community satisfaction and community population? The literature discloses no consensus on this relationship for manufacturers or, for that matter, other community residents. It is thus worthy of further exploration, as are possible relationships between the community satisfactions of manufacturers and such characteristics as plant employment, age of plant, and type of industry.

NEBRASKA CASE STUDY

Much of the remainder of this discussion describes a study by Lonsdale, Kinworthy, and Doering (1976) that explored the above issues in the context of nonmetropolitan manufacturing in Nebraska.[18] As a study area, non-metropolitan Nebraska is representative of a region where industrialization has contributed to population growth in recent years following decades of decline. The discussion outlines the methodology as well as the findings of the study in order to better demonstrate the value of techniques of attitude and opinion measurement for studies of industrial location.

Methodology

Data were obtained in the spring of 1975 from a mail-back questionnaire survey of the 355 manufacturers listed in the 1974–75 *Nebraska Manufacturers Directory* who (1) had 10 or more employees, (2) were located in or near towns with populations under 10,000, and (3) were outside Nebraska's metropolitan areas (the Omaha, Lincoln, and Sioux City SMSAs).[19] Of the 355 manufacturers sent questionnaires, 179 supplied usable responses, yielding a return rate slightly over 50%. Although this created some concern over possible nonresponse bias, a series of difference-in-proportions tests showed no significant differences between the respondents and nonrespondents in terms of such characteristics as the types of products manufactured and the populations of the manufacturers' communities.[20]

The survey respondents completed a questionnaire which asked for some basic characteristics of each manufacturing plant, including its Standard Industrial Classification (SIC), the town in or near which the plant was located, approximate number of years in operation, and employment size. However, the bulk of the questionnaire consisted of a series of 35 questionnaire statements called Likert items measuring opinions on various community factors and to which the manufacturers had five possible responses, ranging from strongly disagree to strongly agree.[21] The responses to the Likert items were gathered for use in constructing a summated scale of community satisfaction as well as to gauge the majority opinions on individual items, while the previously mentioned data on firm characteristics were gathered to eventually test relationships with the scores of the respondents on the constructed satisfaction scale.

The satisfaction scale was constructed following the item analysis procedures commonly used with attitude scales.[22] Sixteen of the original 35 statements were selected for use in the scale, representing those statements which had the highest item to scale-minus-item correlations (Table 1). While none of the statements were found to have a high correlation with the total scale, each nevertheless contributed to a scale that was judged to have an acceptable level of internal consistency. This was indicated through two measures of reliability (internal consistency): a split-half procedure, which yielded a reliability coefficient of .66, and Cronbach's Alpha, which produced a reliability coefficient of .71.

The frequency distribution of responses to each of the 16 Likert items was examined to assess the existence and strength of majority opinions on individual items. Each manufacturer's responses to the statements were then summed to produce an overall satisfaction score. Finally, a series of one-way analyses of variance were conducted to see if there were any significant and discernible relationships between the overall satisfaction scores and the firm characteristics mentioned earlier.

Results

The results of the analysis indicate that while the determinants of a nonmetropolitan manufacturer's satisfaction with his community may be thought to be like those of the general populace in many respects, they do show noticeable differences in the inclusion of a number of operational factors, especially labor. In particular, the three Likert statements with the highest item to scale-minus-item correlations were all labor-related: one dealing with labor quality, the second dealing with labor cost, and the third dealing with labor availability. On these statements, a slight majority of the responding manufacturers (55.4%) agreed or strongly agreed that they had problems obtaining properly qualified labor, while a much larger majority (81.0%) believed that they received more value for labor than they would in a large city (Table 2). There was no majority opinion, however, on the statement dealing with labor availability. The finding that these labor items are important in determining whether or not a manufacturer is satisfied with his community is consistent with other investigations of manufacturing in nonmetropolitan areas that stress labor considerations as important location factors.[23]

The two statements with the next highest item to scale-minus-item correlations both dealt with the attitudes of others in the community. The first showed a majority of the respondents (60.4%) agreeing or strongly

Table 1. Likert Items Comprising Manufacturers' Community Satisfaction Scale

Likert item	Response (% of total)					Item to scale-minus-item correlation
	Strongly disagree	Disagree	Undecided	Agree	Strongly agree	
1. "We have had problems in obtaining properly qualified labor for our firm."	1.6	36.3	6.7	45.3	10.1	.41
2. "In our community, we receive more value per dollar for labor than we would in a large city."	1.1	3.9	14.0	66.5	14.5	.38
3. "We have had problems in attracting a sufficient number of labor applicants for our firm."	8.5	41.3	8.9	31.8	9.5	.37
4. "Local community or county leaders show a willingness to listen to our complaints or concerns and consider corrective action to assist us."	6.1	15.1	18.4	52.5	7.9	.37
5. "The people in this town take pride in their community."	2.2	9.5	7.3	60.3	20.7	.36
6. "We find electric power rates to be reasonable."	9.0	19.6	14.0	55.3	2.1	.34
7. "We find community support facilities (repair shops, legal aid, electricians, etc.) inadequate for the needs of our firm."	4.0	45.8	10.6	31.8	7.8	.32
8. "The public educational facilities in our area are adequate."	2.8	6.7	4.5	66.5	19.5	.32
9. "Our community or county has adopted zoning and/or land-use planning legislation which is causing problems for our firm."	12.8	62.6	17.9	5.0	1.7	.30
10. "Our company finds local taxes too high."	1.7	39.1	21.2	32.4	5.6	.28
11. "The recreational–entertainment facilities in this area are adequate."	7.3	33.0	5.6	47.5	6.7	.28
12. "The availability of suitable housing constitutes a problem for our employees."	3.4	26.8	6.7	43.0	20.1	.28
13. "We feel our firm is adequately assisted by local bank(s) in providing money for existing or new operations."	6.7	7.8	11.7	55.3	18.5	.25
14. "We have problems in obtaining sufficient natural gas to meet our needs."	9.0	57.5	9.5	18.4	5.6	.25
15. "We find rail transportation facilities and services a disadvantage in our present location."	13.5	53.6	10.6	15.6	6.7	.22
16. "The medical facilities and services are adequate in our area."	6.7	25.1	3.9	52.0	12.3	.21

Table 2. Majority Opinions on Likert Items (Percent in Agreement
or Disagreement)[a]

Statement	Majority opinion	%
1. "We have had problems in obtaining properly qualified labor for our firm."	Agreement	55.4
2. "In our community, we receive more value per dollar for labor than we would in a large city."	Agreement	81.0
3. "We have had problems in attracting a sufficient number of labor applicants for our firm."	None	
4. "Local community or county leaders show a willingness to listen to our complaints or concerns and consider corrective action to assist us."	Agreement	60.4
5. "The people in this town take pride in their community."	Agreement	81.0
6. "We find electric power rates to be reasonable."	Agreement	57.4
7. "We find community support facilities (repair shops, legal aid, electricians, etc.) inadequate for the needs of our firm."	None	
8. "The public educational facilities in our area are adequate."	Agreement	86.0
9. "Our community or county has adopted zoning and/or land-use planning legislation which is causing problems for firm."	Disagreement	75.4
10. "Our company finds local taxes too high."	None	
11. "The recreational–entertainment facilities in this area are adequate."	Agreement	54.2
12. "The availability of suitable housing constitutes a problem for our employees."	Agreement	63.1
13. "We feel our firm is adequately assisted by local bank(s) in providing money for existing or new operations."	Agreement	54.2
14. "We have problems in obtaining sufficient natural gas to meet our needs."	Disagreement	66.5
15. "We find rail transportation facilities and services a disadvantage in our present location."	Disagreement	67.1
16. "The medical facilities and services are adequate in our area."	Agreement	64.3

[a] Agreement—Sum of agree and strongly agree > 50%
Disagreement—Sum of disagree and strongly disagree > 50%
None—No majority opinion (neither agreement nor disagreement)

agreeing that local community and county leaders were responsive to their needs, while the second showed a much larger majority (81.0%) believing that the townspeople took pride in their community. Unlike the labor items mentioned previously, these items would also be expected to be important determinants of community satisfaction among the general populace.

Likewise, 7 of the remaining 11 Likert statements comprising the satisfaction scale would seemingly be important to the general populace as well as to the manufacturers. These include the items dealing with housing; local educational, recreational-entertainment, and medical facilities; and, to lesser extent, local banks, taxes, and community support facilities. In none of these items except one—that dealing with housing availability—was a majority opinion recorded that was unfavorable to the community. However, the fact that 63.1% of the respondents agreed or strongly agreed that the availability of suitable housing was a problem for their employees brings out an often overlooked constraint on nonmetropolitan development, but one that would be particularly acute for those firms desiring to transfer large numbers of employees into an area.

The other four items contained in the satisfaction scale covered electric power rates; community zoning and land use planning; natural gas supplies; and rail transportation facilities. On all of these statements, majority opinions were recorded that were favorable to the community. These items are akin to the labor items mentioned earlier, in that they are regarded as traditional operational factors of an industrial location, which would likely be only minor determinants of the community satisfactions of the general populace.

When combined to form the summated scale, the 16 items yielded satisfaction scores that had values ranging from 31 to 72, with a mean of 51 (the maximum possible range was 16 to 80). These scores were then related to various plant characteristics through a series of one-way analyses of variance. In these analyses, five independent (treatment) variables were used: (1) population of town in or near, (2) industry type (SIC), (3) years of operation in the community, (4) plant employment size, and (5) organizational status.[24] Only one of these variables—town population—was found to have a statistically significant relationship with community satisfaction, producing an F ratio significant at the .02 level. The relationship in this case was found to be a positive one, with the community satisfactions of the manufacturers increasing with town size, at least up to the 10,000 population level. This differs from what Rojek et al. found for the general population of a community, perhaps again reflecting the greater concern among the manufacturers than the general populace with operational factors such as labor, transportation, etc., which would normally be expected to be in greater quantities in the larger communities. Certainly, this is consistent with the traditional studies of industrial location, which stress the importance of scale economies and interindustry linkages in entrepreneurial decision-making.

The other independent variable whose relationship with community satisfaction may be speculated on despite a somewhat disappointing level of significance is years of operation in the community (F ratio significant at the .20 level). The group (category) means on this variable indicate something of a cyclical relationship between a manufacturer's length of operation in a community ánd his level of satisfaction. Specifically, the mean satisfaction scores were found to be relatively high for the responding manufacturers who had been operating in the community four years or less, but low for those in the 5-9 year group. The scores then tended to increase for the manufacturers in the succeeding age groups, reaching their highest levels for those manufacturers who had been at their current locations 35 years or longer. These data suggest that the most critical period for a manufacturer in deciding whether or not to remain in a community occurs during his second 5 years in operation. However, as the results of the analysis of variance show, this is far from being a proven hypothesis.

Overall, this Nebraska case study shows how new insights into nonmetropolitan industrialization can be gained by analyzing a manufacturer's community satisfaction. Personal and social relationships that in the past have sometimes been overlooked because of their subjectivity can and should be brought into the analysis with the more objective operational considerations. This can be accomplished through the use of Likert summated scales and other techniques of attitude and opinion measurement.

CONCLUSIONS

A general impression gained from this discussion is that manufacturers in nonmetropolitan areas are more development conscious than the general populace. This is not surprising, considering the vested interest the manufacturer has in the economic health of the community. A partial manifestation of this development consciousness is the manufacturer's community satisfaction, which presumably reflects his general view of local working and living conditions. This view is determined by the interplay of a number of factors, foremost among which appear to be labor factors (especially labor quality, productivity, and availability). Also noteworthy is the apparent positive relationship between community satisfaction and town population—a relationship brought on by a probable desire for greater scale economies and interindustry linkages as well as greater quality of life advantages accruing from more educational opportunities, better recreational-entertainment facilities, improved health care, etc.

It has recently been stated that nonmetropolitan industrial development should be treated as a third type of social change alongside industrialization and modernization.[25] This stems from the fact that nonmetropolitan industrialization is not an evolutionary process but rather a spatial redistribution of economic activity within an already industrialized society. To plan adequately for such change, consideration should be given to a number of sources of information, including a broad sampling of public opinion. This not only includes sampling the attitudes and opinions of the general populace but also those of existing and prospective manufacturers. Since, as this chapter has shown, the opinions of the manufacturers may differ in some respects from those of the general public, it is important that all sides be given fair and considered attention in the formulation of the final development strategies.

NOTES

[1] Well-known examples are Edgar M. Hoover, *The Location of Economic Activity* (New York: McGraw-Hill, 1968); Walter Isard, *Location and Space-Economy: A General Theory Relating to Industrial Location, Market Areas, Land Use, Trade and Urban Structure* (Cambridge: M.I.T. Press, 1956); Benjamin H. Stevens and Carolyn A. Brackett, *Industrial Location: A Review and Annotated Bibliography of Theoretical, Empirical, and Case Studies* (Philadelphia: Regional Science Research Institute, 1967); Gerald J. Karaska and David F. Bramhall, eds., *Locational Analysis for Manufacturing: A Selection of Readings* (Cambridge: M.I.T. Press, 1969); and David M. Smith, *Industrial Location: An Economic Geographical Analysis* (New York: John Wiley & Sons, 1971).

[2] Niles M. Hansen, "Factors Determining the Location of Industrial Activity," in Larry R. Whiting, ed., *Rural Industrialization: Problems and Potentials* (Ames: Iowa State University Press, 1974), p. 41.

[3] Calvin L. Beale, *The Revival of Population Growth in Nonmetropolitan America,* Economic Research Bulletin No. 605 (Washington: U.S. Department of Agriculture, 1975).

[4] David M. Smith, *The Geography of Social Well-Being in the United States* (New York: McGraw-Hill, 1973), pp. 52-61.

[5] Angus Campbell, Philip E. Converse, and Willard L. Rogers, *The Quality of American Life* (New York: Russell Sage Foundation, 1976), p. 2.

[6] Ibid., p. 466.

[7] Roger Durand and Dennis R. Eckart, "Social Rank, Residential Effects, and Community Satisfaction," *Social Forces,* Vol. 52 (1973), pp. 74-85.

[8] Robert W. Marans and Willard Rodgers, "Toward an Understanding of Community Satisfaction," in Amos H. Hawley and Vincent P. Rock, eds., *Metropolitan America in Contemporary Perspective* (New York: John Wiley & Sons, 1974), pp. 299-352.

[9] Ibid., p. 305.

[10] Notable studies of residential preferences are Don A. Dillman and Russell P. Dobash, *Preferences for Community Living and their Implications for Population Redistribution,* Washington Agricultural Experiment Station Bulletin 764 (Pullman: Washington State University, 1972); Niles M. Hansen, *Location Preferences, Migration, and Regional Growth: A Study of the South and Southwest United States* (New York: Praeger, 1973), pp. 64-133; and James J. Zuiches and Glen V. Fuguitt, "Public Attitudes on Population Distribution Policies," *Growth and Change,* Vol. 7 (1976), pp. 28-33.

[11] Clinton J. Jesser, "Community Satisfaction Patterns of Professionals in Rural Areas," *Rural Sociology,* Vol. 32 (1967), pp. 56-59.

[12] Vernon Davies, "Development of a Scale to Rate Attitude of Community Satisfaction," *Rural Sociology,* Vol. 10 (1945), pp. 246-255.

[13] Ronald L. Johnson and Edward Knop, "Rural-Urban Differentials in Community Satisfaction," *Rural Sociology,* Vol. 35 (1970), pp. 554-548; and Dean J. Rojek, Frank Clemente, and Gene F. Summers, "Community Satisfaction: A Study of Contentment with Local Services," *Rural Sociology,* Vol. 40 (1975), pp. 177-192.

[14] M. J. Taylor and P. J. McDermott, "Perception of Location and Industrial Decision-Making. The Example of New Zealand Manufacturing," *New Zealand Geographer,* Vol. 33 (1977), p. 27.

[15] Melvin L. Greenhut, *Plant Location in Theory and in Practice* (Chapel Hill: University of North Carolina Press, 1956).

[16] Robert Foster, "Economic and Quality of Life Factors in Industrial Location Decisions," *Social Indicators Research,* Vol. 4 (1977), pp. 247-265.

[17] Ibid., p. 260.

[18] Richard E. Lonsdale, John C. Kinworthy, and Thomas R. Doering, *Attitudes of Manufacturers in Small Cities and Towns of Nebraska* (Lincoln: Nebraska Department of Economic Development, 1976).

[19] Nebraska Department of Economic Development, *A Directory of Nebraska Manufacturers and Their Products, 1974-1975* (Lincoln: Nebraska Department of Economic Development, 1975).

[20] For a discussion of differences-in-proportions tests, see George A. Ferguson, *Statistical Analysis in Psychology and Education* (New York: McGraw–Hill, 1966), pp. 176-181.

[21] A classic article on the Likert technique is Rensis Likert, "A Technique for the Measurement of Attitudes," *Archives of Psychology*, No. 140 (1932), pp. 1-55.

[22] A clear presentation of item analysis procedures is George W. Bohrnstedt, "Reliability and Validity Assessment in Attitude Measurement," in Robert Summers, ed., *Attitude Measurement* (Chicago: Rand McNally, 1970), pp. 80-99.

[23] Locational aspects of labor are discussed by Richard E. Lonsdale, "Rural Labor as an Attraction for Industry," *American Industrial Development Council Journal*, Vol. 4 (1969), pp. 11-17; Collete Moser, ed., *Labor Market Information in Rural Areas* (East Lansing: Michigan State University Center for Rural Manpower and Public Affairs, 1972); and Steven Kale, "Predicting Labor Availability in Rural Areas: A Methodological Inquiry," *Great Plains–Rocky Mountain Geographical Journal*, Vol. 3 (1974), pp. 60-67.

[24] The data for these variables were grouped as follows: 4 categories of town population (0-999, 1,000-2,499, 2,500-4,999, and 5,000-9,999); 6 categories of industry type (food products–SIC 20; nonelectrical and electrical machinery–SIC 35 and 36; wood products, furniture and fixtures, and fabricated metal products–SIC 24, 25, and 34; printing and publishing–SIC 27; stone, clay, glass, and concrete products–SIC 32; and all other SIC categories); 5 categories of years in operation (0-4, 5-9, 10-19, 20-34, and 35 or more); 5 categories of employment size (10-24, 25-49, 50-99, 100-199, and 200 or more); and 4 categories of organizational status (national, regional, local, and other).

[25] Gene F. Summers, Sharon D. Evans, Frank Clemente, E. M. Beck, and Jon Minkoff, *Industrial Invasion of Nonmetropolitan America* (New York: Praeger, 1976), p. xv.

PART II

THE IMPACT OF NONMETROPOLITAN INDUSTRIALIZATION

Chapter 6

DIMENSIONS OF SOCIAL AND ECONOMIC CHANGE:
The Impact of Nonmetropolitan Industrialization

H. L. Seyler

INTRODUCTION

Earlier chapters have sketched the outlines of a remarkable transformation of the American economic landscape. While there are regional differences in the pace and magnitude of change, redistribution of industrial activity is a national phenomenon involving locational dispersal to less-urbanized, more peripheral areas as well as relocation or expansion within the shadow of metropolitan concentrations. The raw numbers of plants involved and the relative immobility of fixed capital suggest that the shift toward deconcentration is not a short-term departure from earlier agglomeration trends.

Analysts, after inspecting the empirical ledger, could conclude that the contemporary spatial reallocation of industry to nonmetropolitan areas is but a sequence in an unfolding process of deconcentration that began, at the latest, about the middle of this century. Chinitz and Vernon, for example, observed a broad regional redistribution occurring in the 1950s.[1] Later studies confirmed a shift that obtained within regions, particularly the gains enjoyed by nonmetropolitan and decidedly rural areas.[2] A detailed inventory noted that over the period 1947 to 1955, industrial redistribution was largely confined to the existing northeastern industrial belt, and somewhat restricted to suburbanization.[3] From 1958 to 1963, however, greater dispersal of industry to areas outside more heavily industrialized counties, and less-urbanized areas began to accelerate.[4] More recent efforts by Haren illuminate an industry shift that is indeed areally extensive with pronounced gains in areas that are nonmetropolitan and nonadjacent to metropolitan complexes.[5]

Given the range of foreign and domestic influences that could arrest or reverse the dispersal process, prediction of its continuation is certainly hazardous. However, a recent analysis estimated that substantial increases in the future national share of manufacturing will occur in nonmetropolitan areas.[6] After reporting that non-SMSA portions of the country contained 16.9, 16.9, and 19.3% of national manufacturing (based on earnings) in 1950, 1962, and 1970, respectively, shares for these areas were projected to be 21.2, 21.9, and 24.4% in 1980, 1990, and 2000, respectively.[7] The forecast is based upon estimated growth of different two-digit industrial classifications and their probable locational distribution given the experience of the more recent past.

If these estimates are reasonably accurate, resulting social and economic repercussions will be far-reaching. Even if the projections of impressive future expansion are inaccurate, the empirical findings detailing recent changes alone prompt a host of questions about the social and economic impacts on nonmetropolitan areas resulting from the marked relative and absolute gains in industrial activity. Accordingly, the following chapters address a series of highly interrelated questions about the relationship between industrialization and social and economic dimensions in affected nonmetropolitan areas.

Before introducing these assessments, it is essential to set them in a broader, national context. Industrial dispersal is to a degree coincident with a general population redistribution now enveloping the country. It is also inextricably part and parcel of a continuing concern with, and a groping toward, a national growth and development strategy.

A PARALLEL SHIFT

Concomitant with the observed redistribution of industrial activity are strong indications of a fundamental locational shift in national population growth. As Sternlieb and Hughes have stated,[8]

> The changes that have occurred since 1970 are unprecented in scope. From 1970 to 1974, large metropolitan areas were transformed into settings of slow growth, experiencing a average annual rate of increase of 0.3 percent. During the same period, smaller metropolitan areas led the way with an average annual growth of 1.5 percent. Yet the latter are being challenged by the marked resurgence of nonmetropolitan growth, where population increases averaged 1.3 percent annually.... the twenty largest metropolitan areas experienced a net migration outflow of 1.2 million people, while nonmetropolitan territories had a net migration inflow of 1.5 million.

The word "net" in the citation is important, for there is evidence that earlier net migration data masked some sweeping population changes. Morrison has noted that the recent phenomenon of declining or slowly growing metropolitan areas could have been anticipated if researchers had examined migration and birth data more closely.[9] With a drastically lowered birth rate in the country, the effects of migration from large metropolitan areas, particularly but not exclusively in the northeastern quadrant of the country, became strikingly apparent in the 1970s.

During the 1960s, roughly 4 of 10 SMSAs registered more out than inmigration, but the outflows were balanced by natural increases.[10] But, "...that configuration of demographic forces has now changed, bringing growth to an abrupt halt in many areas."[11] In a period of slower national population growth nonmetropolitan areas, for the first time in decades, are experiencing growth at rates exceeding those of metropolitan areas as migration streams have changed.[12] The revealed trend was, in Morrison's words,[13]

> ... so utterly without precedent that a common first reaction to these latest (1970-1973) figures is sheer disbelief.

Presumably, consumers of studies reporting current population trends have recovered from any initial incredulity. The data are real. Just as nonmetropolitan areas are recording absolute increases in their level of manufacturing when that activity is at best expanding slowly, these areas that were formerly plagued by outmigration have been visited by a reversal when national population growth has also slowed. Moreover, the reversal is most impressive:[14]

> ... in those counties with the least commuting to metropolitan areas and in those classified rural nonadjacent. That ... carries the clearest message: the more remote kinds of places—those that as a group used to be regarded as 'nowhere'—have today become somewhere in the minds of many migrants.

The pervasiveness of the altered locational configuration of population change, and its impressive magnitude, has been labelled "counterurbanization" by Berry.[15] He argues that the U.S. is amidst a transformation in the locational organization of population and economic activity that will yield patterns profoundly different from those flowing from the industrial revolution.[16] Perhaps as a harbinger of change in other economically advanced countries, the U.S. will, for the indefinite future, enjoy continued dispersal of population and economic activity as people elect to realize behavioral preferences for lower-density built environments.[17]

The population reversal and industrial dispersal sketched above must necessarily affect social and economic profiles of both the larger metropolitan and nonmetropolitan landscape. Increasingly larger metropolitan areas are, and will continue to be, faced with adjustments to slowly growing, stable, or declining populations and a different, perhaps distressing, economic situation.[18] After decades of population loss, stability, or meager growth, most nonmetropolitan areas seem destined to be recipients of both growth and the stresses and benefits of coping with it.

A DEVELOPMENTAL PERSPECTIVE

Roughly attending, but not temporally coincident with, the locational redistribution of industrial activity is an ever expanding dialogue, volume of research, and array of programs devoted to understanding and effecting change in the locational configuration of economic well-being. The persistence of economically depressed or stranded areas, the presence of poverty in less-urbanized areas, and the perceived rural–urban disparities in other aspects of well-being have prompted an enlarged role for government in the developmental process. After years and layers of legislation creating programs to treat locational imbalances in economic well-being, most appraisals of the effectiveness of such efforts generally conclude they have been ineffectual.[19]

Despite the negative judgments flowing from program assessments, they have not been dismantled or substantially altered in their thrusts. Programs continue to be procedurally and locationally fragmented, and oriented toward "worst first" areas.[20] While there is some flirtation with a national growth policy, area development programs are not conceived or executed with respect to a national plan.[21]

A central feature in programs designed to enhance economic vitality in disadvantaged areas is a heavy emphasis on manufacturing development. A major provision of the Rural Development Act of 1972, for example, commissions the Farmers Home Administration to aid in the financing of nonmetropolitan industrialization for places up to 50,000 population,[22]

> ...though special consideration is given to the open countryside, villages, towns, and small cities up to 25,000 population.

This represents an institutionalization of a sentiment expressed by Heady:[23]

> The solutions to rural community development lie in restoring equity in the distribution of cost and benefits from national growth and technological change.
>   Initially, the recipe for doing so seemed to be rural industrialization. This avenue for restoring employment opportunities, improving income, and providing a more favorable social milieu is a positive possibility for many rural communities and *should be pursued with zest.* (emphasis added)

Further embodying this line of thinking, though more sceptically, Tweeten has observed that:[24]

> ...although the spector of 15,000 local development corporations chasing something on the order of 1,000 new firms each year invites scepticism, communities in large numbers will continue to enhance their economic base through new industry.

And in what amounts to an endorsement of a growth center policy for nonmetropolitan industrialization, other analysts have argued that the core of a cost effective policy for nonmetropolitan development would be industrial growth, if the assumed difficulty of inducing the poor to migrate to metro areas is not resolvable.[25]

Thus there is a curious disjointedness in the nexus of industrial dispersal, population redistribution, and the programs and dialogue addressing area development. Areas that were once being emptied of people are amidst a resurgence of growth. Industrial activity is shifting into these areas as well. Yet critiques of governmental programs, at least at the federal level, suggest programs have been ineffective in redirecting the distribution of industrial activity to more disadvantaged areas. Since the programs are oriented to "worst first" areas, they cannot have had a role in the growth of industrial activity in areas that fail to meet federal guidelines for developmental assistance. Meanwhile, programs focusing on industrial development continue to be advocated as an avenue for reducing locational imbalances in economic well-being in spite of their declared failure.

Advocates of industrialization as a central feature of area developmental policy and the programs resulting from their urging seem to be out of phase with the flow of events represented in the available empirical record. Firms are generally electing to locate, relocate, or expand in nonmetropolitan areas in response to their perception of the economic milieu, and the behavior appears to be unrelated to federal programs conceived to effect such an eventuality. Put another way, if there had been no developmental programs emphasizing industrial growth, there is every reason to assume the redistribution of industry would have taken a form much as it has.

What is more important is the widely held belief that industrial expansion will provide a basis for economic development of less-urbanized areas. Thus a key question invites attention. If developmental programs were wrought anew to be efficacious in directing industry to target areas, and if these programs were conceived in a manner that recognized probable population trends, would benefits accrue as anticipated by advocates of such programs? Thus two issues are joined. First, the locational restructuring of the economic landscape now underway provokes efforts to assess its meaning for nonmetropolitan areas on its own merits. Second, appraisals of the impacts on social and economic components of nonmetropolitan areas are essential for an enlightened dialogue about appropriate modes of governmental action.

SOCIAL AND ECONOMIC IMPACTS OF NONMETROPOLITAN INDUSTRIALIZATION

To resolve these joined issues, one must address three facets. First the anticipated developmental benefits of industrial growth should be briefly articulated. Then the relationship between growth and developmental indices can be examined with respect to expectations. A third facet is the necessity of incorporating the influence of population shifts. The latter helps insure that the role of industrialization as a change-inducing process is properly weighed.

Industrial Growth and Developmental Expectations

There is a tendency to confuse growth and development when discussing expectations from economic change. Clearly, industrial dispersal has created jobs in nonmetropolitan areas. When industry expands without an offsetting employment decrease in other sectors, aggregate incomes from wages and salaries and property will grow to some extent in a host area. Depending on households' spending patterns and consumption by a new or enlarged industrial firm(s), a multiplier effect will also increase aggregates, including income, sales, and local government revenues. A net gain in employment could also affect population aggregates (i.e., stabilize or increase total population, or specific age or occupation categories).

Developmental change, however, connotes structural transformations in economic composition and related alterations in household or individual welfare. Positive change implies improved household or individual income levels, better per capita public services, and enhanced private services such as a broader array of shopping goods and personal services. An element that is definitionally elusive, but an important dimension of well-being, can be labelled as "quality-of-life." The critical question here is does growth in aggregates promote the kinds of structural changes that yield welfare improvements, including an elevated quality-of-life? In the tersest expression, does growth generally produce development?

ASSESSING THE IMPACTS OF INDUSTRIALIZATION

Setting aside any consideration of the possible merits of no growth, chapters which follow probe the association of industrialization and area development. Five questions are raised and resolved in an effort to enrich our understanding of the impacts of nonmetropolitan industrialization in the general context developed above. Shaffer opens the analysis by asking, what are the general economic repercussions associated with nonmetropolitan industrial growth? He critically examines the realities of change, as opposed to expectations, to set a stage for subsequent assessments. Fuguitt and Heaton address the link between population resurgence and industrial expansion through an inspection of industrial growth and net migration on a national scale. The impact of industrial activity and inmigration is researched by Kuehn with special emphasis on an area that is a model of an historically disadvantaged region.

Economic and social impacts of industrial growth are treated in two chapters which conclude the appraisal segment of this volume. In a case study of the northern interior plains, Seyler attempts to clarify the relationship between increased industrial employment and household income change. Finally, Summers, Beck, and Snipp examine the probable effects on the public sector of expanded industrial activity.

Important topics had to be ignored, given the limits imposed in a one-volume treatment. The impact of nonmetropolitan industrialization on environmental quality is a notable omission.[26] Will industrial dispersal transfer pollution problems to an ever larger locational arena? Will those people electing a nonmetropolitan locale bring with them the very problems perceived to be an unacceptable feature of the metropolitan areas they left or avoided? Are the evolving, more dispersed patterns of population and industry more or less environmentally stressful in the long run? Are current trends inviting more or less demands for energy and other natural resources?

Longer-term economic considerations were also omitted. Will nonmetropolitan industrialization relieve or intensify economic cycles of boom and bust that have been a condition experienced by areas dependent on primary activities? Will industrial dispersal introduce more or less stability in employment, reduce or enlarge under- and unemployment? And if developmental gains from industrialization are limited in their present form, what kinds of acceptable governmental intervention will help achieve longer-range developmental improvements?

Since the focus here is no nonmetropolitan areas, effects produced in metropolitan areas were ignored. But questions invite the attention of researchers. If, as it seems, nonmetropolitan areas are absorbing an increasing national share of industries that require unskilled or semiskilled workers, does this not shift employment opportunity away from a relatively immobile and inefficiently used laborforce in inner-city areas? Is industrial dispersal transferring, rather than ameliorating, economic disparity? Does inmigration, including returnees, to nonmetropolitan areas drain away the human resource base of metropolitan areas, further compounding problems and inhibiting the economic resurgence that is required in some of the larger? If, as has been argued above, nonmetropolitan industrialization should be approached as part of a national transformation, can any future policy initiative be framed without tracing the implications for older and larger metropolitan concentrations?

These omissions notwithstanding, and as selective as the impact analyses must be, they do provide a perspective on the developmental effects of nonmetropolitan industrialization. The implications of developmental strategy highlighted by the findings and appraisal of their meaning for nonmetropolitan communities are discussed in the final chapter.

NOTES

[1] Benjamin Chinitz and Raymond Vernon, "Changing Forces in Industrial Location," *Harvard Business Review,* Vol. 38 (1960), pp. 126–136.

[2] See Daniel Creamer, *Manufacturing Employment by Type of Location* (New York: National Industrial Conference Board, 1969); and Yehoshua S. Cohen and Brian J. L. Berry, *Spatial Components of Manufacturing Change, 1950–1960* (Chicago: Department of Geography, University of Chicago, Research Paper No. 172, 1975).

[3] Creamer, ibid.

[4] Ibid.

[5] Claude C. Haren, "Location of Industrial Production and Distribution," in L. R. Whiting, ed., *Rural Industrialization: Problems and Potentials* (Ames: Iowa State University Press, 1974), pp. 3–26; see also chapter 2 above.

[6] U.S. Department of Commerce, Regional Economic Analysis Division, *OBERS Projections, Economic Activity in the U.S.: Volume 6, Non-SMSA Portions of BEA Economic Areas* (Washington, D.C.: U.S. Government Printing Office, 1974).

[7] Ibid., pp. 5–7.

[8] George Sternlieb and James W. Hughes, *Current Population Trends in the United States* (New Brunswick, N.J.: Center for Urban Policy Research, 1978), pp. 69–70.

[9] Peter A. Morrison, "The Current Demographic Context of National Growth and Development," in L. S. Bourne and J. W. Simmons, eds., *Systems of Cities: Readings on Structure, Growth, and Policy* (New York: Oxford University Press, 1978), pp. 473–479.

[10] Ibid., p. 473.

[11] Ibid., p. 475.

[12] Ibid., p. 476.

[13] Ibid., p. 477.

[14] Ibid., p. 478; for substantiation that this is indeed a national phenomenon with participation by all regions, see Brian J. L. Berry, "The Counterurbanization Process: How General?," in Niles M. Hansen, ed., *Human Settlement Systems* (Cambridge: Ballinger, 1978), pp. 25–49. esp. pp. 34–41.

[15] Berry, ibid.

[16] Ibid.

[17] Ibid., pp. 41–47.

[18] Recognition and adjustment to these changes are addressed in Charles L. Levin, ed., *The Mature Metropolis* (Lexington: Lexington Books, 1978).

[19] See, "Center for Political Research," *Federal Activities Affecting Location of Economic Development, Vol. I* (Washington, D.C.: Economic Development Administration, U.S. Department of Commerce, 1970); Economic Development Administration, *Program Evaluation: The EDA Growth Center Strategy* (Washington, D.C.: U.S. Department of Commerce, 1972); and Peter A. Morrison et al., *Review of Federal Programs to Alleviate Rural Deprivation* (Santa Monica: Rand Corp. Report, R-1651-CF, 1974).

[20] For a critique, see Niles M. Hansen, *Rural Poverty and the Urban Crisis* (Bloomington: Indiana University Press, 1970). esp. pp. 152–159; and Sol A. Levitan and Joyce K. Zickler, *Too Little But Not Too Late* (Lexington: D.C. Heath, 1976), esp. pp. 141–145.

[21] For a review of the dialogue about a national growth policy, see James L. Sundquist, *Dispersing Population; What America Can Learn from Europe* (Washington, D.C.: The Bookings Institution, 1975), pp. 1–36; for a representative sketch of private sector reservations about a national policy, see "Task Force on Economic Growth and Opportunity," *Rural Poverty and Regional Progress in an Urban Society* (Washington, D.C.: Chamber of Commerce of the U.S., 1969), pp. 4–18.

[22] James G. Maddox, *Towards A Rural Development Policy* (Washington, D.C.: National Planning Association, 1973), p. 20.

[23] Earl O. Heady, "Foreword," in L. R. Whiting, ed., *Communities Left Behind: Alternatives for Development* (Ames: Iowa State University Press, 1974).

[24] Luther Tweeten, "Enhancing Economic Opportunity," in L. R. Whiting, ibid., p. 92.

[25] Luther Tweeten and Neal Walker, "Economic Cost of Poverty," in R. O. Coppedge and C. G. Davis, eds., *Rural Poverty and the Policy Crisis* (Ames: Iowa State University Press, 1977), pp. 45–69.

[26] See Michael Greenberg et al., *A Primer on Industrial Environmental Impact* (New Brunswick: Center for Urban Policy Research, 1978).

Chapter 7

THE GENERAL ECONOMIC IMPACT OF INDUSTRIAL GROWTH ON THE PRIVATE SECTOR OF NONMETROPOLITAN COMMUNITIES

Ron E. Shaffer

Earlier chapters have documented the shift of industry to nonmetropolitan areas. Communities have welcomed the change because of its perceived potential for generating local jobs, additional income, increased sales revenue, and many other economic improvements. The general consensus has been that manufacturing development was necessary to diversify local economic bases, to replace the decline in resource based activities, e.g., agriculture, mining and forestry, and to preserve an economically viable nonmetropolitan America.

In general, nonmetropolitan communities did experience increases in income and employment and other associated indicators of economic activity as local manufacturing expansion occurred. But one result of the recent success of nonmetropolitan communities in attracting manufacturing growth is the question: Is the change generally beneficial? We have now accumulated a research base that permits us to provide some tentative answers, although much research is still necessary.

The question addressed in this chapter is, "How are the economic components of nonmetropolitan communities affected by industrial growth?" Economic impacts have received a much larger share of researchers' attention than other industrial development impacts. No doubt the reason is because industrial development has been pursued as a policy to induce economic changes in nonmetropolitan areas.

In the remainder of this chapter I will discuss the types of economic change that might occur in a community and provide some empirical evidence for these expectations. The types of impact examined will be limited to income, sales and employment, fully recognizing that other important community changes are not examined. My discussion will emphasize two basic concerns. The first is how industrial development might affect economic dimensions of the community where a plant is located, i.e., the host community, rather than some broader geo-political entity. The second is how industrial development might affect specific socioeconomic groups within that community.

The impact from a new manufacturing plant can be divided into the primary or direct and secondary changes. While this is almost a platitudinous statement, we all tend to succumb to glibly stating a multiplier and glossing over the community and plant characteristics that actually influence those impacts and determine that multiplier. Even a brief review of the ltierature, which I will not repeat here, will verify the absence of *a* multiplier for rural industrial development.[1]

INCOME

Income is the most frequently mentioned impact from new manufacturing plants. The income impact can vary depending on the wage scales paid and previous income earned by the workers. It can be expressed as changes in the distribution of income, type of income received as well as the amount of income received. For the community, the income impact is sensitive to where and how workers spend their new income.

Variation in Income Change for Individuals

While most studies have found significant aggregate income changes resulting from industrial development, the income impact on individuals is highly variable.[2] Three case studies are illustrative. A study of the impact of 33 manufacturing plants on Appalachian communities indicated that 53% of those employed at the time they took their present job reported an increase in earnings, while 12% reported a decline in earnings.[3] Of 110 Texans reporting income levels both before and after industrial development, 17% took jobs at wage levels that were equal to their previous wage levels, 20% experienced a decrease in their income, and the balance (63%) earned more in their present than in their previous job.[4] In a different areal setting, 39% of the household heads who migrated into rural Ozark areas to accept manufacturing jobs experienced an income loss.[5] This income decline was substantial in some of the Ozark cases, and for most of these families (95%) income dropped below poverty thresholds as a result of the move. Family income averaged $6,314 before moving; after the move it was only $3,413. However, care must be taken in extrapolating the Ozark data to other situations for two reasons. First, 81% of the income losers were return migrants and noneconomic motives may have weighed heavily in their decision. Second, official poverty levels were used and no adjustments were made for cost of living differences.

Gross Payroll Does Not Equal Change in Community Income

The payroll at a new plant is the most obvious and frequently mentioned income impact of industrial development. However, gross payroll does not equal the actual take-home pay of workers. The gross payroll is reduced by withholding for federal and state income taxes, social security, and the employee's contribution to insurance and retirement programs.[6] A worker with a $10,000 a year job may leave the factory gate with only $8,000 of take-home pay. Gross payroll overestimates the initial income impact on the community. Wadsworth and Conrad, for example, estimated that only $491 per week was new income to the host community despite the weekly payroll of $6,000.[7] A study of 11 Ohio plants found that only 21% of the annual payroll was spent in the community the first time.[8] Reinschmiedt and Shaffer estimated that 57% of the gross payroll from 9 Texas plants and 12 Oklahoma plants, respectively, was spent by plant workers in the host community.[9]

Not only is the amount of income entering a community likely to be less than anticipated, but even without these adjustments the long-run income impact may be less than expected. A study of the income effects of industrial development in four depressed regions estimated the present value of the wage increment over the remaining employable years of the worker, when discounted at 8%, averaged only $12,880 per worker and varied from $9,833 to $22,239.[10] If the worker had been previously employed, the average present value of the income increase was $6,555 and ranged from $5,442 to $10,829. If the worker had previously been unemployed, the average presnt value of the increase in wages averaged $41,726 per worker and ranged from $36,869 to $53,555.

Variation in the Type of New Spending by Households

The next critical income impact question is how the new dollars are or are not spent. How the new dollars are spent refers to different types of direct and more immediate purchases made by employees. They may use the new dollars for additional spending on durables (appliances, housing, and cars) or nondurables (food, entertainment, recreation, and clothes). How income changes are spent is heavily influenced by whether new jobs are for male or female workers.[11] A female work force is likely to increase family consumption in the form of more and higher priced cars, more convenience food purchases, more household services performed outside the home (laundry, dry cleaning, child care), more eating out, more and higher quality women's clothing, more furniture purchases, remodeling and trading up in houses rather than more houses. In contrast, a male work force would generally be associated with increased purchases of lower-cost food items (those what would be cooked at home), more restaurant sales (but not as much as if it were women working), and increased tavern and bowling alley business.

Employees may also use the added dollars they earn not for new spending, but to retire existing debts or to increase savings. The retirement of debts means no new spending will occur in a community. New spending may occur some time in the future, but it will not be immediate. Wadsworth and Conrad found that 8.9% of the gross payroll from a new plant was used for savings or to retire debts.[12] Andrews and Bauder in their study of an Ohio plant found that 64% of the families used part of the income increase for savings and life insurance purchases.[13] Kaldor et al., reported that 20% of the farm families with someone taking a job at a new plant used their income increments to pay off debts or for savings.[14] The increase in savings may imply additional housing and business investment, but there is evidence suggesting that the additional savings need not result in additional local investment.[15]

Effect of Workers' Prior Income on Community Income Gains

When examining the income impact of manufacturing development, the income loss from previous jobs must be considered in calculating community income changes. This income loss can come from local or nonlocal jobs and public assistance. If a person leaves an $8,000 a year job to take one paying $10,000, a community may gain only $2,000 of income if the worker left a job that was not refilled. There is evidence that up to 20% of vacated jobs in rural areas with high underemployment may not be refilled.[16] A study of 21 manufacturing plants in Oklahoma and Texas found that the communities lost an average of $16,367 in primary income and another $13,325 in secondary income per plant from unrefilled previous jobs.[17]

The creation of local manufacturing jobs can provide an opportunity for community residents to work in their home community rather than commute to jobs elsewhere. If a former commuter takes a local job, the community will lose the income formerly brought into the community. A study of a chair factory in rural Indiana estimated that about one-half of the plant's $6,000 a week payroll simply replaced the income of workers who formerly commuted to jobs elsewhere.[18] A less direct measure of this impact are the estimates of the location of prior jobs held by community residents. In a study of Eastern Oklahoma, researchers found 45% of the workers held jobs outside their community, and in Kentucky commuting out of a county declined by 40% when new manufacturing jobs were created between 1960 and 1970.[19]

If the majority of new industrial workers were previously unemployed or on public assistance, the community need not experience a major income increase for two reasons. First, individuals who are persistently unemployed typically do not possess the skills necessary to earn substantial wages. Therefore, the jobs that they take will earn them only a minimal income. Second, since the public assistance dollars are now replaced by manufacturing wages, only the difference between the former public assistance income level and the new income level is a net addition to the community's income. Ignoring political persuasions, a community should view public assistance dollars as similar to a manufacturing payroll, because these dollars are paid by someone else and flow into this community from elsewhere just as payrolls generated from exported manufacturing production.[20] The end result of both of these phenomena is a reduction in the amount of new income generated in the host community.

Locational Variation in New Spending

Where the worker spends the new income has a tremendous influence on the local economic impact from a new manufacturing plant. In analyses that use counties or larger geo-political units as the impact area, the "where new spending occurs" question is seldom asked. However, studies that examine the community impact of new manufacturing plants must be very conscious of where the impact occurs. Because of different geographic patterns in which the income is spent, identical amounts of take-home pay can result in different community impacts. Dollars spent for new household appliances obviously will not affect the host community if those purchases are made in another community.

Geographic spending patterns of consumers are influenced by at least three factors. The first is the size of the community, measured by the types of consumer goods and services available. The usual proxy for this is population. The size of the community influences where money is spent, because the larger community offers a more complete range of goods and services that will keep the workers' dollars in the community. The second factor is the location of a community with respect to a larger, more complete shopping center. The local merchant must compete with larger stores which offer a wider choice of goods and services. Thus, spending is influenced by the ease of access individuals have to larger shopping areas. If access is difficult, increasing isolation, then more dollars are more likely to be spent locally. The initial income level of the community also affects the amount of income that will remain within the community. A critical factor which must be considered occurs when, and if, an income level is reached that gives people discretionary income beyond the basic necessities. The higher the pre-industrial development income level, ceteris paribus, the more income that will be spent on items not supplied by merchants in smaller nonmetropolitan communities.

There has been a limited amount of research on how additional income is spent among different communities. An examination of the influence of industrial development on Iowa farm families found that 50% of the families increased their shopping in the community in which the plant had located, and of those who increased their shopping, 74% also decreased the amount of spending previously made in other communities.[21] The amount of income spent in the host community by a worker is influenced by a worker's place of residence (Table 1). A new manufacturing plant locating in rural Texas or South Dakota and drawing its work force from the surrounding villages and farms would cause a primary income increment in the host communities of less than half the plant's gross payroll. The communities in any one of the three states would experience only 60 to 77% of the gross payroll as a primary income increment even if all the workers lived in the host community.

Table 1. Proportion of Total Income Spent in Community where
Plant is Located by Worker's Place of Residence
(% of income)

Worker's place of residence	Texas	Oklahoma	North Dakota
In host community	77.3	60.5	75.7
Outside host community, but in county	48.9	62.7	38.1
Outside county	25.4	44.4	34.1

Source: Adapted from various studies. See note 22.

Income Sources Change

Rural industrial development can also affect the type of income received in the community. The new plant will have an obvious effect on the wages and salaries paid in a community, but an often overlooked impact is the effect on property income. An analysis of income sources for four industrializing Oklahoma counties found that the contribution of property income to total income increased by 2.2 to 4.4% over previous levels, while in the state and nation the increase was 2.4 and 1.0% respectively.[23] When Scott and Summers compared income increases for individuals 65 and older in a county with industrial development to income increases in adjacent counties without industrial growth, they found that property income increased 82% in the industrialized county and only 38% in the adjacent counties.[24] They attributed this to differences in business activity, the value of assets and increases in sales and rental of real estate.

Industrial Growth and Poverty Levels

Rural industrial development has been advocated as a means to help the poor, but the results are mixed. A study of 121 household heads, previously in the labor force, migrating into the rural Ozark area found that of the 55 household heads receiving an income increase, 13 had previously been in poverty and 11 of these escaped proverty as a result of the new job.[25] A study of new industrial jobs in the economically depressed areas of the Four Corners, Appalachia, the Ozarks, and the Delta found that 22% of the 5,122 jobs were filled by residents who were previously in poverty.[26] Of 26% who had been in poverty, only 64% escaped poverty by taking the new job, and 3.1% of the new jobs resulted in people moving into poverty. Poor individuals and families suffered from two income limiting factors. First, their annual incomes remained low because of low wages received. Second, jobs that they filled were often seasonal jobs. The dominant characteristic of families escaping poverty was that 53% had two workers, while only 26% of the families that remained poor had two workers.

Effects on Income Distribution Vary

Manufacturing development can affect not only the income level but the distribution of income. Most studies of rural industrial development have not discussed income distribution beyond suggesting that income distribution should be improved. Clemente and Summers found that those under 65 had a greater percentage increase in income than those over 65 in a county that experienced industrial development.[27] Thus, the elderly were relatively worse off, and this was reemphasized when they found that the income change of those over 65 in an industrializing county was $602 less than the increase for those over 65 in a nonindustrialized county. In their before and after comparison, Clemente and Summers found that households headed by females received an average income of $3,292 less than households with male heads in 1966. After industrial development, households headed by females received an average of $5,116 less than those with male heads. Thus the relative economic condition of households with female heads actually worsened with industrial growth.

West's study of counties in Missouri found no significant improvement in the equalization of income distribution with the occurrence of manufacturing development.[28] However, a study of nonmetropolitan areas with industrial gains in Texas concluded a somewhat more equal income distribution resulted from manufacturing development.[29] A study in Oklahoma yielded similar findings.[30]

A more precise estimate of income distribution can be derived from the relative mean income of various segments of the population. This essentially measures the mean income of a specific population segment relative to the mean income for the entire population. A study of four Oklahoma counties found that in 1960 the lowest quartile's mean income ranged from 10 to 32% of the mean income in the counties.[31] By 1970, the lowest quartile's mean income had increased to a range of 28 to 50% of the respective counties' average. The second quartile over the same period increased from 40 to 50%, in 1960, to 50 to 82% in 1970. Thus, the relative mean income for the lowest two quartiles either remained constant or gained relative to the population average. A comparison of the relative mean income for the highest quartile showed that it declined for all four counties from a range of 215 to 244% in 1960 to only 180 to 215% in 1970. A study of nonmetro areas in Texas registering industrial growth found that the mean income of the lowest quintile increased 24%, from 41 to 51% of the population mean income.[32] While this suggests an improvement, the highest quintile also increased from 181 to 190% of the population mean. The three middle quintiles experienced declines of 1 to 15%. Obviously, the evidence of a more equalized income distribution is somewhat mixed.

SALES BY LOCAL MERCHANTS

A new manufacturing plant injects money into the local community in two fashions. The first is through the wages and salaries of its workers, further compounded by the amount they spend locally. The second is the nonlabor inputs purchased within the community by the plant. The amount of local purchases can vary by type of ownership, the type of manufacturing plant and the type of existing business services. The more inputs a new manufacturing plant purchases locally, the greater the local economic benefits to the community. These inputs can range from raw materials to legal services.

The degree of local purchases by the plant is a function of ownership structure and the local services available. Local ownership is likely to result in a higher proportion of the inputs being purchased within the community, though this is highly variable. A nonlocally-owned business, such as a branch plant, will probably make fewer purchases locally, because nonlabor inputs are more likely to be purchased at some central location and distributed to the plant.[33] Regardless of the type of ownership, the degree of local purchases by the plant is dependent upon the availability of required goods and services within the community. A community seeking to maximize economic impact of a new manufacturing plant needs to attract plants what will utilize existing businesses.[34] Deaton's study of a pallet plant in Tennessee emphasizes the importance of these backward linkages.[35] He found that the primary employment at the plant was only one-third of the employment created in logging, sawmills, and trucking which provided inputs to the pallet plant. However, many rural communities provide only minimal nonlabor inputs to new plants. A study of 49 new plants in eastern Tennessee found only 8 purchased as least one-half of their inputs from within the study area.[36] Nine Texas plants reported an average of only 27.5% of their inputs were purchased from businesses in the host community.[37] Local purchases ranged from a low of just over 1% to a high of 80%. Erickson found that manufacturing plants tended to purchase their nonlabor inputs from larger communities in non-metropolitan areas.[38] The result of limited nonlabor inputs purchased in host communities is a reduction in the potential local economic impact.

EMPLOYMENT

Nonmetropolitan industrial growth has been advocated as a policy to provide the jobs necessary for economically displaced workers and new laborforce entrants. Empirical evidence indicates that outcomes are highly variable. The employment impact depends as much on who as how many are employed. Are men or women employed? Are workers currently in the workforce? Are the unemployed hired? What types of jobs are created?

Inmigrants and New Jobs

One of the major considerations affecting the employment generated by a new plant is the number of inmigrants attracted to the community. This takes two forms. The first is people who have never lived in the community, but who migrate in response to job opportunities. The second form is former residents returning when the opportunity to work appears in their "home-place." Kuehn and associates found that inmigration of new residents into four different multicounty areas ranged from 4.3 to 18.8% of a new plant's labor force.[39] Helgeston and Zink found 37% of the employees at four new plants changed their residence to take the job.[40] Half of these workers moved to Jamestown from other North Dakota communities beyond the immediate region, and a third moved to these jobs from urban areas outside the host state.

Another phenomenon often associated with nonmetropolitan industrial growth is the return of former residents when a new plant moves into a community. Many of these individuals left the community originally because local jobs or the type of jobs desired were unavailable when they entered the labor force. These return migrants often bring with them critical labor skills acquired in their previous jobs. The result is a larger pool of skills making the community more attractive for future development.

Analysts have attempted to estimate the number of people migrating to a community who had previously resided there. One study found that return migration ranged from 3.8 to 13.1% of a county's work force in new industries. An average level of 11% was observed for counties in the study area.[41] These inmigrants move in response to employment opportunities, but they substantially preempt local residents. A study in the Ozark region compared some of the employment characteristics of inmigrants with longer term residents, and found the imigrant to be more educated with more related job experience than residents.[42]

The net result of inmigration, including returnees, is a reduction in the employment prospects for longer-term residents, not only in total, but in terms of occupational advancement. It is also possible that inmigrants may take jobs that do not fully utilize their skills. In this case nonmetropolitan industrial growth may actually perpetuate the underemployment that has plagued these areas historically.

The amount of inmigration is largely a function of the skills required in relation to the skills possessed by existing residents. Research directly addressing this issue is limited. However, Miernyk's study of manufacturing growth in Appalachia found 94% of all workers lived within 50 miles of their current job at the time they applied for it.[43] A higher proportion of the semiskilled and unskilled than skilled workers lived within the 50 mile radius.

Impact of Commuting

One of the immediate responses to a new plant in a nonmetropolitan area is a dramatic increase in commuting. This can be attributed to the prevailing low density settlement and the opportunity for off-farm employment for youth and women. While workers commuting from beyond the host community dissipates the employment impact, it also reduces the adverse employment adjustments should the plant close. When, for instance, an army ordnance in Baraboo, Wisconsin (population 8,300) employing 875 workers closed, businesses in the community faced minimal losses. The total direct and indirect income impact was only 10% of total personal income in the community.[44]

Studies of commuting also reveal a wide variation in different areas. Case studies have reported a range from 9 to over 80% of employees commuting to plants outside their county of residence (Table 2). Perhaps typical is a Kentucky study that found 28% of the increase in manufacturing jobs between 1960 and 1970 had been taken by intercounty commuters. Over the same period, commuting to adjacent counties from counties experiencing manufacturing growth increased an average of only 7%.[45]

Table 2. Workers' Place of Residence Relative to Job Location
(% of labor force)

Residence	North Dakota	Oklahoma	Kentucky	Illinois	Iowa
In community	68.1	58.7	27	a	a
In county	23.1	30.8	57	a	a
Outside county	8.9	10.5	20	82	50

[a]Data not available.
Source: Adapted from various studies. See note 49.

In many cases the commuting distance can be significant. Clemente determined that workers at an Illinois steel plant had an average one-way commute of 19.1 miles with a maximum of 57 miles.[46] Miernyk found that one-third of the workers commuted at least 20 miles in Appalachian areas gaining industrial activity.[47] Similar findings appear in a study by Kuehn and associates where 15% of the workers commuted at least 20 miles.[48]

Laborforce Participation Rates

The occurrence of new industrial job opportunities in nonmetropolitan areas invariably results in a labor force increase. This increase is due to the combined effects of inmigration and new entrants. New entrants can have a stunning impact on the size of a nonmetropolitan labor force. A representative example from a study of Jamestown, North Dakota reported the 1963 labor force potential.[49] It was estimated that 31% more people (1,543) were available for work in that community than were counted in the 1960 Census of Population.[50] The potential for such remarkable surges in the size of labor forces is largely related to the length of time in which the area has experienced a declining demand for labor and the types of jobs created. For example, four studies of labor force change resulting from manufacturing growth in Appalachia found the average proportion of workers who were new entrants to be 17, 22, 37, and 59%.[51]

A plant hiring female workers will have a greater impact on labor force participation than a plant of similar size hiring males. Comparison of 1959 and 1969 labor force participation rates for males and females in Iowa found no statistically significant correlation between the male labor force participation rate and manufacturing growth.[52] However, there was a significant association between manufacturing growth and female participation. Miernyk concluded that 36% of the women employed on manufacturing had entered the formal labor force with these jobs.[53] Sixty-three percent of these women had dropped out of the labor force at least once in the preceding 5 years, and 92% of the dropouts had remained out of the labor force for at least 2 years.

Effects on Unemployment and Underemployment

Industrial development is often advocated as a policy to reduce unemployment and poverty in nonmetropolitan areas. This is assumed to occur in two ways. First, new or expanding plants can directly hire the unemployed and/or poor. Evidence reported here suggests that the proportion of unemployed workers hired is quite restricted, and even after the poor take new jobs many remain poor. Another way industrial growth can assist the unemployed and poor is through the availability of nonmanufacturing jobs vacated when other workers take a job at a new plant.[54] Evidence collected by Bender and associates shows that this phenomenon is not as strong as once believed.[55] The local job shifting process can be dampened by inmigration. Furthermore, studies of 21 plants in Oklahoma and Texas estimated that a fifth of jobs vacated were not refilled.[56]

The record of the impact of industrial growth on unemployment is mixed, but it tends to indicate unemployment need not decline. Jordan's study of an Arkansas plant largely staffed by a female work force discovered a 60% increase in unemployment within 3 years of the plant's appearance.[57] He concluded that this was due to an unemployed husband remaining in the community, a fairly rapid turnover of women at the plant, and new female entrants into the labor force. Rodgers et al., study of Iowa communities found no significant association between female unemployment and gains in manufacturing.[58] A study of industrial growth in Appalachia found evidence that the unemployment situation did improve.[59] Forty-three percent of the workers at Area Redevelopment Administration supported plants were unemployed at the time they were hired. An additional 12% had experienced some unemployment in the 5 years preceding their current job, and 15% had been unemployed for a year or more. Other plants in the area reported 8 to 35% of their workers had been unemployed before their current job. Almost 8% of the workers at 12 Oklahoma plants and 30% of those at 9 Texas plants were unemployed when they started work.[60]

New manufacturing jobs offer the prospect of reducing underemployment. In Miernyk's analysis, for example, 12% of the males and 9% of the females at a new plant had previously held part-time jobs.[61] He also determined that 22% of the males hired had dropped out of the labor force at least once in the ppreceeding 5 years. Eighty-six percent of these employees had dropped out for as long as 2 years. A study of plants in Oklahoma and Texas noted 16% of the work force had previously held part-time jobs.[62]

Occupational Changes

One of the changes likely to occur in nonmetropoiitan areas registering industrial expansion is a growing diversity of occupations and a greater movement of individuals between job categories. Research has found mixed results concerning the upgrading of occupations as measured by the general shift from blue to white collar jobs. An Ohio inquiry found the rate of increase in blue and white collar jobs for both a more and less industrialized county to be essentially the same.[63] Similarly, a study of communities in Iowa determined there were no significant associations between the change in manufacturing employment and the change in percentages of employment in blue and white collar jobs.[64] In contrast, a study of Putnam County, Illinois, which gained a major steel rolling plant, found that employment in white collar occupations increased by about one-third over a 5-year period from 1966 to 1971.[65]

Manufacturing growth in Iowa communities produced no significant changes in male occupations between 1960 and 1970.[66] However, a study found a positive correlation of female employment in managerial and proprietor occupations and a negative correlation of females employed in service occupations. This latter relationship suggests that manufacturing provided alternatives for females in a nonmetropolitan setting. A comparison of two Illinois counties observed that occupational mobility was similar in a county that had experienced industrial growth to another that had not.[67] However, in the county with industrial growth occupational movers had moved to a wider variety of job types than in the less industrialized county. Thus, although the rate of occupational mobility may be the same, occupational diversity can be quite different. In support of this contention, an Ohio study indicated that over a 5-year period from 1957 to 1962, a more industrialized county exhibited a 20% increase in the number of occupational categories, while a less industrialized county recorded no significant changes.[68]

SUMMARY AND CONCLUSIONS

Industrial development in nonmetropolitan areas definitely affects economic components, specifically income, sales, and employment. However, the overview of general themes executed in the preceding pages indicates the impacts are frequently much different in form and magnitude than often assumed. The income impact is less a function of plant payroll than workers' geographic spending patterns and business purchases. All too frequently lower income families are least affected by manufacturing growth and they can even be placed in a relatively worse economic position. In nonmetropolitan areas, especially rural communities, new manufacturing plants with minimal economic linkages to the host community beyond the local labor hired have reduced area impacts. Multiplier effects can be decidedly small.

The location of a new manufacturing plant invariably produces an increase in local employment, but local residents and the unemployed need not be among those hired. Inmigrants and commuters willing to travel inconvenient distances reduce the job impact for local residents. Both the inmigrants, including returnees, and those commuting from the outside often possess skills and experience levels that cannot be matched by local residents. The net effect of this disadvantageous situation is largely a function of the types of skills required and available, but it appears to fall heavily upon smaller places.

This chapter has identified many areas where research is warranted to resolve conflicting findings. One aspect that needs to be addressed is the distributional impact of manufacturing development. This can be divided into two separate questions. We now have only rudimentary estimates of how various socioeconomic sectors of nonmetropolitan areas are affected by industrial growth. Obviously these estimates need to be improved. The second part involves the national economic implications of suboptimal location decisions by manufacturing firms. Resolving both questions is essential before we can support a national policy of industrial dispersal.

NOTES

[1] Gene F. Summers et al., *Industrial Invasion of Nonmetropolitan America* (New York: Praeger, 1976), p. 56.

[2] Ibid., pp. 64–67.

[3] William H. Miernyk, "Local Labor Market Effects of New Plant Locations," in John F. Kain and John R. Meyer, eds., *Essays in Regional Economics* (Cambridge: Harvard University Press, 1971), p. 175.

[4] Lynn Reinschmiedt, "An Evaluation of Economic Benefits and Costs of Industrialization in Rural Communities in Texas," unpublished doctoral dissertation, Texas A & M University, 1976, p. 96.

[5] Lloyd D. Bender, Bernal L. Green, and Rex R. Campbell, "Trickle Down and Leakage in the War on Poverty," *Growth and Change*, Vol. 2 (1971), p. 38.

[6] Likewise, if workers substitute company paid insurance or retirement programs for personal programs, this suggested measure of take home pay underestimates the worker's income.

[7] Henry A. Wadsworth and J. M. Conrad, *Impact of New Industry on a Rural Community* (West Lafayette, Indiana: Agricultural Experiment Station, Purdue University, Research Bulletin No. 811, 1966), p. 8.

[8] Leroy J. Hushak and Alan Osman, *The Economic Impact of Manufacturing Plants in a Five County Region of Southeast Ohio* (Columbus: Department of Agriculture and Rural Sociology, Ohio State University, Report ESO-406, 1977).

[9] Reinschmiedt, op. cit., p. 69; see also Ron E. Shaffer and Luther Tweeten, *Economic Changes from Industrial Development in Eastern Oklahoma* (Stillwater: Agricultural Experiment Station, Oklahoma State University, Bulletin B-715, 1974), p. 8.

[10] John A. Kuehn et al., *Impact of Job Development of Poverty in Four Developing Areas* (Washington, D.C.: U.S. Department of Agriculture, Agricultural Economic Report No. 225, 1972), p. 13.

[11] John T. Scott, Jr. and Gene F. Summers, "Problems and Challenges Faced by Rural Communities with Industrial Development," in L. R. Whiting, ed., *Problems and Potentials of Rural Industrialization* (Ames: Iowa State University Press, 1974), pp. 102-104.

[12] Wadsworth and Conrad, op. cit., p. 7.

[13] Wade H. Andrews and Ward W. Bauder, *The Effects of Industrialization on a Rural County: Comparison of Social Change in Monroe and Noble Counties of Ohio* (Columbus: Agricultural Research and Development Center, Ohio State University, Series A.E. 407, 1968), p. 65.

[14] D. R. Kaldor, Ward W. Bauder, and M. W. Trautwein, *The Impact of New Industry on a Rural Community* (Ames: Agricultural and Home Economics Experiment Station, Iowa State University, Special Report No. 37, 1964), p. 9.

[15] Ron E. Shaffer, "Wisconsin Commercial Banks Effects on Community Economic Development," in Department of Agricultural Economics, Univ. of Wisconsin, *Economic Issues,* No. 15 (1977).

[16] Reinschmiedt, op. cit., p. 70; and Shaffer and Tweeten, op. cit., p. 8.

[17] Reinschmiedt, op. cit., p. 70; see also Ron E. Shaffer and Luther G. Tweeten, "Measuring Net Economic Changes from Rural Industrial Development: Oklahoma," *Journal of Land Economics,* Vol. 50 (1974), p. 264.

[18] Wadsworth and Conrad, op. cit., p. 7.

[19] Shaffer and Tweeten, op. cit., note 9, p. 8; and Eldon D. Smith and Gene F. Summers, *How New Industry Affects Rural Areas—A Review of Research* (Mississippi State: Southern Region Rural Development Center, Mississippi State University, forthcoming), p. 21.

[20] Helmberger estimated the foregone income from less than national participation in the Food Stamp Program was $1.6 million in Dane County, Wisconsin. See Peter G. Helmberger, "Farms and Food Stamps—the 1977 Farm Bill," in Department of Agricultural Economics, Univ. of Wisconsin, *Economic Issues,* No. 16 (1977).

[21] Kaldor, Bauder, and Trautwein, op. cit., pp. 9-10.

[22] Adapted from Reinschmiedt, op. cit., p. 28; Shaffer and Tweeten, op. cit., note 9, p. 8; and Dwight G. Uhrich, "Economic Impact of New Industry on the Brookings Community: 3M A Case Study," unpublished master's thesis, South Dakota State University, 1974, p. 61.

[23] Ron E. Shaffer, "Rural Industrialization: A Local Income Analysis," *Southern Journal of Agricultural Economics,* Vol. 6 (1974), p. 99.

[24] Scott and Summers, op. cit., p. 98.

[25] Bender, Green, and Campbell, op. cit., p. 39.

[26] Kuehn et al., op. cit., pp. 6-8.

[27] Frank Clemente and Gene F. Summers, *Large Industries in Small Towns: Who Benefits* (Madison: Center for Applied Sociology, University of Wisconsin, Working Paper RID 73.9, 1973), p. 9.

[28] Jerry G. West and Roselee Maier, "Income Distribution Consequences of Rural Industrialization," a paper presented at the annual meeting of the Agricultural Economics Association, August, 1975.

[29] Reinschmiedt, op. cit., p. 99.

[30] Shaffer, op. cit., note 23, p. 99.

[31] Ibid.

[32] Reinschmiedt, op. cit., p. 102.

[33] John H. Britton, "The Influence of Corporate Organization on Linkage of Industrial Plants: A Canadian Inquiry," *Economic Geography*, Vol. 52 (1976), pp. 311–324; Willard F. Mueller, "Impact of Changing Industrial Organization on Community Development," unpublished manuscript, Department of Agricultural Economics, University of Wisconsin–Madison, August, 1972; Alan Pred, "On the Spatial Structure of Organizations and the Complexity of Metropolitan Interdependence," *Papers and Proceedings of the Regional Science Association*, Vol. 34 (1975), pp. 115–142; and Walter Stohr and Franz Todtling, "Spatial Equity–Some Anti-Theses to Current Regional Development Doctrine," *Papers and Proceedings of the Regional Science Association*, Vol. 38 (1977), pp. 33–54.

[34] Daniel Z. Czamanski and Stan Czamanski, "Industrial Complexes: Their Typology, Structure and Relation to Economic Development," *Papers and Proceedings of the Regional Science Association*, Vol. 38 (1977), pp. 93–111.

[35] Brady Deaton, "C.D.C's: A Development Alternative for Rural America," *Growth and Change*, Vol. 6 (1975), pp. 31–37.

[36] Ted Klimanski, "A Schema for Planning Industrial Development in the Rural Border South," in *Planning Frontiers in Rural America* (Washington, D.C.: Subcommittee on Rural Development of Committee on Agriculture and Forestry, U.S. Senate, 94th Congress, 2nd Session, 1976), p. 41.

[37] Reinschmiedt, op. cit., p. 31.

[38] Rodney A. Erickson, "Sub-regional Impact Multipliers: Income Spread Effects of A Major Defense Installation," *Economic Geography*, Vol. 53 (1977), pp. 287–288.

[39] Kuehn et al., op. cit., p. 5.

[40] Delmar L. Helgeson and Maurice J. Zink, *A Case Study of Rural Industrialization in Jamestown, North Dakota* (Fargo: Department of Agricultural Economics, North Dakota State University, Agricultural Economics Report No. 95, 1973), p. 40.

[41] Kuehn et al., op. cit., p. 5.

[42] Bender, Green, and Campbell, op. cit., p. 37.

[43] Miernyk, op. cit., p. 177.

[44] Erickson, op. cit., pp. 283–294.

[45] Smith and Summers, op. cit., p. 21.

[46] Frank Clemente and Gene F. Summers, *Rural Industrial Development and Commuting Patterns* (Madison: Center for Applied Sociology, University of Wisconsin, Working Paper RID 73.15, 1973).

[47] Miernyk, op. cit., p. 177.

[48] Kuehn et al., op. cit., p. 13.

[49] Uhrich, op. cit., p. 62; Shaffer and Tweeten, op. cit., note 9, p. 8; Smith and Summers, op. cit., p. 16; Clemente and Summers, op. cit., note 46, p. 5; and Kaldor, Bauder, and Trautwein, op. cit., pp. 26–27.

[50] Helgeson and Zink, op. cit., p. 16.

[51] Miernyk, op. cit., pp. 171–172, 181.

[52] David L. Rogers, Willis Goudy, and Richard O. Richards, "Impacts of Industrialization on Employment and Occupational Structures," *Journal of the Community Development Society*, Vol. 7 (1976), pp. 54–55.

[53] Miernyk, op. cit., pp. 171–172.

[54] M. W. Reder, "The Theory of Occupational Wage Differentials," *American Economic Review*, Vol. 45 (1955), pp. 839–852.

[55] Bender, Green, and Campbell, op. cit., pp. 39–40; Bruce Weber, *Trickling Down: Are Rural and Rural Poor Family Incomes Responsive to Economic Growth?* (Madison: Institute for Research on Poverty, University of Wisconsin, Discussion Paper 210-74, 1974).

[56] Reinschmiedt, op. cit., p. 62; and Shaffer and Tweeten, op. cit., note 9, p. 8.

[57] Max F. Jordan, *Rural Industrialization in the Ozarks: Case Study of a New Shirt Plant at Gassville, Arkansas* (Washington, D.C.: U.S. Department of Agriculture, Agricultural Economic Report No. 123, 1962), pp. 12-13.

[58] Rogers, Goudy, and Richards, op. cit., p. 54.

[59] Miernyk, op. cit., pp. 171-172, 181.

[60] Shaffer and Tweeten, op. cit., note 9, p. 8; Reinschmiedt, op. cit., p. 62.

[61] Miernyk, op. cit., pp. 171-173.

[62] Shaffer and Tweeten, op. cit., note 9, p. 8.

[63] Andrews and Bauder, op. cit., p. 33

[64] Rogers, Goudy, and Richards, op. cit., p. 56.

[65] Gene F. Summers, *Large Industry in A Rural Area* (Madison: Center for Applied Sociology, University of Wisconsin, Working Paper RID 73.19, 1973), p. 11.

[66] Rogers, Goudy, and Richards, op. cit., p. 55.

[67] Elwood M. Beck, Jr., *Industrial Development and Occupational Movers and Stayers: An Interim Report* (Madison: Center for Applied Sociology, University of Wisconsin, Working Paper RID 72.17, 1972), p. 13.

[68] Andrews and Bauder, op. cit., p. 35.

Chapter 8

NONMETROPOLITAN INDUSTRIAL GROWTH AND NET MIGRATION

Tim Heaton and Glenn Fuguitt

Industrial development in nonmetro areas has been viewed by many as a viable solution to problems generated by long-term declines in the demand for labor in the agricultural sector. Displacement of farm workers may lead to population stagnation and impoverishment of rural families, and the creation of new employment opportunities in manufacturing is often assumed to be essential in order to retain potential outmigrants and to improve the standard of living. At the same time that it has been perceived as a solution to social and economic problems, industrial employment has grown in nonmetropolitan settings.[1] As types of industrial production reach a mature stage in larger urban areas, skilled labor and agglomeration economies become less essential, while available low-wage labor in rural areas allows for significant reductions in production costs. Thus, slow-growth industries may "filter down" from major industrial installations in and around large cities to more remote nonmetropolitan areas.[2] This filtering down process is facilitated by improvements in transportation and communication networks which reduce the friction of space, so that a more remote location may be economical provided other production costs are relatively low. A recent review of case studies on industrial growth in nonmetropolitan areas, however, shows that the consequences of industrial growth are not always beneficial for the local community.[3] Because of the importance placed on industrial development, and the actual expansion of industry in nonmetropolitan areas, it is necessary that the consequences of the shift over the recent past be critically examined.

This research will focus on the relationship between levels of employment in manufacturing and population change through net migration in

119

nonmetropolitan areas. First a model is proposed which allows the level of manufacturing activity to generate net migration growth in two ways: by inducing additional industrial expansion, thus creating more job opportunities, and by encouraging or discouraging growth of the population not engaged directly in manufacturing. Then we examine variations in the basic model. More specifically, the model is tested for both high- and low-wage manufacturing over time periods 1950-60, 1960-70, and in part with the more limited data available for 1970-75. Also, we show how effects vary by location in the urban hierarchy and by region.

THE BASIC MODEL

Evidence relating manufacturing to population change or migration has not yielded consistent generalizations. Duncan and Reiss found that levels of manufacturing, both in terms of the percentage employed and value of products sold, were negatively associated with population growth for various types of cities.[4] They concluded that manufacturing may still account for population growth in many cities, but where the level of manufacturing is already high little additional growth may occur. Also, their comparison of different cities showed that growth from manufacturing is not as great as that from services. Similarly, the southern towns examined by Tarver which specialized in manufacturing had lower growth than service centers, and the growth in these manufacturing centers was less in the 1960s than in the 1950s.[5] In a study of nonmetropolitan counties, Groth, on the other hand, found a positive effect of specialization in manufacturing on migration, particularly for high-wage manufacturing.[6] A recent analysis of southern cities suggested that capital-intensive industry attracts population while labor-intensive industry does not.[7] A review of case studies by Summers and associates concluded that new industry in rural areas can reduce outmigration as well as attract inmigrants.[8] In a model similar to our own, Flora and Thomas examined the effects of both level and change in manufacturing on migration in the North Central region of the United States.[9] They found that each had a positive effect on migration, and that the correlation between levels and growth in manufacturing was positive in the West North Central region but negative in the East North Central region. In the model developed below, we attempt to make more explicit some assumptions which link together the three basic variables: level of manufacturing, growth in manufacturing, and migration.

One assumption which may be implicit is that growth of new manufacturing employment will occur where the level of manufacturing is already high. This might occur for various reasons. Much employment growth results from expansion of existing firms rather than from establishment of new plants. Also, the presence of manufacturing implies that factors already exist which attract industry, such as raw materials, transportation networks, a labor supply, or other factors creating agglomeration economies. On the other hand, various factors may discourage additional employment growth in industrial areas. For example, market oriented firms can often capture a larger share of the market by locating in new areas.[10] Firms in search of cheap labor may find that wages have risen too high in industrial communities.[11] The correlation between levels of manufacturing and employment growth will depend on which of these two opposing tendencies dominates, but as long as both positive and negative forces are operating the correlation will be small.[12]

A second related assumption is that these new jobs in manufacturing will reduce outmigration and/or attract inmigrants. Migration is the relevant component of population change, since birth rates and death rates are not as responsive to employment opportunities as is the migration rate.[13] Even the migration rate, however, is not always highly sensitive to employment opportunities. Low-wage and female jobs absorb under- and unemployment, perhaps deterring outmigration slightly, but the effect on inmigration may be negligible. Also, if there is a reduction in employment, outmigration may not follow. Evidence shows that migrants are frequently not responsive to local employment conditions.[14] Thus, the link between employment change and migration should not be taken for granted.

The economic base theory supposes another way in which levels of, or growth in, manufacturing can affect migration. Wages paid for "basic employment" will generate nonbasic employment, generally in services. In any cross-section of communities, we expect to find some with high levels of manufacturing due to recent growth which have not yet established all of the services demanded by the new labor force. Continued nonbasic growth will occur, creating opportunities for potential inmigrants. On the other hand, high levels of manufacturing may detract from the quality of life to the extent that dissatisfied persons leave and potential inmigrants choose to live elsewhere. Air pollution, noise pollution, water pollution, and unattractive plant sites are all undesirable. Because of these positive and negative factors associated with industry there could be an effect of level of manufacturing on migration which is independent of subsequent growth or decline in manufacturing employment.

The preceding discussion establishes a model with the rate of net migration as a dependent variable, the level of manufacturing as the exogenous variable, and growth in manufacturing as an intervening variable. Levels of manufacturing can affect migration either via additional growth or decline in industrial job opportunities, or by means independent of change in the level of employment (see diagram in Fig. 1). In the following paragraphs we outline ways in which this model might vary depending on the type of manufacturing, the location of the area, the region, and the time period.

High- vs. Low-Wage Employment

Some previous research has shown the effect of manufacturing on population growth to be more positive for high-wage than for low-wage employment, and for capital-intensive than for labor-intensive production.[15] Obviously, the

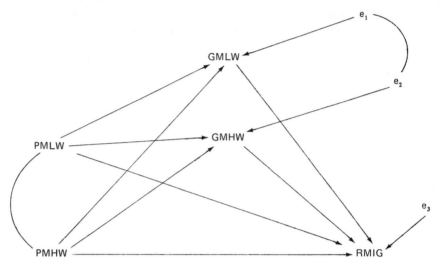

Fig. 1. Path diagram of the basic model.[a]

[a]Definitions: PMLW = percentage in low-wage manufacturing, PMHW = percentage in high-wage manufacturing, GMLW = growth in low-wage manufacturing, GMHW = growth in high-wage manufacturing, and RMIG = migration rate.

greater the wages paid the greater is the potential for growth in nonbasic services. Also, jobs offering higher wages are more attractive to potential inmigrants. Indeed, skills required in high-wage industries may not be available in the local labor force. It is not clear, however, whether new firms will be attracted to high-wage areas, especially if cheap labor is an important production factor. Migration is hypothesized to be more responsive to levels of, and growth in, high-wage than low-wage employment. Because low-wage industries are said to be attracted to new areas having an available unskilled labor supply, additional low-wage growth is expected to be less in areas already having a concentration of industry than is high-wage growth.

Location in the Urban Hierarchy

Location and size of the county could also alter the effect of manufacturing.[16] Sparsely settled, remote areas are theoretically least successful in attracting "trickle down" industries and, even when successful, they should receive firms in slowly growing or declining industries. Conversely, capital-intensive, high-wage plants would be expected to concentrate in more accessible urban settings when the advantages of proximity to related enterprises outweigh the attraction of a low-cost, unskilled labor force.[17] Yet the greater potential these types have as service centers could mean that among urban and accessible counties those specializing in manufacturing experience slower growth. Our analysis will compare the effects of manufacturing in different types of counties in order to determine where industry poses the greatest potential for population growth. Both distance from a metropolitan center and size of largest city in the county are used to characterize types of counties.

Region

We would expect regional differences in the effect of manufacturing employment on migration, and within the limited scope of this chapter there is particular interest in examining the distinctions between the South and the rest of the nation. Industrial development in the South seems to follow the northern pattern, but at a later date.[18] Also, much of the manufacturing attracted to rural areas there tends to be of a low-wage variety.[19] Even so, southern manufacturing may lead to more migration than in other regions because of its relative advantage over other types of economic activity. In the South, it is likely that desirable alternatives have been more restricted than in other regions. There is also a greater potential for return migration in the South because of its past history of outmigration.

Temporal Change

The shift toward a service economy has reduced the importance of manufacturing in the growth process. Furthermore, reductions in the friction of space have increased the range of external economies, thus reducing the pull of established industrial centers. At the same time, a new pattern of net migration has emerged in recent years, favoring nonmetropolitan areas, but particularly those which include resort and recreational activities.[20] Recent growth in nonmetropolitan employment has been concentrated largely in the service sector. In all, we expect the effect of levels of manufacturing on population change via net migration to decrease over time. Finally, as transportation and communication networks integrate the national economy, we should expect a convergence in the regional and locational differences observed in this research.

To summarize, the basic model is expanded to include both high- and low-wage manufacturing employment. Regional and locational variations will be shown for three time periods: 1950–60, 1960–70, and 1970–75. Unfortunately, data on employment change between 1970 and 1975 are not available, so only a part of the model can be estimated for the most recent time period.

DATA AND METHODS

The basic units of this research are nonmetropolitan counties in the conterminous United States. Data deficiencies necessitated omission of Alaska and Hawaii. Counties are classified as nonmetropolitan according to their status at the beginning of each decade considered. For 1950–60, non-metropolitan counties are those not in 1950 SMAs; for 1960–70, they are counties not in 1960 SMSAs as modified in 1963 following the results of the 1960 census; and for 1970–75, they are those not in 1970 SMSAs as updated in 1973. There are advantages in using current metropolitan status, par-ticularly in the interpretation of location variables. For example, were one to use the 1970 metropolitan–nonmetropolitan distinction throughout, there would be a built-in bias for an increasing adjacency effect, since many of the 1970 SMSAs are based on cities which were comparatively small in 1950. On the other hand, because of definition changes, this classification falls short of representing exactly those counties that would have been metropolitan in 1950 and 1960 according to the 1970 definition.

The location code classifies nonmetropolitan counties at the beginning of each time interval considered according to whether they are adjacent to metropolitan counties, and by the presence or absence of an incorporated place over 2500 in the county.

Employment data for industry were obtained from the Department of Commerce, Office of Business Economics, based on the Censuses of Popu-lation for 1950 and 1960, and from the U.S. Census Fourth Count for 1970. Unfortunately, data do not exist at the county level which would allow us to ascertain proportion of employment which pays above or below average wages. Thus, the distinction between low-wage and high-wage industries is based upon a classification by Philip Groth using national average income levels by industry.[21] Low-wage industries include apparel and textiles, food processing, lumber, and furniture, and all other manufacturing is classified as high-wage. This distinction undoubtedly fails to capture substantial variation in the distribution of wages between areas and regions (e.g., both types of manufacturing probably tend to pay lower wages in the South), but it is still an improvement on a single variable which combines all types of manu-facturing. Since the data are from the Census of Population, employees are recorded by place of residence rather than place of employment. This is most appropriate since our dependent variable, net migration, also is a residence variable. In interpreting the results, however, it should be remembered that with the increase in commuting over the 25-year period examined, there has undoubtedly been a decrease in the extent to which change in the industrial employment of residents in a county reflects change in the number of jobs located in that particular county.

The percentage of the total labor force engaged in manufacturing will be used to indicate the level of manufacturing. When percentages are used in regression models, some care must be taken in the interpretation of param-eters. Since the percentage in manufacturing and the percentage in non-manufacturing employment must sum to 100, both cannot be used as independent variables in the same equation. When manufacturing is in the equation, its unstandardized regression coefficient shows the effect on migra-tion if an additional 1% of the labor force is in manufacturing instead of nonmanufacturing. Thus, due to this interdependence between industrial and nonindustrial employment, introduction of controls for nonindustrial employment is not feasible, and indeed is statistically impossible when these two categories are exhaustive of all employment. While it would be possible to control for certain types of activity such as agriculture, the primary concern of this chapter is to compare manufacturing to all other types of employment. Therefore, no attempt is made to explicitly control for the existence of nonindustrial jobs. Change in manufacturing is computed as the percentage growth or decline in the total existing labor force due to gains or losses in manufacturing jobs, i.e., the number in manufacturing at time two minus the number in manufacturing at time one, divided by the total labor force at time one and multiplied by 100.

The amount of net migration for 1950-60 was taken from data for each county published by the U.S. Census, and comparable data for 1960-70 were obtained from a computer tape furnished by the Census Bureau.[22] Net migration for 1970-75 is taken from the Bureau of the Census federal/state cooperative series of county population estimates for 1975.[23] The annualized net migration rate used is the estimated number of net migrants divided by the product of the mid-decade population and the time interval (10 for 1950-60 and 1960-70, and 5.25 for 1970-75) and multiplied by 100.

The technique of path analysis is used to evaluate the model.[24] Path analysis enables us to partition direct and indirect effects. In this particular instance, we are concerned with the direct effect of the relative importance of manufacturing at the beginning of the period on net migration, and the indirect effect through the growth of manufacturing employment.

RESULTS

The means and standard deviations of the variables considered are displayed in Table 1 by location and region for each of the three time periods. In 1950, low-wage employment was the dominant type of manufacturing but high-wage jobs have grown at a much faster pace. The average high-wage employment gain was more than three times that of low-wage employment in the 1950s, and more than five times the average in the 1960s. Thus, by 1970 high-wage manufacturing had become more prevalent in nonmetropolitan industrial employment. This shift to an economic system emphasizing types of employment that are growing, i.e., manufacturing and services, should have some effect on population change. Indeed, concomitant with the growth of manufacturing, the data indicate a reversal of migration patterns from net outmigration to net inmigration.

Levels and growth of manufacturing and migration rates vary by type of county and region. In general, urban counties have higher levels of manufacturing than rural counties, and adjacent counties have higher levels than nonadjacent counties. But these differences are much greater for high-wage than for low-wage employment. As the "trickle down" theory predicts,

Table 1. Means and Standard Deviations for Levels and Growth of
Manufacturing, and for Migration Rates[a]

Variable	Year	By type of county					By region	
		Total	Adjacent		Nonadjacent		North	South
			Urban	Rural	Urban	Rural		
MEANS								
PMLW	1950	7.8	8.9	8.6	8.0	6.7	5.5	10.6
	1960	9.1	9.4	10.1	9.1	8.3	5.9	12.7
	1970	9.1	9.5	10.4	9.0	8.1	5.3	13.7
PMHW	1950	5.9	11.2	4.8	6.2	2.4	7.6	4.0
	1960	8.2	13.4	7.3	8.0	4.2	9.5	6.8
	1970	11.5	15.6	11.0	10.8	6.7	11.7	11.1
GMLW	1950–60	1.1	.9	1.1	1.0	1.4	.7	1.6
	1960–70	.8	.5	.8	.7	1.2	–.3	2.1
GMHW	1950–60	3.5	6.3	5.1	2.8	2.1	3.4	3.5
	1960–70	5.1	6.6	6.1	4.7	4.0	3.9	6.5
RMIG	1950–60	–1.4	–.4	–1.2	–1.3	–2.1	–1.1	–1.7
	1960–70	–.7	–.2	–.4	–.8	–1.2	–.7	–.7
	1970–75	.5	.6	1.0	.3	.5	.6	.5
STANDARD DEVIATIONS								
PMLW	1950	8.7	9.6	8.7	8.6	8.0	6.6	9.9
	1960	9.3	9.8	9.6	8.7	9.3	6.2	10.8
	1970	9.8	9.7	9.9	9.6	10.0	6.3	11.2
PMHW	1050	7.9	10.6	5.8	7.7	3.5	9.4	5.1
	1960	8.8	10.8	6.9	7.9	5.1	10.2	6.5
	1970	10.7	10.7	8.5	9.9	10.4	12.7	7.6
GMLW	1950–60	4.2	3.3	4.1	3.4	5.4	3.6	4.7
	1960–70	4.3	3.5	4.8	3.9	5.3	2.9	5.3
GMHW	1950–60	5.3	7.2	6.2	4.3	3.8	5.1	5.5
	1960–70	5.7	6.1	6.6	5.4	5.2	5.	6.2
RMIG	1950–60	1.9	1.8	1.8	1.7	1.8	1.7	1.9
	1960–70	1.5	1.5	1.7	1.4	1.5	1.5	1.6
	1970–75	1.7	1.5	2.0	1.4	2.0	1.7	1.7
N of	1950	2792	563	213	1129	887	1495	1297
counties	1960	2656	684	257	982	733	1416	1240
	1970	2440	806	283	771	580	1337	1103

[a]Manufacturing levels are represented by percentages of the total labor force.

Note: PMLW = percentage in low wage manufacturing; PMHW = percentage in high wage manufacturing; GMLW = growth in low wage manufacturing; GMHW = growth in high wage manufacturing; RMIG = rate of net migration.

low-wage employment grew faster in rural and in nonadjacent counties, so that differences between groups of counties in proportion of low-wage manufacturing employment decreased over time and by 1970 the highest proportion was for rural adjacent counties. On the other hand, high-wage employment grew most rapidly in urban and in adjacent counties over both decades. Turning to migration, in the 1950s all areas experienced net outmigration, especially rural and nonadjacent counties. Subsequently, the reversal to net inmigration occurred in all four types of counties but particularly in nonadjacent and rural counties. By the 1970s rural counties were growing faster than urban counties, but adjacent areas still maintained an advantage over nonadjacent areas.

Southern counties, on the average, have levels of low-wage manufacturing about double those of other areas, while high-wage manufacturing is less prevalent. Southern counties also experienced more rapid growth of low-wage employment in both decades, and of high-wage employment in the 1960s, than did the remainder of the nation. Within the South, however, high-wage employment had at least twice the average growth rate of low-wage employment over both decades. In spite of its more rapid industrial growth, the South does not have greater attraction to migrants. Southern outmigration was higher than in other regions in the 1950s, but in the latter two time periods regional differences in migration were minimal.

Regression coefficients for the model with all counties included are presented in Table 2. The standardized coefficients indicate the relative importance of a variable, i.e., the expected change in the standardized (Z - score) value of the dependent variable given a unit change in the standardized value of the independent variable. Unstandardized coefficients indicate the expected change in the actual value of the dependent variable given unit change in the independent variable. We will focus on unstandardized coefficients since they are more appropriate for comparison across decades, types of counties, and regions (see Duncan for a discussion of comparing coefficients across populations[25]).

As was expected, growth of low-wage employment is more likely to occur where high-wage employment is minimal, but the negative association is small for both time periods. The level of low-wage employment and the growth of low-wage employment were negatively associated in the 1950s, but by the 1960s the association had shifted to positive. For high-wage employment, growth was identified more with areas already containing high-wage employment than with low-wage areas in the 1950s. In the 1960s, however, the reverse was true. Thus, the data show that in the most recent decade low-wage areas were attractive sites for additional employment growth, both low- and high-wage. In both decades, agglomeration economies connected with the presence of high-wage manufacturing were a positive force in the location of new high-wage employment.

The effects of levels of manufacturing on migration if employment growth is not included in the equation are indicated by the third column of Table 2. Comparing the migratory response to industrialization over the three periods,

Table 2. Standardized (betas) and Unstandardized (bs) Regression
Coefficients for the Model Predicting Migration Rates:
1950–1960, 1960–1970, and 1970–1975[a]

Predetermined variable	Year	Dependent variable			
		GMLW	GMHW	RMIG	RMIG
PMLW b	1950–60	−.016	.064	.010	.001
beta		−.035	.105	.045	.004
PMHW b	1950–60	−.056	.206	.075	.047
beta		−.107	.308	.321	.200
GMLW b	1950–60	−	−	−	.103
beta		−	−	−	.046
GMHW b	1950–60	−	−	−	.149
beta		−	−	−	.427
R²		.013	.106	.105	.276
PMLW b	1960–70	.075	.185	.020	.004
beta		.159	.299	.120	.025
PMHW b	1960–70	−.029	.166	.046	.031
beta		−.058	.254	.261	.179
GMLW b	1960–70	−	−	−	−.002
beta		−	−	−	−.007
GMHW b	1960–70	−	−	−	.086
beta		−	−	−	.322
R²		.029	.148	.080	.169
PMLW b	1970–75	−	−	.007	−
beta		−	−	.045	−
PMHW b	1970–75	−	−	−.001	−
beta		−	−	−.005	−
R²		−	−	.002	−

[a]See Table 1 legend for definitions of variables

we find that in the 1950s the presence of low-wage manufacturing has a small positive effect, while high-wage manufacturing has a moderate positive effect. A decade later, the low-wage effect increases and the high-wage effect declines. By the 1970s, both effects are reduced to values near zero and the high-wage effect is negative. But because these effects reflect migration resulting from continuing job expansion, they are reduced when growth in manufacturing is added to the equations (see column 4). As predicted, growth in the number of high-wage jobs has a substantially larger effect on migration than does growth in the number of low-wage jobs in both decades, and the effects of employment growth become smaller over time.

Using techniques described by Alwin and Hauser, we can decompose the total effect of levels of manufacturing on net migration (column 3 of Table 2) into a direct effect (column 4 of Table 2) and an indirect effect (the product of the effect of levels of manufacturing on manufacturing growth, and of manufacturing growth on migration).[26] The indirect effect shows the extent to which the association between initial industrial concentration and net migration works through a related increase in industrial jobs. The direct effect reflects any multiplier benefits that may accrue to industrial areas and result in higher levels of net migration. Total, direct, and indirect effects are reported in Table 3.

Table 3. Decomposition of Effect of Level of Manufacturing
on Migration Rates[a]

Predetermined variable	Year	Total effect	Direct effect	Indirect effect VIA	
				GMLW	GMHW
PMLW b	1950–60	.010	.001	−.001	.010
beta		.045	.004	−.004	.045
PMHW b	1950–60	.075	.047	−.003	.031
beta		.321	.200	−.011	.132
PMLW b	1960–70	.020	.004	.000	.016
beta		.120	.025	−.001	.096
PMHW b	1960–70	.046	.031	.000	.015
beta		.261	.179	.000	.082
PMLW b	1970–75	.007	−	−	−
beta		.045	−	−	−
PMHW b	1970–75	−.001	−	−	−
beta		−.009	−	−	−

[a] Derived from Table 2.

We have seen that throughout the 1950s and 1960s high-wage manufacturing had a larger total effect on net migration than low-wage manufacturing. In Table 3 we see that in each decade the total effect for the initial level of high-wage manufacturing on net migration is through both multiplier benefits (direct effect) and, to a lesser extent, through the related growth of high-wage jobs (indirect effect). Note also that for both decades the initial levels of low-wage manufacturing generate net migration almost entirely due to growth of the number of *high-wage* manufacturing employees. Consequently, the higher association between the level of high-wage manufacturing and net migration, as compared with the association of the level of low-wage manufacturing and net migration, is due to the larger direct effect for high-wage manufacturing. Unfortunately, a lack of information on employment change since 1970 makes it impossible to specify changes in direct and indirect effects which led to a decline in the total effects of manufacturing.

To summarize, some ideas developed above do receive empirical support. The level of high-wage manufacturing has a larger effect on net migration primarily because it generates more migration independent of continued manufacturing employment growth. Also, growth of high-wage jobs has a greater impact on net migration than does growth of low-wage jobs. Low-wage employment growth is repelled in areas of high-wage concentration; but high-wage growth is occurring in high-wage areas, and in the 1960s high-wage employment also is more likely to grow in low-wage areas. Finally, since 1970, levels of manufacturing have virtually no effect on migration. We attribute this latter finding to the increasing importance of service employment. Furthermore, it is possible that recent industrial growth is more decentralized than in the past, so that initial levels of manufacturing will be negatively associated with employment growth.

Differences by Type of County

In Table 4 we show how effects vary by type of county. For simplicity, we do not report standardized coefficients nor do we include all of the paths in the model. The results generally parallel those of Table 3, but some differences by type of county bear comment. First, focusing on levels of high-wage manufacturing, the direct effect is greater for nonadjacent than for adjacent counties, and greater for rural than for urban counties in both decades. It seems plausible that in the more remote rural areas high-wage manufacturing requires the creation or expansion of services and infrastructure that leads to higher levels of net migration, whereas this type of support already exists in more central urban areas. Second, for high-wage areas in the 1950s and for both high- and low-wage areas in the 1960s, the indirect effect via growth in high-wage employment is greater in adjacent than in nonadjacent counties. Apparently, proximity to a larger city is an advantage in attracting migrants through additional high-wage employment in industrial areas.[27] Third, the indirect effects realized through growth in high-wage employment are larger in rural than in urban counties, whether or not these counties also are adjacent to metropolitan areas. We interpret this rural–urban difference in indirect effects to mean that in rural areas where opportunities are more limited, manufacturing acts as a greater stimulus to retain potential out-migrants and to attract potential inmigrants than in more developed urban areas.

The total effects reflect a combination of the above trends. Until 1970, levels of employment in high-wage industry make a bigger difference than in low-wage industry in all types of counties, but in the 1970s this high-wage advantage is neutralized, and, in fact, slightly reversed. For high-wage industry in the 1950s, the adjacent–nonadjacent differential in total effect is slight. This is because the larger direct effect for nonadjacent counties is balanced by the larger indirect effect for adjacent counties. In the 1960s, however, the total effects are larger in nonadjacent than in adjacent counties. Up until 1970 the total, direct, and indirect effects of high-wage industry were larger in rural

Table 4. Decomposition of Effect of Level of Manufacturing on Migration Rate by Type of County (bs Only)[a]

Variable	Total effect	Direct effect	Indirect effect VIA	
			GMLW	GMHW
Adjacent: 1950-60				
Urban: PMLW	−.007	−.008	−.002	.003
PMHW	.041	.020	−.004	.025
Rural: PMLW	.006	.002	.000	.004
PMHW	.140	.061	.000	.079
Nonadjacent: 1950-60				
Urban: PMLW	.004	−.005	−.001	.010
PMHW	.042	.034	−.002	.010
Rural: PMLW	.009	.001	.001	.007
PMHW	.132	.087	−.003	.048
Adjacent: 1960-70				
Urban: PMLW	.005	−.007	−.003	.015
PMHW	.016	.000	.001	.015
Rural: PMLW	.004	−.012	.000	.016
PMHW	.086	.060	.001	.025
Nonadjacent: 1960-70				
Urban: PMLW	.021	.010	.000	.011
PMHW	.034	.029	.000	.005
Rural: PMLW	.022	.007	.001	.014
PMHW	.084	.068	.000	.016
Adjacent: 1970-75				
Urban: PMLW	−.001	—	—	—
PMHW	−.018	—	—	—
Rural: PMLW	−.017	—	—	—
PMHW	−.019	—	—	—
Nonadjacent: 1970-75				
Urban PMLW	008	—	—	—
PMHW	.004	—	—	—
Rural: PMLW	.018	—	—	—
PMHW	.018	—	—	—

[a]See Table 1 legend for definitions of variables.

than in urban counties. But this rural advantage accrued only in the nonadjacent counties in the 1970s. In fact, the total effects for adjacent counties were all negative in 1970-75, indicating that the newer migration trend in adjacent counties favors areas with lower proportions of their labor force in either low- or high-wage manufacturing.

Comparison across decades of differences among county groups in these direct effects supports the hypothesis that locational differences are diminishing. Moreover, most of this convergence is due to the reduction of association between levels of high-wage industry and net migration in rural areas.

Regional Differences

When the South is compared with the rest of the country (Table 5), several differences appear. Perhaps the most notable regional deviation from the overall pattern is that the high-wage advantage over low-wage areas exists only in the South. Together the direct and indirect effects combine to produce a larger total effect on migration for high-wage than for low-wage industry over 1950–60, particularly in the South. This high-wage advantage declines in both regions, so that by 1970–75 the high-wage effect is actually smaller than the low-wage effect in the North. Though the time covered is limited, the evidence does suggest that change in the South is delayed but still follows the northern pattern. Presumably, the high-wage effect was higher at an earlier point and has declined over time in northern counties and the decline is occurring at a later date in the South.

Nevertheless, differences between regional effects for both high- and low-wage industry levels remain about equal over time, except for the higher-wage difference in 1950. Thus, changes in effects have not yet resulted in regional convergence.

Table 5. Decomposition of Effects by Region[a]

Variable	Year	Total effect	Direct effect	Indirect effect VIA	
				GMLW	GMHW
North PMLW	1950–60	.035	.037	−.010	.008
PMHW		.058	.031	−.003	.030
South PMLW	1950–60	.011	.002	.000	.009
PMHW		.099	.059	−.002	.042
North PMLW	1960–70	.040	.040	−.007	.007
PMHW		.040	.021	.000	.019
South PMLW	1960–70	.014	−.001	.000	.015
PMHW		.056	.039	.000	.017
North PMLW	1970–75	.036	−	−	−
PMHW		−.009	−	−	−
South PMLW	1970–75	.003	−	−	−
PMHW		.013	−	−	−

[a]See Table 1 legend for definitions of variables.

CONCLUSION

When applied to nonmetropolitan counties in the United States, our basic model leads to several conclusions. Net migration differentials among counties associated with different levels of manufacturing can either be a result of subsequent industrial contraction or expansion or of positive or negative factors independent of employment change in manufacturing. Because of the dual nature of the association, simple correlations between levels of manufacturing and migration can be misinterpreted. Results for all nonmetropolitan counties, considered together, tend to support the following conclusions: (1) Effects of levels of manufacturing on migration, which are independent of subsequent employment growth, are greater for high-wage than for low-wage employment; (2) agglomeration economies operate for high-wage employment, i.e., high-wage areas have larger gains of additional high-wage employment than other areas; (3) new low-wage industry is not attracted to high-wage areas; (4) high-wage industry is attracted to low-wage areas; and (5) growth of high-wage jobs has a greater impact on migration than growth of low-wage jobs. But locational and regional differences do exist.

When counties are compared in terms of proximity to metropolitan areas and presence of urban centers, the major finding is that the level of manufacturing has a much greater impact on migration in rural areas. But the urban–rural differences have declined, and in 1970–75 they are minimal. Given that urban places function as service centers, the small effect of manufacturing in urban counties is no surprise. Similarly, in recent times the negative impact of the decline in agriculture has lessened, while services have become more important in rural areas. As the economic bases of urban and rural centers become more alike, one may expect convergence in the effects of manufacturing among residence groups.

Regional comparisons also show differences. Low-wage employment has a slightly smaller effect in the South than elsewhere. High-wage employment has a larger effect in the South than elsewhere, suggesting that for persons wanting to remain in or return to the South high-wage industries offer an incentive to do so. Over time, however, the high-wage effect has declined, especially in the South. Apparently the South is following a similar but belated pattern of development compared to the rest of the country.

Writers have been quick to point out that nonmetropolitan industrial expansion is largely of the low-wage, labor-intensive variety. A possible implication may be that this is a poor basis for transforming the economy away from declining extractive activities. Yet we found over the 1950–70 period that growth in employment in high-wage industries outstripped growth in low-wage industries in all groups of counties considered. Analysis showed also that high-wage industrial employment tended to grow in areas already high in the proportion employed in low-wage industries. This suggests that an area may be attractive initially for its relatively unskilled labor force, but that this can be followed by more high-wage industry, thus upgrading the area's labor force.

The major conclusion, however, is that manufacturing may have received more attention than it merits as a solution to the problem of nonmetropolitan population decline. At a time when nonmetropolitan areas experienced a dramatic reversal from outmigration to inmigration, the association between levels of industry and migration dropped to values near zero. Nonmetropolitan centers enjoying industrial expansion can no longer be assured of a more favorable balance between in- and outmigration, on the whole, than other nonmetropolitan areas. Introduction of new industrial employment will, we predict, continue to induce net inmigration into some areas. However, with the growth of a service-oriented economy, manufacturing will further decline in importance. Indeed, Allaman and Birch give some evidence of a decline in the number of rural manufacturing firms since 1970, and Haren shows that employment growth in services far exceeds manufacturing.[28] Traditionally, the service sector has been viewed as nonbasic and, as such, dependent on production in other sectors of the economy. Consequently, direct inducement of growth in the service sector was assumed not to be a viable means of affecting population distribution. In light of the declining migration advantage accruing to industrial expansion in nonmetropolitan areas, the recent slow growth of manufacturing employment, and the rapid expansion of services, potential growth in the service sector should receive greater attention as a possible policy tool in the future.[29]

NOTES

[1] Claude C. Haren, "Rural Industrial Growth in the 1960s," *American Journal of Agricultural Economics,* Vol. 52 (1970), pp. 431–437; Thomas Till, "Extent of Industrialization in Southern Labor Markets in the 1960s," *Journal of Regional Science,* Vol. 13 (1973), pp. 453–459.

[2] Wilbur R. Thompson, "The Economic Base of Urban Problems," in N. W. Chamberlain, ed., *Contemporary Economic Issues* (Homewood, Ill.: Richard D. Irwin, 1969); Rodney A. Erickson, "Nonmetropolitan Industrial Expansion: Emerging Implications for Regional Development," *Review of Regional Studies,* Vol. 6 (1976), pp. 35–48.

[3] Gene F. Summers, Sharon D. Evans, Frank Clemente, E. M. Beck, and Jon Minkoff, *Industrial Invasion of Nonmetropolitan America* (New York: Praeger, 1976).

[4] Otis D. Duncan and Albert Reiss, *Social Characteristics of Urban and Rural Communities* (New York: John Wiley & Sons, 1956), pp. 197–200.

[5] James D. Tarver, "Patterns of Population Change Among Southern Nonmetropolitan Towns, 1950–70," *Rural Sociology,* Vol. 37 (1972), pp. 53–72.

[6] Philip G. Groth, "Population Change in Counties Classified by Economic Function," *Growth and Change,* Vol. 8 (9177), pp. 38–43.

[7] Leonard F. Wheat, *Urban Growth in the Nonmetropolitan South* (Lexington, Mass.: Lexington Books, 1976), pp. 37–46.

[8] Summers et al., op. cit., note 3, pp. 24–29.

[9] Cornelia B. Flora and Don Thomas, "Migration and Nonmetropolitan Industrialization in the North Central Region," in J. Allan Beegle and Robert L. McNamara, eds., *Patterns of Migration and Population Change in America's Heartland* (East Lansing, Mich.: Michigan State University Agricultural Experiment Station, Research Report 344, 1978), pp. 32–39.

[10] David M. Smith, *Industrial Location* (New York: John Wiley & Sons, 1971), pp. 62–66.

[11] Wheat, op. cit., note 7, pp. 37–46.

[12] For a more complete discussion of factors which encourage or discourage industrial location in nonmetropolitan areas, see the chapters in this volume by Kale and Lonsdale, and Doering and Kinworthy.

[13] David F. Sly, "Migration and the Ecological Complex," *American Sociological Review*, Vol. 37 (1972), pp. 615–628; W. Parker Frisbie and Dudley L. Poston, Jr., *Sustenance Organization and Migration in Nonmetropolitan America* (Iowa City: The University of Iowa, 1978), pp. 2–3.

[14] Ira S. Lowery, *Migration and Metropolitan Growth: Two Analytical Models* (San Francisco: Chandler, 1966), pp. 30–33; Michael J. Greenwood, "An Analysis of the Determinants of Geographical Labor Mobility in the United States," *Review of Economics and Statistics*, Vol. 51 (1968), pp. 189–204.

[15] Groth, op. cit., note 6; Wheat, op. cit., note 7.

[16] For a discussion of the differing effects of manufacturing on economic welfare in more vs. less-urban counties, see the chapter by Seyler in this volume.

[17] Barry M. Moriarty, "Manufacturing Wage Rates, Plant Location, and Plant Location Policies," *Popular Government* (Institute of Government, University of North Carolina at Chapel Hill), Spring 1977, pp. 48–53.

[18] Clifford H. Patrick and P. Neal Ritchey, "Changes in Population and Employment as Processes in Regional Development," *Rural Sociology*, Vol. 39 (1974), pp. 224–237.

[19] Till, op. cit., note 1; Moriarty, op. cit., note 17; J. O. Wheeler, "Regional Manufacturing Structure in the Southeastern United States, 1973," *Southeastern Geographer*, Vol. 14 (1974), pp. 67–83.

[20] Calvin L. Beale and Glenn V. Fuguitt, "The New Pattern of Nonmetropolitan Population Change," CDE Working Paper 75-22 (Center for Demography and Ecology, University of Wisconsin–Madison, 1975).

[21] Groth, op. cit., note 6.

[22] U.S. Bureau of the Census, "Components of Population Change, 1950 to 1960 for Counties, Standard Metropolitan Statistical Areas . . . ," *Current Population Reports*, Series P-23, No. 7 (November 1962).

[23] U.S. Bureau of the Census, "Federal State Cooperative Program for Population Estimates," *Current Population Reports*, Series P-26, Nos. 75-1 to 75-50 (1976); and "Population Estimates and Projections," *Current Population Reports*, Series P-25, Nos. 624 (Washington); 629 (Maryland); 631 (New York); 633 (Massachusetts); 637 (Texas); and 638 (Alaska) (1976).

[24] See Otis D. Duncan, *Introduction to Structural Equation Models* (New York: Academic Press, 1975), for an introductory discussion of the statistical techniques we use.

[25] Ibid., pp. 54–57.

[26] Duane F. Alwin and Robert H. Hauser, "The Decomposition of Effects in Path Analysis," *American Sociological Review*, Vol. 40 (1975), pp. 37–47.

[27] Note that some of this growth in employment could be the movement of people to adjacent counties who hold or obtain manufacturing jobs in the metropolitan-based firms.

[28] Peter M. Allaman and David L. Birch, "Components of Employment Change for Metropolitan and Rural Areas in the United States by Industry Group: 1970–72," report prepared at the Joint Center for Urban Studies of the M.I.T. and Harvard University (1975). See also the chapter by Haren in this volume.

[29] Research for this chapter has been supported by the Economic Development Division, Economic Research Service, U.S. Department of Agriculture, and by the College

of Agricultural and Life Sciences, University of Wisconsin-Madison, through a cooperative agreement, as well as by the Regional Research Institute, West Virginia University. Analysis was aided by a "Center for Population Research" grant, No. HDO5876, to the Center for Demography and Ecology, University of Wisconsin-Madison, from the Center for Population Research of the National Institute of Child Health and Human Development.

Chapter 9

NONMETROPOLITAN INDUSTRIALIZATION AND MIGRATION:
An Overview with Special Emphasis on the Ozarks Region

John A. Kuehn

As earlier chapters in this book have substantiated, two trends of importance for nonmetropolitan growth and change have emerged during the 1960s. First, the manufacturing sector is dispersing nationally and regionally with expanding production in nonmetropolitan areas. Second, many nonmetropolitan areas are experiencing population growth and net inmigration after decades of population decline and net outmigration. This chapter examines some of the relationships between industrialization and migration by integrating several case studies as they relate to recent industrial activity in nonmetropolitan counties in the Ozarks Economic Development Region.

RECENT TRENDS IN THE LOCATION OF
MANUFACTURING AND POPULATION

Manufacturing employment has shifted toward and dispersed within nonmetropolitan areas during the 1960s. Of the nearly 3,000,000 workers added by manufacturing nationally, 43% were located in nonmetro areas, especially in the South and North Central regions of the nation. This share of the nation's net gain contrasted sharply with the nonmetropolitan share of 22% of total manufacturing workers in 1960. Gains in manufacturing employment accounted for 45% of the net increase in total nonmetropolitan employment during the 1960s. About 29% of the nonmetropolitan counties gained 500 or more manufacturing workers during the decade, and an additional 26% gained 100 to 500 employees.[1] During the 1970s, the importance of manufacturing in less urbanized areas has been eclipsed by growth in the trades, services, and government sectors.[2] Between 1970 and 1977, manufacturing accounted for only 8% of the total nonmetropolitan growth in nonfarm employment.[3] However, nonmetropolitan areas fared better than metro areas in manufacturing employment. Nonmetropolitan areas gained more than 300,000 workers while metro areas lost over 1,000,000 workers in manufacturing. Most of the nonmetropolitan growth in manufacturing was in the South.

The Ozarks Region participated in the national decentralization of manufacturing during the 1960s and has maintained this growth during the early 1970s. During the period 1967 through 1974, Kuehn and Braschler identified 2,617 new manufacturing plants located in the Ozarks Economic Development Region which includes Arkansas, Kansas, Louisiana, Missouri, and Oklahoma.[4] Sixty percent of these new operational plants were located in nonmetropolitan areas, especially in towns of less than 25,000 population.[5] The general locational disposition of the new plants is summarized in Figure 1. Fifteen percent of 2,617 new plants located in nonmetropolitan counties adjacent to urbanized metro cores, 4% in nonadjacent counties containing a city of 25,000 or more people in 1970, and 40% in nonadjacent counties having no large cities. There was no strong tendency for larger plants to perfer larger cities or smaller plants to prefer smaller towns. New nonmetropolitan plants were very diversified with 286 different industries represented. They were widely dispersed among towns. Within nonmetropolitan areas, 497 towns acquired new plants employing 10 or more workers; 241 of these towns had populations below 2,500 in 1970. A shift to a more dispersed locational form was even more pronounced in the 1972 to 1974 period than over a span from 1967 to 1971.

The long established trend of increasing population concentration into large metro areas was reversed during the early 1970s, and this reversal was not confined to mere urbanized sprawl nor to nonmetropolitan counties with large towns.[6] Nonmetropolitan counties, both adjacent and not adjacent to metro areas, had higher population growth rates and greater inmigration than metro areas between 1970 and 1976. As a group, nonmetropolitan counties adjacent to metro areas had 1,328,000 net inmigrants from 1970 to 1976, while nonmetropolitan counties not adjacent to metro areas had 928,000 net inmigrants. Over the same period, metropolitan areas gained only 545,000 net inmigrants, mainly in areas of less than 750,000 population. Much of the net inmigration into nonmetropolitan areas has occurred in less urbanized counties with towns of less than 25,000 population. Beale has attributed much of this population turnaround to the growth of recreation, retirement, manufacturing, trade, and services in nonmetro areas.[7]

Many individuals and families apparently are realizing their preferences to live in small towns. A recent national survey by Fuguitt and Zuiches revealed that 68% of the respondents preferred to live in small towns or rural areas rather than in metro areas, no matter the distance to larger cities.[8] For these respondents, differences in earnings could be less important than often difficult-to-quantify amenities. Dollar earnings are easily quantified, but are

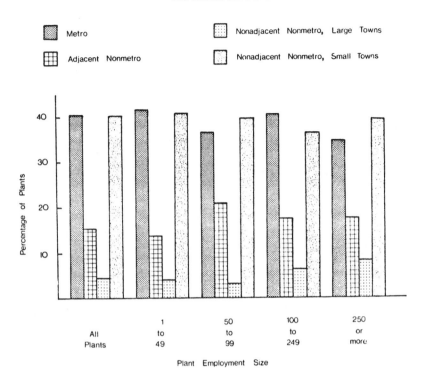

Fig. 1. Distribution of new plants by type of location, Ozarks region, 1967–74.

only one ingredient of behavior that attempts maximization of individual welfare. Trade-offs exist between earnings and amenities, including amenities associated with residential preferences. Thus it should come as no surprise to witness that some inmigrants experience an earnings decline with their move. Area amenities combined with job opportunities may likely be more important than absolute earnings differentials in explaining recent migration reversals. Indeed, some of the previous movement to large urbanized areas may have been "forced migration" caused by the *scarcity* of even comparatively low paying jobs in nonmetropolitan areas.[9] Past choices confronting previous rural to urban migrants may well have been between rural unemployment and high urban earnings and not between low rural earnings and high urban earnings.[10] The basic suppositions of this chapter are that the growth of nonmetropolitan job opportunities has enabled many workers to trade earnings differentials for area amenities and that inmigrants contribute to the stock of human capital in nonmetropolitan areas.

SELECTED MIGRATION STUDIES

The population shifts noted above direct attention to related migration studies. A study by Matson used data from the Continuous Work History Sample to analyze inmigration rates for workers by industry between 1960 and 1970.[11] Inmigrants were defined as those moving into 12 Southeastern states from the remaining regions of the nation. Six percent of the 1970 workers in these 12 states were inmigrants. Manufacturing evidenced a slightly greater propensity to hire inmigrants than all other sectors combined. Approximately 9.4% of the gross additions in manufacturing employment were inmigrants vs. 7.3% of the gross additions in nonmanufacturing employment. Certain industries within manufacturing evidenced a greater propensity to hire inmigrants than others. These included ordnance, transportation equipment, petroleum, electrical machinery, instruments, and nonelectrical machinery. Other sectors with high hiring rates for inmigrants were mining, transportation, and wholesale trades.

Another study by Bender et al. examined characteristics of inmigrants and residents in a sample of rural Ozark households living in towns of less than 2,500 population or in the open countryside.[12] About 12% of the household heads surveyed in late 1966 had migrated across county boundaries since 1961, in most instances from outside the Ozarks mountainous area. On the average, inmigrant household heads were 10 years younger, had an additional year of formal education, held twice as many jobs during the period, and had $479 more in annual household earnings than resident household heads. On the other hand, 39% of the inmigrants had accepted income losses at the time of their move even though they were still in the labor force. Reasons for moving often included lower living costs, family needs, and to avoid what they perceived as urban problems.

Perkinson investigated household migration between 1970 and 1975 into an 8-county rural area of North Carolina's Coastal Plain.[13] Approximately 8% of the surveyed households were inmigrants to the area, and 39% of these inmigrants returned to the same county in which they had lived before. Manufacturing accounted for practically half of the area's total employment growth. About 20% of the new inmigrants and 28% of the returnees worked in manufacturing. On the average, new inmigrants had about $1,100 more in annual household earnings than residents. Returnees and residents earned nearly identical amounts. However, none of the differences in earnings were statistically significant. And, after adjusting for household social characteristics in a multiple regression analysis, Perkinson concluded that new inmigrants had 22% less and returnees 27% less household earnings than residents with comparable socioeconomic profiles.[14] Half of the new inmigrants were professionals or managers, whereas half of the residents and returnees were craftsmen or operatives. In general, new inmigrants were younger and had more formal education than returnees, who in turn were younger and more educated than residents. Twenty-eight percent of the new inmigrants and 68% of the returnees listed family or area living conditions as the major reason for their inmigration. Interestingly, about one-half of the returnees had originally left the area to improve their civilian employment.

In a related study, Olsen and Kuehn investigated migrants' responses to industrialization in four Southern nonmetropolitan areas between 1965 and 1970.[15] These four multicounty areas were selected because of their rapid growth in nonfarm employment, particularly in manufacturing. Areas selected within the Ozarks and Upper Coastal regions had experienced industrial growth for several decades. Recreation and retirement complexes were also important growth sectors in the Ozarks area. Areas selected within the Mississippi Delta and Four Corners regions were relative newcomers to industrialization and had sizeable minority populations. Workers were sampled and interviewed at 26 of the 56 plants which were established or had considerably expanded their operations since 1965.

Overall, new inmigrants and returnees, defined as movers into the multicounty areas, each represented about 11% of the surveyed jobs. Movers within each multicounty area were classified as residents. However, differences among areas were noticeable. The Delta had few new inmigrants or returnees. In the remaining three areas, returnees held one-eighth of the jobs. New inmigrants held one-fifth and residents about two-thirds of the Ozark jobs. In the Upper Coastal area, however, residents held four-fifths of the jobs and new inmigrants were only a small proportion of the surveyed workers.

As indicated in Table 1, new inmigrants in the sample generally had higher salaries, more job mobility, and more formal education than returnees, who in turn ranked above residents. As expected, both new inmigrants and returnees

Table 1. Characteristics of Manufacturing Employees in Four Industrializing Rural Areas, 1970

Percentage in each group with characteristic in 1970	Residents (77%)[a]	New inmigrants (11%)	Returnees (11%)
Weekly salary greater than $80	57	68	62
Decline in real salary from previous job	16	33	38
Three or more civilian jobs 1965 to 1970	22	53	41
Primary reason for leaving previous job[b]			
Monetary	78	74	52
Area living conditions	1	7	18
Less than 30 years old	48	53	54
High school graduates	45	66	56

[a]Percentage is of total plant workers.

[b]Calculated as percentage of workers not unemployed for long periods or not continuously employed at same plant.

Source: Adapted from Olsen and Kuehn.

had proportionately more young people than resident workers. Interestingly, 33% of the new inmigrants and 38% of the returnees experienced real salary declines between their 1970 and first previous jobs. Seven percent of the new inmigrants and 18% of the returnees stated that area living conditions were the *primary* reason for leaving their previous jobs. Salary declines were particularly evident for returnees in the Upper Coastal area and for new inmigrants in the Ozarks area.

MIGRATION IN THE OZARKS REGION

Most studies of migration have relied upon primary surveys to obtain data concerning migrants' characteristics. At the small area level, published Census records reveal only the number of migrants and their ages. In recent years, access to a third source of data has been developed. Data concerning migrants' characteristics were obtained from the Continuous Work History Sample, specifically the longitudinal first quarter file (BEA).[16] This file is a 1% sample of workers covered by the social security program during the first quarter of each year. Workers' histories include data on sex, race, year of birth, and also the state, county, major industry of employment, and estimated annual wages. The sample included 14,393 workers in the nonmetropolitan portions of the Ozarks Region in 1975. These workers and their characteristics were classified according to four migrant groups.

In the newly developed file, migrant status was determined using the first quarters of 1965 and 1975. Of the 14,393 covered workers in 1975, 19% were classified as residents, 21% as new inmigrants, 6% as returnees, and 55% as new entrants or workers with no known work location in 1965.[17] Residents were defined as those workers in 1975 who worked in covered employment in the same county in 1965 and who had no known work history in a different county from 1966 through 1974. New inmigrants were defined as those 1975 workers who worked in covered employment in a different county in 1965. This definition of new inmigrants includes all intercounty changes in work location, even those of very short distances. Returnees were defined as those 1975 workers who worked in covered employment in the same county in 1965 and who did have a known work history in a different county in any year from 1966 through 1974. This definition of returnees can be considered restrictive insofar as no consideration is given work locations prior to 1965 or between 1966 and 1974 for new inmigrants.

Entrants were defined as those 1975 workers who had no covered employment during the first quarter of 1965. Several explanations, besides reporting and coding errors, can account for the large size of this group, 55% of the sampled workers. First, many of this group were likely too young to be employed in 1965; 41% were less than 15 years old in 1965. Second, women have been increasing their participation in the labor force; 52% of the entrants were females. Third, the entrant may not have worked in the first quarter of

1965 or may have worked in certain types of employment not covered by social security, e.g., federal government, some state and local governments, some agricultural workers, and railroads.

Workers covered in the sample were further classified according to two broad industry categories, namely, manufacturing and nonmanufacturing, and according to three types of nonmetro counties in which they were employed. Between 1965 and 1975, manufacturing accounted for 16% of the net increase in total covered employment in nonmetro counties adjacent to metro cores, 22% in nonadjacent counties having cities of 25,000 or more population, and 30% in nonadjacent counties having no large cities. Henceforth, these nonmetro counties are labeled fringe, urbanized, and rural counties, respectively. Clearly, the importance of manufacturing in nonmetro growth increased as urbanization decreased.

Sampling variability constitutes a major limitation in interpreting data from the 1% sample files, particularly with small sample sizes. Relative standard errors become greater as the number of observations decrease within any particular subcategorization. For example, relative standard errors for returnees are greater than those for residents, new inmigrants, and entrants. Approximate standard errors have been calculated by the Social Security Administration for estimated percentages of persons, estimated number of persons with specific characteristics, and for estimated average total earnings.[18] In the analysis to follow, small differences among groups are likely to be insignificant.

As indicated in Table 2, more new inmigrants and returnees worked in rural counties than in urbanized and fringe counties. The geographic distribution of new inmigrants was practically identical to that of residents and entrants. Thirty percent worked in fringe counties, 16% in urbanized counties, and 54% in rural counties. Returnees, on the other hand, were even more oriented to small towns and open country areas distant from metro cores. Only 24% of the returnees worked in fringe counties, 13% in urbanized counties, and 63% in rural counties. This appears consistent with recent polls of residential preferences. Most of the inmigrants chose to work and live in rural counties at some distance from metropolitan concentrations.

Manufacturing played a greater role in providing jobs for new inmigrants and returnees as distance to metro cores increased and the degree of urbanization declined. About 25% of the total sampled workers were employed in manufacturing; among the four migrant groups, only returnees had a greater overall propensity (30%) to be employed in manufacturing. The proportions of residents and entrants employed in manufacturing were practically identical among the three types of counties. However, the proportions of new inmigrants and returnees employed in manufacturing were greater in rural counties than in the other counties, especially fringe counties adjacent to metro cores. Twenty-eight percent of the new inmigrants and 32% of the returnees in rural counties were employed in manufacturing vs. 20 and 25%, respectively, in fringe counties. The importance of manufacturing job opportunities for the realization of residential preferences was greatest in the rural counties, the preferred destination of most movers.

Table 2. Worker Characteristics in Nonmetropolitan Counties of Ozarks Economic Development Region, 1975

Characteristic	Total	Residents	New immigrants	Returnees	New entrants and unknown
Percentage distribution by type of county	100	100	100	100	100
Adjacent to metro core	30	31	30	24	30
Not adjacent to metro core, large city	14	15	16	13	14
Not adjacent to metro core, other	56	54	54	63	56
Percentage employed in manufacturing by type of county					
All nonmetropolitan counties	25	25	25	30	24
Adjacent to metro core	23	25	20	25	23
Not adjacent to metro core, large city	24	26	24	30	22
Not adjacent to metro core, other	26	25	28	32	25
Percentage of population	100	19	21	6	55
Percentage of manufacturing jobs	100	19	21	7	53
Percentage of nonmanufacturing jobs	100	18	21	5	56
Average total dollar earnings, 1975, workers 25 or older					
Manufacturing	8,120	9,628	9,467	8,480	6,164
Nonmanufacturing	7,375	8,161	9,321	7,327	5,725
Manufacturing by type of county					
Adjacent to metro core	9,169	11,248	10,766	7,633	7,037
Not adjacent to metro core, large city	8,725	8,534	10,649	9,992	6,935
Not adjacent to metro core, other	7,481	9,007	8,624	8,436	5,577
Average age of manufacturing workers	36	48	41	43	30
Average age of nonmanufacturing workers	39	52	44	44	32
Percentage of manufacturing workers, male	66	75	78	79	56
Percentage of nonmanufacturing workers, male	54	55	72	66	46

Note: Large city equals a city of 25,000 or more population in 1970 within the county.

On the other hand, this importance was not a result of plants' hiring practices favoring new inmigrants and returnees. Little or no difference occurred in the hiring of migrants between manufacturing and non-manufacturing jobs. About 28% of the manufacturing jobs and 26% of the nonmanufacturing jobs were held by new inmigrants and returnees. These shares are practically identical to the proportion of new inmigrants and returnees in the entire sample, about 27%. Little or no difference existed in hiring rates and population shares when stratified by types of counties. This appears consistent with the study by Matson et al. on the Southeastern states.[19]

Overall, residents, new inmigrants, and returnees working in manufacturing had approximately equal average earnings in 1975 after taking into account sampling error. The overlap among confidence intervals at even the 68% confidence level, one standard error, was substantial. When grouped by migrant status and by type of county, only three very minor differences in manufacturing earnings were revealed.[20] First, new inmigrants working in rural counties earned less than new inmigrants employed in urbanized and fringe counties. Second, residents working in fringe counties earned more than residents working in urbanized and rural counties. Third, within fringe counties, returnees earned less than new inmigrants and residents. Moreover, industry of employment—manufacturing vs. nonmanufacturing—made no difference for new inmigrants and returnees overall or within county groupings. However, residents in manufacturing did earn significantly more than residents not working in manufacturing, mainly in the fringe and rural counties.[21]

These findings are not inconsistent with those made by Perkinson's regression analysis and the sample differences revealed by Bender's and Olsen's analyses. New inmigrants and returnees apparently possessed skill levels at least comparable to those of residents. And if Perkinson's finding of migrant disadvantages is also valid in the Ozarks Region, then it may be surmised that inmigrants and returnees could possess higher skill levels than residents even though earnings are approximately the same.[22]

Also, the premise that job opportunities may be more important than earnings differentials for new inmigrants and returnees was not refuted by this data. Sixty percent of the new inmigrants and 67% of the returnees working in manufacturing moved to rural counties having small towns only. For returnees, these counties offered no statistically significant earnings advantage compared to other county types. And new inmigrants earned somewhat less in these counties than in fringe or urbanized counties.

On the average, new inmigrants and returnees were roughly the same age, about 7 years younger than residents. For each migrant group, average ages exhibited little or no difference between manufacturing and nonmanufacturing employment. Overall, 66% of the manufacturing workers were males. Except for entrants, over three-fourths of the manufacturing workers in each migrant group were males. Given this data, it appears that manufacturing in non-metropolitan areas does not provide jobs primarily for females, but rather for the traditional household head.

IMPLICATIONS OF RURAL INDUSTRIALIZATION FOR INMIGRATION AND ECONOMIC CHANGE

Nonmetropolitan industrialization does furnish job opportunities for new and returning inmigrants, as witnessed by several case studies and recent Ozark industrial activity. This is especially true for those areas preferred by potential movers, i.e., rural counties at some distance from a metropolitan concentration. Manufacturing as a source of growth becomes more important as rurality increases. Second, the development of new job opportunities appears more important than gains or differentials in earnings for many inmigrants. Sizeable proportions of new and returning inmigrants cite area amenities as their primary motive for moving. Third, despite actual or potential declines in earnings and disadvantages associated with migration, new inmigrants and returnees have about the same earnings as residents, indicative of at least comparable skill levels. Fourth, new and returning inmigrants are usually younger, more educated, and exhibit greater job mobility than residents.

In summary, nonmetropolitan industrialization not only benefits residents but also fosters revitalization of human capital within these areas through inmigration. Because of the selectivity of migration, areas that previously experienced prolonged outmovement generally have an underrepresentation of younger, educated adults.[23] Current inmigration with its own selectivity rebuilds the human resource base within rural areas. More importantly, job opportunities in nonmetropolitan areas permit residents, new inmigrants, and returnees to realize their preferences for living conditions. Satisfying residential locations can be attained without inordinate monetary costs, including the cost of total unemployment. For the maximization of individual welfare, trade-offs between nonmonetary amenities and high dollar earnings become feasible and less restrictive as nonmetropolitan job opportunities expand. Indeed, a policy study within the U.S. Department of Agriculture "... suggested that rural development might best be described as a public commitment to maintain opportunities for individuals to choose among a wide range of life styles—urban as well as rural—and to assume that those choices are not so inordinately costly in terms of decent opportunities to live and work that they are available only to the very few."[24]

NOTES

[1] Claude C. Haren, "Location of Industrial Production and Distribution," in L. R. Whiting, ed., *Rural Industrialization: Problems and Potentials* (Ames: Iowa State University Press, 1974), pp. 3–26.

[2] Claude C. Haren and Ronald W. Holling, "Industrial Development," Industrial Development Note No. 66, Extension Service, U.S. Department of Agriculture, October 1977.

[3] The national recession of 1969 to 1972 and the economic decline of 1974 affected manufacturing employment more adversely than nonmanufacturing employment. Also, at least part of the growth in other sectors could be attributed to the impact of prior manufacturing growth.

[4] John A. Kuehn and Curtis Braschler, *New Manufacturing Plants in the Nonmetro Ozarks Region* (Washington, D.C.: Agricultural Economic Report No. 384, U.S. Department of Agriculture, 1977).

[5] The classification of SMSAs in this study conforms to that of the Office of Management and Budget, as announced on February 8, 1974. Metropolitan core counties were defined as those having 20% or more of their population residing within a designated urbanized area.

[6] Calvin L. Beale, "Internal Migration in the United States Since 1970," a statement prepared for the House Select Committee on Population, U.S. House of Representatives, February 8, 1978.

[7] Ibid.

[8] Glenn V. Fuguitt and James J. Zuiches, "Residential Preferences and Population Distribution: Results of a National Survey," in *Where Will All the People Go?*, Committee Print, Subcommittee on Rural Development, 93rd Congress, 1st Session, October 23, 1973, pp. 21–41.

[9] For a discussion of the push hypothesis in outmigration, see Vernon Renshaw, "The Relationship of Gross Migration to Net Migration: A Short Run, Long Run Distinction," *Regional Science Perspectives*, Vol. 5 (1975), pp. 109–124; and Michael J. Greenwood and Eric J. Anderson, "A Simultaneous-Equations Model of Migration and Economic Change in Rural Areas: The Case of the South," *Review of Regional Studies*, Vol. 4 (1974), pp. 37–48.

[10] William E. Laird and Warren F. Mazek, "City-Size Preferences and Migration," *Review of Regional Studies*, Vol. 4 Supplement (1974), pp. 18–26.

[11] The Continuous Work History Sample maintained by the Social Security Administration covers only workers participating in the social security program. Data are on a place of work basis which may vary from the county of residence. It is not possible to determine the origin of new entrants into the social security program; consequently, migrant numbers may be underestimated. Roger A. Matson, Charles E. Trott, and Wesley G. Smith, "The Development of Industrially Differentiated Inmigration Rates for the Southeast, 1960-70," *Review of Regional Studies*, Vol. 4 (1974), pp. 8–17.

[12] Lloyd D. Bender, Bernal L. Green, and Rex R. Campbell, "Trickle-down and Leakage in the War on Poverty," *Growth and Change*, Vol. 2 (1971), pp. 34–41.

[13] Leon Perkinson, "Household Migration into a Small Rural Southern Area," an unpublished report prepared for the Economic Development Division, U.S. Department of Agriculture, n.d.

[14] Migrants were apparently at a disadvantage in local job markets when compared to similar residents. See Leon Perkinson, "Rural Inmigration: Are Migrants Universally Disadvantaged?," unpublished report prepared for the Economic Development Division, U.S. Department of Agriculture, n.d.

[15] Duane A. Olsen and John A. Kuehn, *Migrant Response to Industrialization in Four Rural Areas, 1965-70*, Agricultural Economic Report No. 270, U.S. Department of Agriculture, September 1974.

[16] Data from the CWHS file were acquired from Prof. Jack Gilchrist of Montana State University who developed GRASP programming system to access this massive data base.

[17] Attention is focused on the gross inmigration of workers participating in the social security program rather than net migration. The U.S. Bureau of the Census estimated that nonmetropolitan Ozark counties had 133,327 net inmigrants between 1970 and 1975, and had 56,606 net outmigrants between 1965 and 1970.

[18] Bureau of Economic Analysis, *Regional Work Force Characteristics and Migration Data: A Handbook on the Social Security Continuous Work History Sample and its Application* (Washington, D.C.: U.S. Government Printing Office, 1976).

[19] Matson, op. cit., note 11.

[20] The highest t-value for testing differences between average earnings was only 1.49 within a migrant group by type of county or within a type of county by migrant group.

[21] Overall t-value was 2.12; t-values were 1.46 and 1.57 for fringe and rural counties, respectively. Also, an additional significant finding was that within nonmanufacturing sectors new inmigrants earned more overall than returnees ($t = 3.13$) and residents ($t = 2.19$).

[22] See Perkinson, op. cit., note 14.

[23] Beale, op. cit., note 6.

[24] Kenneth R. Farrell, testimony before the Agricultural Research and General Legislation Subcommittee, Committee on Agriculture, Nutrition and Forestry, U.S. House of Representatives, May 4, 1978.

Chapter 10

INDUSTRIALIZATION AND HOUSEHOLD INCOME LEVELS IN NONMETROPOLITAN AREAS

H. L. Seyler

The locational redistribution of industrial activity reported earlier in this book certainly invites attention to related social and economic change. Authors in Part II have attempted selectively to gauge the impacts of industrialization upon nonmetropolitan areas. In keeping with that orientation, this chapter examines the relationship between industrial growth and household income levels for a sample of nonmetropolitan areas during the period 1965 to 1974. A question is posed: Has industrial growth in nonmetropolitan areas been accompanied by a significant improvement in levels of household income?

As will be substantiated below, the literature addressing the question is contradictory. Clarification of the relationship is essential if inferences are to be extended about the impact of industrialization on one dimension of area development—household income, and all of the welfare connotations associated with it. By extension, a tentative assessment can be rendered about the efficacy of developmental strategies emphasizing industrial growth as a means of improving individual welfare, as distinct from aggregate economic change. Since this chapter is not designed to be suspenseful, a preliminary answer to the question should be offered. The analysis that follows supports an answer in the negative. There is a very weak positive relationship between industrial expansion and household income levels for a special class of more-urbanized nonmetropolitan areas. The relationship is, however, statistically insignificant. For most nonmetropolitan areas, evidence suggests industrial growth has no appreciable impact upon household income levels. Moreover, the findings appear to be consistent with theoretical expectations,

149

and in agreement with other empirical studies when important differences in the characteristics of nonmetropolitan areas are considered. Before articulating the relationship between gains in nonmetropolitan industrial activity and income levels, the areal setting and empirical and theoretical context for the study should be described.

THE CONTEXT OF INDUSTRIAL CHANGE

Summary observations above are based upon an examination of 242 nonmetropolitan counties in the West North Central census region registering gains in manufacturing employment between 1965 and 1973. The sampled counties were drawn from an area experiencing areally extensive increases in manufacturing activity both generally and in most nonmetropolitan portions. Magnitudes and proportions of change are displayed in Tables 1 and 2,

Table 1. Manufacturing Employment in Plains States, Selected Years, 1951–1973

State	Less-urban nonmetro-area counties[a]	Nonmetro-area counties with larger places[b]	State	Less-urban nonmetro-area counties[a]	Nonmetro-area counties with larger places[b]
Minnesota			South Dakota		
1951	25,215	28,865	1951	2,257	3,639
1962	27,641	32,539	1962	2,958	4,508
1965	28,873	34,688	1965	2,309	4,250
1973	43,947	41,921	1973	3,276	7,169
Iowa			Nebraska		
1951	13,801	27,626	1951	4,942	5,718
1962	17,672	26,463	1962	5,954	8,075
1965	17,672	30,033	1965	6,039	8,814
1973	33,999	31,020	1973	17,059	20,000
Missouri			Kansas		
1951	–	–	1951	8,193	13,450
1962	–	–	1962	7,478	14,051
1965	39,343	30,926	1965	9,509	25,848
1973	55,901	39,103	1973	12,724	27,665

[a]Nonmetro counties with largest settlement less than 10,000 and at least one county removed from the core county(s) of an SMSA.

[b]Nonmetro counties with a place of 10,000 or larger and at least one county removed from the core county(s) of an SMSA.

Source: Taken or estimated from information provided in *County Business Patterns*, selected years, Office of Business Economics, U.S. Department of Commerce.

Table 2. Share of Manufacturing Employment in Nonmetro Plains Counties, Selected Years, 1951-1973

State	Less-urban nonmetro-area counties[a]	Nonmetro-area counties with larger places[a]	State	Less-urban nonmetro-area counties[a]	Nonmetro-area counties with larger places[a]
Minnesota			South Dakota		
1951	12.8	14.6	1951	20.3	32.8
1962	12.2	14.3	1962	21.8	33.3
1965	11.7	14.0	1965	18.6	34.2
1973	14.0	13.4	1973	17.3	37.9
Iowa			Nebraska		
1951	8.6	17.2	1951	9.6	11.2
1962	10.8	16.1	1962	9.6	13.0
1965	10.4	16.4	1965	9.1	13.2
1973	14.9	13.6	1973	18.7	22.0
Missouri			Kansas		
1951	–	8.0	1951	7.5	12.4
1962	–	7.6	1962	–	–
1965	9.6	7.6	1965	8.1	12.8
1973	12.2	8.5	1973	8.3	18.0

[a]Percent of State Manufacturing Employment.
Source: Taken or estimated from information provided in *County Business Patterns*, selected years, Office of Business Economics, U.S. Department of Commerce.

respectively. In both tables, nonmetropolitan counties are differentiated by size of their largest settlement, a distinction that is important for the analysis that follows. At this point, however, attention is directed to the range of change and the share of state employment present in nonmetropolitan areas when counties adjacent to SMSA core counties are excluded.[1] Inclusion of data for cross-sections as early as 1951 highlights the acceleration of change occurring between 1965 and 1973. In an environment of industrial growth, nonmetropolitan counties in the study area have fared well, gaining over 85,000 manufacturing employees from 1965 to 1973. While enjoying absolute gains, less-urban counties enlarged their share of activity in all study-area states except South Dakota. Shares of employment in more-urban counties increased in three states.

Another measure of change further evidences a locational transformation. During the period 1970 to 1975, increases in aggregate personal income attributable to manufacturing ranged from 32% in Missouri to 82% in South Dakota for areas other than SMSA core counties.[2] Excepting Iowa (−.8%), counties other than SMSA core counties increased their share of this measure in all study-area states. Gains varied from 1% in Kansas to 10% in South

Dakota. This shift occurred while all study-area states were registering an impressive aggregate income gain in manufacturing of over 1.8 billion dollars.[3]

INDUSTRIAL GROWTH AND INCOME CHANGE

The magnitude of expansion described above must necessarily induce other changes in affected areas. Growth of existing firms and/or entry of new firms into nonmetropolitan areas set forces in motion that can alter a host of characteristics, reshaping the social and economic landscape. As industrial gains vary in amount and type, resulting changes in aggregate activity can and have been imperfectly charted.[4] Increases in manufacturing without offsetting losses in other sectors inevitably enlarges aggregate income as direct and indirect effects reverberate through an area's economy. When a student of area development turns to the impacts on individual or household welfare, however, evidence is more fragmentary and conflicting. An overview of the relevant literature on the association of household income change and industrial expansion is instructive.

For example, in an analysis of manufacturing growth between 1950 and 1960 for 11 nonmetropolitan counties, Lindsey found that median household income rose from 64% of the national level in 1949 to 72% in 1959.[5] However, in addition to a very limited sample size, he selected only counties that had at least doubled their manufacturing employment, and their gain had to be at least 1,000 employees. The sample was restricted to more urban counties with magnitudes of change that were representative of only a small subset of more populous nonmetropolitan areas.

A later case study, intriguing in many respects, spawned a series of publications reporting on an array of social and economic changes· produced by the construction of a large new steel plant near Hennepin, Illinois. Household income was among the many facets of community development examined. Comparison of the county in which the new facility was located and a control county without industrial growth produced findings that bear upon the question raised in this chapter. For example, Scott and Summers concluded there was some reduction in the degree of income inequality.[6] Another report based on the case study by Beck et al. observed, "There was no statistically significant difference in income gains by heads of households in the industrially developing and control area."[7] Yet another paper drawing on the case study concluded: "However our expectation that industrial development, which increases the local labor demand, would result in an accentuation of the income gap between persons in a position to respond to the demand and those less able was not supported."[8] Thus those residents with age or other limitations who might have been relatively disadvantaged by inability to share in industrial expansion were unaffected, in this case, as income gains by participants in the expansion were insignificant.

Contrasting with these findings is a study by West and Maier where they found a substantial reduction in the percentage of poor in a sample of

Missouri counties with large percentage increases in manufacturing employment from 1960 to 1970.[9] Evidence of a positive effect on income also appears in Till's study of the nonmetropolitan South. He noted that industrial growth might, in areas with serious unemployment, produce a reduction in the number of households with incomes below a designated poverty level.[10]

The studies cited above are representative. There are gaps and inconsistencies in our empirical awareness of the income effects of industrial growth, particularly household or per capita impacts. The ledger is clearer when theoretical or expected impacts are examined.

THEORETICAL CONSIDERATIONS

After reviewing the recent history of nonmetropolitan growth in the South, Hansen observed that since "... the rural South's attractiveness seems to lie largely in its large pool of underemployed labor, the growth of low-wage sectors will not bring the incomes of rural southerners up to the level of the nation as a whole."[11] He further concluded: "In brief then, until nonmetropolitan areas, particularly those not in proximity to SMSAs, are able to capture firms earlier in the life cycle of their industries, they will continue in too many cases to run along the treadmill of trading dying industries for mature, low-skilled, low-wage industries."[12]

The concept that industries "trickle down" to less populous and peripheral areas originated with Thompson who argued that "These smaller industrial novices also struggle to raise per capita income over the hurdle of industries which pay the lowest wage rates."[13] Thus the "trickling down" or "filtering down" concept, to the extent that it is operative, has nonmetropolitan areas gaining a mixed blessing as "... industry slides down the learning curve ... the more industrially sophisticated areas become superfluous. The aging industry seeks out industrial backwaters where cheaper labor is now up to the lesser demands of the simplified process."[14] The net effect of the process is to sustain lower incomes in nonmetropolitan areas. Their role in an ongoing redistribution of industrial activity is one of continuing disadvantage.

In addition to the trickling down effect, industrial growth can affect migration decisions. Increased industrial employment is seen as an inducement retaining people who would normally migrate. They forsake higher incomes in other places for lower wages that are just high enough to defer relocation.[15] This serves to sustain the number of households with low incomes.

Other expectations of income impacts are based upon a reading of trends in industrial organization. Increasingly, it is argued, branch plants will require a small managerial staff as the multiplant firms concentrate managerial functions in metro areas while decentralizing production facilities.[16] Hansen, by example, found that fewer than 150 families were transferred when branch plants were established in 34 nonmetropolitan communities in Minnesota and Wisconsin.[17] As fewer managerial personnel are required in the future, the lower number of higher-income households would dilute the impact of industrial development on household incomes in areas where plants are located.

Yet another consideration linked to income effects of industrial change involves the nature of income multipliers. Since nonmetropolitan areas by definition have smaller and less diversified collections of people and activity, there are significant "leakages" of income that reduce income multipliers.[18] Purchases outside of an economy by households and by firms would limit the round-by-round linkages and lessen the impact of increased industrial activity.

The joint effect of low-wage, slow-growing, or nationally declining industries, retention at low wages of those who would have migrated without industrial growth, centralization of higher-income managerial workers, and diluted multiplier impacts would seriously limit income gains at the household level. However, nonmetropolitan areas are far from a homogeneous population. If counties, for example, are units of observation, they range from those that are more economically diversified and that just fail to meet the population criteria for official designation as metropolitan, to those having no official urban place and depending upon highly specialized primary activity.

As the size of settlements and their economic activity concentrations vary over the nonmetropolitan landscape, the potential impacts should differ as well. Areas having larger places and a more diverse array of economic activity should experience less income leakage. Income multipliers should be higher, perhaps high enough to support the establishment of additional higher-order tertiary functions as well as the expansion or duplication of existing tertiary establishments. Owners or managers of new or expanded businesses could realize midrange or higher incomes compared to the community norms. With larger size and service bases, the probability of interindustry linkages should be higher. The larger places should enjoy an advantage in attracting larger new firms and/or support greater expansion of existing firms.[19] The larger firms should require more managerial workers and a wider range of skills among production workers. Taken together, the latter considerations could increase the number of households with higher incomes.

The matter of trickling down of low-wage industries is more difficult to handle. One could argue that larger, more diverse areas would attract a mix of industries, only some of which have attributes fitting Thompson's description. There are indications that nonmetropolitan areas are getting a share of higher-wage operations. In his study of nonmetropolitan areas in the South, for example, Till found evidence of growth in higher-wage, less labor-intensive industry.[20]

The expectations sketched above simply transfer to nonmetropolitan centers the process of economic change that is used to characterize larger urban or metropolitan economies.[21] Thus, nonmetropolitan places, as their populations and activity complexes enlarge, would progressively enjoy thresholds allowing not only aggregate expansion and diversification, but also household income gains. Following this line of reasoning, areas with smaller settlements, especially those that are decidedly rural, would experience little or no income gain. Since there are far more smaller than larger communities, household income gains from industrial growth should be areally restricted.

ASSESSING THE RELATIONSHIP

To assess the relationship between household income and industrial growth in view of the empirical and theoretical considerations discussed above, several operational decisions were made to simplify a complex set of inter-dependencies. Exclusion was employed to control, to an extent, confounding influences. The sample of nonmetropolitan counties selected for this study excluded core counties of SMSAs (containing some part of the core metropolis) and a tier of surrounding counties. In the latter, suburbanization or exurbanization of population and economic activity could be expected to affect household income. Counties in the northern half of Minnesota, the Black Hills of South Dakota, and southern Missouri were excluded to control for the possible influences of forestry, mining, and recreational activity.

Exclusions noted above and areas that had to be omitted because of the census "disclosure rule" yielded a sample of 242 counties in 6 states with an increase in manufacturing employment. The sample comprised 43% of all counties in the study-area states, and over 80% of all counties beyond the shadow of SMSA core counties.

Other confounding influences were partially controlled by categorization and the mode of analysis adopted. Counties were first grouped by size of their largest settlement. Those without a settlement of at least 10,000 were classed as "less urban." Counties with places of 10,000 or larger were designated "more urban." These classes were elected to reflect the differing impact potentials associated with industrial growth in areas with varying socio-economic attributes. The classification procedure produced 193 less-urban and 49 more-urban counties.

Another important distinction is addressed in the question: When is industrial growth substantial enough to induce change in other area characteristics, especially household income? A wide variation in the level of industrial expansion is less-urban counties necessitated another control. While a gain of one additional manufacturing employee qualified a county for inclusion in the less-urban classification, a subcategory was used to identify less-urban counties with employment gains of 100 or more employees. Accordingly, 108 less-urban counties were identified that had registered larger employment increases.

An attempt was also made to control a more troubling element, the role of agricultural activity. Direct and indirect effects attributable to agriculture are basic to the economy of the study area and its constituent parts. Therefore, aggregate personal income from agriculture for each county was included as an independent variable in the regression model used to assess the relationship between income and industrial growth.

The last operational decision involved selection of acceptable indices for household income, the dependent variables in the analysis. Median household effective buying income in 1974, the percentages of households with effective buying income of less than $5,000 in 1974, the percentage of households with effective buying income above $10,000 in 1974, and the absolute change in median household effective buying income from 1965 to 1974 were chosen.[22] Effective buying income is an estimate that incorporates differences in the cost of living and is, therefore, superior to estimates published by the Bureau of the Census, as the latter can understate the purchasing power of non-metropolitan residents. Thus, the indices differentiate an income norm, lower incomes, higher incomes, and change in an income norm, respectively.

With the elements of the model specified, the analytical procedure can be illuminated. Sixteen regressions were conducted using the gain in numbers of manufacturing employees from 1965 to 1973 and aggregate personal income attributed to agriculture as independent variables. The independent variables were regressed with the four income indices for four county categories to produce partial correlations between manufacturing change and household income while controlling for the agricultural income variable.

To be more specific, if industrial growth and income change are positively related, the following should obtain. Those counties registering larger gains in manufacturing employment from 1965 to 1973 will have:

(1) Higher median incomes in 1974
(2) A smaller percentage of households with incomes below $5,000 in 1974.
(3) A larger percentage of households with incomes above $10,000.
(4) Recorded larger absolute change in median household income from 1965 to 1974.

Given the theoretical expectations sketched earlier, relationships expressed by partial correlations should be stronger for more-urban, nonmetropolitan counties than the less-urban category.

FINDINGS

Despite the inevitable limitations of the operational assessment, several generalizations can be advanced. For the sample as a whole, industrial growth appeared to generate little improvement in household income, however much it may affect aggregate levels of income or a host of other factors. The areally extensive expansion of industrial activity did not induce a coextensive welfare impact (Table 3). Relationships expressed by the partial correlation co-efficients in Table 3 generally coincide with expectations but for one major exception. While relationships are generally stronger in more-urban than less-urban counties, the coefficients are statistically insignificant. An inspection of the last two columns is especially revealing. The relationship between gains in manufacturing employment and household income indices for less-urban counties is very weak. Technically, the partial correlations are insignificantly

Table 3. Partial Correlations between Change in Manufacturing Employment, 1965–1973, and Household Income Measures for Nonmetro Plains Counties while Controlling for Farm Income[a]

Income measures	Total sample (N = 242)	Less urban[b] All (N = 193)	Less urban[b] LG[c] (N = 108)	More urban[d] (N = 49)
1. Median household effective buying income, 1974[e]	.24	.02	.10	.17
2. Percentage of households with effective buying income below $5,000, 1974.[e]	−.20	−.04	−.12	−.09
3. Percentage of households with effective buying income above $10,000, 1974.[e]	.19	−.05	.04	.18
4. Change in median household effective buying income, 1965–1974.[e]	.10	−.03	.02	.18

[a]Aggregate personal income attributed to farming in 1974 is controlled for income measures 1, 2, and 3. Change in this variate 1970–1974 is controlled for the fourth income measure. Data were obtained from *Local Area Personal Income, 1970–75* (Regional Volumes), Bureau of Economic Analysis, U.S. Department of Commerce, Washington, D.C.; and from *County Business Patterns,* 1965 and 1973, Office of Business Economics, U.S. Department of Commerce, Washington, D.C.
[b]Counties with no place as large as 10,000.
[c]LG denotes less urban counties gaining 100 or more jobs.
[d]Counties with a place of 10,000 or larger.
[e]Data taken from *Survey of Buying Power,* 1965 and 1974, Sales Management, Inc., New York, New York.

different from zero at a .30 significance level. Correlations are slightly stronger for the more-urban counties. Excepting the percentage of households with low incomes (where the sign of the coefficient matches expectations), correlations are significant only if one accepts a confidence level of just over 80%, a hazardous decision. Thus while correlations are stronger, they are also statistically insignificant for more-urban, nonmetropolitan counties.

EQUIVOCATIONS AND IMPLICATIONS

An obvious objection to the assertions above would be vested in criticism of analytical procedures. It can be argued that important confounding factors were uncontrolled. The impacts of the tertiary sector and transfer payments were not controlled directly. Categories used in the study do represent partial control of the service sector, however. The less-urban counties, since they are defined by the presence of a smaller settlement, should be dominated by central-place tertiary activities serving a restricted tributary area. As these are support activities, income changes would normally originate in primary or secondary activity. Thus, the effects of confounding influences should be lessened for the less-urban counties. The presence of at least some tertiary establishments providing goods and services beyond a localized tributary area is a feature most characteristic of the more-urban counties with larger settlements. Partial correlations reported for the more-urban counties may not express the relationship as satisfactorily as would be the case for the less-urban areas.

Other criticisms could be directed to the adequacy of sample categories. It could be argued that 25,000 or 30,000 population would be a more appropriate lower, community-size category to gauge the influence of developmental thresholds. That is, there is a necessary and sufficient lower level of population and mix of economic activity that permits household incomes to rise in most income classes. If this premise has merit and the more urban category is adjusted accordingly, support is provided for the expectation of minimal household income impacts from industrialization in most of the nonmetropolitan landscape.

A pointed reservation involves the magnitude measure of industrial growth. How much additional employment is required to induce income change? If a lower limit of 200, 500, or 1,000 employees is used to identify a sample, most of the nonmetropolitan landscape would be omitted from an impact appraisal. While it should be acknowledged that small increases in manufacturing employment can represent a minor share of total employment and dependent households, surely the larger the gain, the greater the potential impact.

Exception can also be taken with the welfare measures used in this study. Some might argue there are intangible factors more important than money income. This introduces the issue of implications of developmental strategies. If area development strategies have as goals improved levels of individual and household welfare, this study indicates industrial growth may not contribute substantially to realization of those objectives. Moreover, it is difficult to separate well-being from disposable income, both for direct consumption of goods and services and the range of public services that depend upon household income. Some may insist, however, that industrial growth, even with lower income levels than might be earned through migration, preserves community vitality and enables people to remain in more "liveable" settings. A related argument could be that without industrial dispersion into nonmetropolitan areas incomes would be even lower in these areas than they are today. That is, nonmetropolitan industrialization can be viewed as a holding action that has softened the negative impact of economic forces in areas that are unlikely to successfully enlarge and diversity their economic bases.

Finally, the results of this analysis could be challenged by questioning the length of the study period. It could be argued that contemporary industrialization, while not inducing household income gains in the short term, could provide a foundation from which longer-range benefits will be realized.

Despite these reservations, this assessment of the impact of industrialization on household income indicates a limited developmental effect, if any. In the study area industrial growth did not significantly reduce the share of households with lower incomes, increase the share of households with higher incomes, or elevate the general level of household income. If confounding factors were at least partially controlled, the study suggests that developmental policies and programs might achieve more success in raising household incomes by emphasizing changes in nonmanufacturing sectors. If, however, emphases continue to be placed upon the enlargement or attraction of manufacturing, developmental agencies should consider a systematic intervention in the process of industrial redistribution to alter the composition of activity expanding or relocating in nonmetropolitan areas.

NOTES

[1] SMSA core counties are those containing some portion of the core metropolis.

[2] Data were obtained from *Local Area Personal Income 1970-75, the Plains* (Washington, D.C.: Bureau of Economic Analysis, U.S. Department of Commerce, 1977).

[3] Ibid.

[4] For an overview, see Luther Tweeten and George L. Brinkman, *Micropolitan Development: Theory and Practice of Greater-Rural Economic Development* (Ames: Iowa State University Press, 1976), pp. 226-255.

[5] Fred D. Lindsey, *What New Industrial Jobs Mean to a Community* (Washington, D.C.: Chamber of Commerce of the U.S., 1962).

[6] John T. Scott and Gene F. Summers, "Problems in Rural Communities After Industry Arrives," in *Rural Industrialization: Prospects, Problems, Impacts, and Methods,* a series of papers compiled by the U.S. Senate Subcommittee on Rural Development (Washington, D.D.: U.S. Government Printing Office, 1974), p. 21.

[7] E. M. Beck, Louis Dotson, and Gene F. Summers, "Effects of Industrial Development on Heads of Households," *Growth and Change,* Vol. 4 (1973), pp. 16-19; citation p. 17.

[8] Gene F. Summers and Frank Clemente, "Industrial Development, Income Distribution, and Public Policy," *Rural Sociology,* Vol. 41, (1976), pp. 248-268; citation p. 263.

[9] Jerry G. West and Roselee Maier, "Income Distribution Consequences of Rural Industrialization," a paper presented at the Annual Meeting of the Agricultural Economics Association, August 1975.

[10] Thomas E. Till, "Industrialization and Poverty in Southern Nonmetropolitan Labor Markets," *Growth and Change,* Vol. 5 (1974), pp. 18-24.

[11] Niles M. Hansen, *The Future of Nonmetropolitan America* (Lexington, Mass.: D. C. Heath, 1973), p. 14.

[12] Ibid.

[13] Wilbur R. Thompson, "The Economic Base of Urban Problems," in N. W. Chamberlain, ed., *Contemporary Economic Issues* (Homewood, Illinois: Richard D. Irwin, 1969), pp. 1-47.

[14] Ibid., p. 9.

[15] Tweeten and Brinkman, op. cit., note 4, pp. 244–245.

[16] G. B. Norcliffe, "A Theory of Manufacturing Places," in Lyndhurst Collins and David Walker, eds., *Locational Dynamics of Manufacturing Activity* (New York: John Wiley, 1975), pp. 19–57 (esp. pp. 32–37).

[17] Hansen, op. cit., note 11, pp. 74–75.

[18] Tweeten and Brinkman, op. cit., note 4, pp. 235–237.

[19] Norcliffe, op. cit., note 16, pp. 40–43.

[20] Till, op. cit., note 10, p. 19.

[21] See Wilbur R. Thompson, "Economic Growth and Development: Processes, Stages, and Determinants," *A Preface to Urban Economics* (Baltimore: The John Hopkins Press, 1965), pp. 11–60.

[22] Estimates for the income variables were obtained from the *Annual Survey of Buying Power* (New York: Sales Management Corporation, annual issues).

Chapter 11

COPING WITH INDUSTRIALIZATION

Gene F. Summers, E. M. Beck,
and C. Matthew Snipp

Nonmetropolitan development depends to a very great extent upon the attraction of additional capital to resident communities. While there are several methods by which new capital can be introduced into communities, manufacturing growth is favored by many development planners and theoreticians.[1] This choice of policy instrument rests upon several factors; among the most apparent are its export base character, its presumed multiplier effects, and the belief that nonmetropolitan communities can be made attractive sites for branch and expansion locations of manufacturing firms. We share the view that increasing the amount of available capital is essential to most community economic development, but refrain from endorsement of manufacturing as the universally most appropriate policy instrument.[2] Nevertheless, it is often the vehicle for introjecting new capital into local economies and that fact alone demands that its effects on the community be examined and understood.

THEORETICAL MODEL AND RELATED RESEARCH

In a recent publication, we reviewed an extensive body of case study reports showing the impacts of industrial growth on several aspects of the local community, and developed a flow model linking new industry and the public sector through several exchange processes involving units of the private sector, the population, as well as the nonlocal public sector and the physical infrastructure inventory of the local community.[3]

161

Manufacturing is sought by many public officials because they believe industrial development will ease the fiscal burden in small communities by enlarging their tax base. Increased value of real property is the key to the expected relief, but also included are increased aggregate consumable income, a greater volume of retail sales, direct payments by industry, and larger state and federal transfer payments. It is important to note that the anticipated public sector benefits depend upon growth in the private sector and upon increased returns to labor supplied by the resident population of the community. The logic supporting this expected payoff from the chain of transactions linking new industry and the public sector is found in the export base multiplier theory of money flows in the local economy.[4] According to this formulation, local industries can be divided between those which market their products and services outside the local economy, and thereby generate a net money flow into the community, and those which market their output within the community.[5] The net inflow resulting from "basic" industries stimulates the internal circulation of money. This is accomplished mainly through exchanges between the basic and nonbasic industrial firms, among the nonbasic firms, and between the population and both types of firms. These exchanges produce aggregate gains in income through higher wages and greater utilization of local labor, increased valuation of the existing inventory of real property, additions to the inventory of real property, and expansion of industrial output—all of which contribute directly and indirectly to the local public sector's ability to generate revenue.

Case studies generally provide evidence which is consistent with this model of exchange networks.[6] One study revealed that 28 communities reported real income gains following the location of new industry, while none experienced a decline.[7] In every community studied, the assessed valuation of property was expanded and property tax receipts were increased.[8] Retail sales consistently increased, producing sales tax receipts collected by the state and transferred back to the community. Indeed, total intergovernmental transfer payments were increased.[9] In some instances, there was suggestive evidence that local officials were shifting a greater share of public sector costs to the state and federal levels, creating a more dependent relationship than existed previously.

But this is only the evidence linking new industry to public sector revenues. Public sector expenditures are equally important, since the hoped for relief is nonexistent if costs to the public sector rise at a rate equaling or exceeding the revenue gains. The expansion of manufacturing through the location of new firms creates demands upon the public sector for services and facilities.[10] Some of the pressures for additional expenditures come directly from the new firms for items such as site purchase and preparation, access roads, road connections, and utilities.[11] Further pressures come from the growth of residential, industrial, and commercial properties which even in the planning stages require the time and efforts of public officials and employees, and after construction demand the delivery of basic public services. Finally, and perhaps of greatest fiscal consequence, the increased utilization and expansion of the population add to the costs of new industry to the public sector.[12] Clearly, communities' public sectors are confronted with the fact that previously existing relations with their population and with private sector units are likely to be strained to the point of requiring adjustments and realignment.

Most case studies have stressed the benefits derived from new industry; only a few have examined costs as well.[13] Those analyses which have explicitly calculated public sector net gains associated with new industry have consistently reported small or negative net effects. This remained true even when secondary impacts were analyzed.

Other studies comparing estimates of private sector net gains and those of the public sector also found sharp contrasts. In particular, one study of 12 communities reported average private sector gains of $153,000. The local governments of these same communities had an average net gain of only $520, and their school districts $400.[14]

In summarizing evidence from these case studies, it is reasonable to assert that industrial location in the nonmetro community can bring employment, population growth, and economic prosperity to the area; but as the studies have shown, these benefits do not come automatically nor do they apply in all cases. In some instances the structure of the community and the character of the particular industry merge to the benefit of both parties. More often the industry clearly gains, while having a negligible or even negative effect on the host community over the long run.[15]

But case studies have an inherent limitation. All change is attributed to the new industry. Obviously this is unreasonable since many things besides new industry may have occurred within the community, state, and/or nation that affect local conditions. But, unfortunately, with only case study data one cannot distinguish between the effects of new industry and other possible sources of change.

In order to separate community public sector changes associated with industrial growth from other possible causal forces, we have turned to an analysis of a random sample of nonmetropolitan counties. Data reflecting changes over a period of years were examined to locate covariation between changes in the level of manufacturing and the county public sector. The statistically reliable covariation was then analyzed following the causal implications of the export base multiplier theory.

METHODOLOGY

The question of how the public sector copes with industrialization was examined by using changes in public sector revenues, selected expenditures, and functional allocations of personnel as criterion variables. Our first effort was to ascertain the extent of covariation between public sector changes and the net gains in the number of manufacturing plants. To understand the network of exchanges which cause, or produce, such an association, we turned to the export base multiplier model. Unfortunately, it could not be utilized fully because data were not available to trace all the linkages specified by the model. Thus, a simplified form was used which permits interpretation of coping behavior but leaves unused much of the richness inherent in a more complete application of the multiplier model. Nevertheless, by examining major factors which are presumed to intervene between new industry and public sector changes, we came to at least a partially verified interpretation which isolates manufacturing from other factors. Changes in net migration, education, and income are examined as explanatory variables.

It is well known that amount of change in a system is partially determined by the state of the system at the beginning of the period over which observations are made. Therefore, it was necessary to control for the initial level of all variables before proceeding to the causal interpretation. This was accomplished by making the initial level of each endogenous variable explicit in its estimation equation.[16]

Sampling Procedure

Nonmetropolitan counties of the U.S. constitute the population of geo-political units studied as social systems. One might reasonably refer to these units as communities.[17] From the universe of counties with nonmetro status in 1950, a stratified 10% random sample was drawn by grouping all nonmetro counties according to major census region, as defined by the U.S. Bureau of the Census. Within each region, each county was assigned a number drawn from a table of random digits. From these numbers a 10% sample within each region was selected, again using a table of random numbers.

The choice of 1950 was largely determined by the fact that a data file was to be created for the sample counties which would permit several analyses of post-World War II changes in "rural" America.[18] The data file contains 276 counties, some of which are currently of metropolitan status. Removing the metro counties does not disturb the random sampling quality of the remaining counties, since all 1978 nonmetro counties had an equal probability of being included in their regional sample.

Data

All data were derived from publications of the U.S. government. Capital migration was measured by net gains in the number of manufacturing plants located within the county, as reported in the 1967 and 1972 Census of Manufacturers (Vol. III, Table 9). Net gains in numbers of manufacturing plants was our choice for measurement of capital input in the manufacturing sector of the local economy. The choice was made necessary by the fact that new capital expenditures by manufacturing firms is suppressed to avoid disclosure in a large proportion of the nonmetro counties. The same constraint of disclosure violations prevents the use of numbers of manufacturing jobs or wages paid in manufacturing as alternative indicators of capital inflows due to manufacturing.

Public sector changes were derived from the 1967 and 1972 Census of

Governments. Total revenue is general revenue of all local governments in the county for the fiscal years 1966–67 and 1971–72.

Total expenditures and subcategories of welfare, police protection, corrections, and natural resources were derived from the 1967 and 1972 Census of Governments. It is important to note that these figures refer only to the county government, not to all local governments, and therefore one cannot derive net gains to the public sector by subtraction. Within county government expenditures, we selected welfare, police protection, and corrections, which case studies have indicated may be affected by new industry. In addition, we selected natural resources expenditures because of their apparent connection to potential environmental costs.

Net migration is a direct indicator of increased human capital supply within the local system and was measured by the net migration (1965–70) in the county as reported in the 1970 Census of Population. The quality of the labor supply within the resident population is measured by the median years of schooling completed by males. This choice of indicator is based on our knowledge that males have completed fewer years of schooling than women in the nonmetro areas and that women are less active in the labor force. Therefore, capital inputs have a greater likelihood of affecting the quality of the male segment of the labor supply than the female component. In other words, we deliberately made a measurement choice which favors the logical model. The measures were derived from the 1960 and 1970 Census of Population.

A satisfactory index for returns to labor are wages and salaries, but we were forced by the practical matter of data availability to use the aggregate of family income in an approximate measure for the theoretical construct. Thus, income gains were also derived from the 1960 and 1970 Census of Population.

RESULTS

According to the theory outlined in the above discussion, net gains in the number of manufacturing plants is an indication of capital migration which is expected to stimulate economic, human capital, and social changes within the community that must be dealt with by the officials in the public sector. Measurable changes in the revenues, expenditures, and allocation of public sector personnel are regarded as evidence of how the community copes with industrialization.

Evidence of Change

The data reported in Table 1 indicate that between 1967 and 1972 the 240 counties experienced an average net gain of 1.6 manufacturing plants.[19] As is evident in the standard deviation, there was considerable variance among them in the number of plants gained. There also is evidence of considerable growth in the public sector. The average net gain in revenues aggregated for all local

Table 1. Mean Changes in Selected Characteristics of
Nonmetro Counties (N = 240), 1967–1972

Variable	Change	
	Mean	Standard deviation
Manufacturing plants (No.)	1.596	11.595
Revenues of local governments ($)	4,460,354	7,230,170
Expenditures of county governments ($)	1,321,738	2,364,063
Employees (FTE) of county governments	139.74	207.05

governmental units was $4.46 million. Net gains in expenditures of the county governments also was quite large; the average was $1.13 million. County governments also experienced an average net gain of full-time employees.[20] All three measures of public sector activity have standard deviations which suggest negative net gains. This was verified by inspection of the actual distribution of changes.

Specifically, we found that 91 counties had a net loss of manufacturing plants, 28 had experienced no net change, and 121 were "gainers." At this point, we set aside those counties with net losses and no gains in order to concentrate on the effects of new industry. This is necessary because the export base theory and its derived multiplier effect are not symmetrical with

Table 2. Evidence of Curvilinearity Between Change in Manufacturing
and Public Sector Changes Among 240 U.S. Counties, 1967–1972

Change in number of manufacturing plants	Public sector changes			
	Revenue	Expenditures	Employees (FTE)	Counties (no.)
Losses				
> 10	8,712,050	2,403,235	213.100	17
1–10	2,838,795	679,676	93,936	74
No change	2,240,536	539,821	62.000	28
Gains				
1–10	3,685,518	896,711	121,491	97
> 10	11,486,460	3,275,417	373.542	24
Correlation				
(ungrouped data)	.200	.162	.275	
Grand mean	4,388,035	1,132,738	137.252	

regard to the effects of changes in net capital inputs. The theory takes as a premise that there is a positive net gain in the "basic" industries and it is this gain which stimulates the local economy. This is unfortunate because a symmetric theory of community change, one which explained the effects of decline as well as growth, would be more parsimonious and therefore preferred. The limitation of the export base multiplier theory is manifested clearly in the data shown in Table 2. Those counties with net losses of more than 10 plants had public sector gains in revenue, expenditures, and personnel changes almost equal those of the heavy gainers. Obviously, net gain in manufacturing plants has a curvilinear relation with public sector changes. We will not explore possible explanations of this curvilinearity, but rather note two points. First, growth in manufacturing is not the only means by which local communities can increase revenues (or expenditures) since the heavy losers of plants are large "gainers" in the public sector. Second, we wish to be explicit about the empirical necessity of our decision to examine only those counties with net gains in manufacturing. To do otherwise would result in conclusions of "no effect" of growth while real effects were hidden by the curvilinearity. We turn, then, to those counties which had net gains in manufacturing plants.

Table 3 indicates positive net gains in manufacturing and public sector variables much larger than those reported in Table 1. Note also that the standard deviations are still larger than the means. In the restricted case of "gainers," this fact indicates a strong positive skew in the distribution rather than negative net change.

Table 3. Mean Changes in Selected Characteristics of Nonmetro
Counties with Net Gains in Manufacturing
(N = 121), 1967-1972

Variable	Change	
	Mean	Standard deviation
Manufacturing plants (No.)	7.793	12.400
Revenues of local governments ($)	5,267,273	8,967,225
Expenditures of county governments ($)	1,368,521	2,937,471
Employees (FTE) of county governments	172.26	243.08

Evidence of Covariation

The evidence of correlation between manufacturing growth and public sector changes is positive, but rather weak. Inspection of Table 4 shows that

Table 4. Correlations Between Net Gains in Manufacturing and
Public Sector Changes (*N* = 121), 1967–1972

Public sector changes	Manufacturing changes			
	Number of plants	Jobs	Capital expenditures	Wages paid
Revenue	.330**	.078	.184	−.003
Expenditures	.238*	.044	.227*	−.015
Employees (FTE)	.422**	.163	.168	.042

*P < .01.
**P < .001.

the net gain in the number of new manufacturing plants is correlated with revenue gains, *r* = .330; with expenditures, *r* = .238; and with personnel gains, *r* = .422. These coefficients should be regarded as maximum limits of causal effects since some, or even all, of the observed covariation could be spurious due to manufacturing gains being correlated with an unmeasured variable, such as lagged effects of manufacturing which existed prior to 1967. This possibility is examined explicitly in the next section.

Table 4 also reports the correlation coefficients for other indicators of manufacturing gains and public sector changes. Only one of the nine coefficients is statistically significant. However, as was already noted, these data are incomplete due to suppression by the Bureau of the Census to protect confidentiality. Therefore, they can be regarded only as suggestive. But they are not without value since (1) suppression occurs only among counties with small gains, and (2) they are consistently insignificant. Thus, the weight of their effect is to support the statement that evidence indicates a positive, weak correlation between gains in manufacturing and public sector changes.

A partial decomposition of net gains in county expenditures can be observed in Table 5. Public welfare, police protection, corrections, and resources were selected because of their relevance to the public sector function(s) of maintaining order, securing the quality of the human capital resources of the community, and conserving the physical environment. Moreover, these aspects of the local system were reported in case studies as important areas of impact. It is evident by inspection that public welfare ($332,645) accounts for the largest percentage of the total increase in expenditures. Police protection accounts for only about 4% of the increases, and corrections accounts for about 1%. Together the two social control categories of expenditures account for slightly over 5% of the average increases. Expenditures for maintenance of the physical environment account for a surprisingly small amount of the net increase, just over 1%.

Table 5. Change in County Government Expenditures and Their Correlation with Gains in Manufacturing ($N = 121$), 1967–1972

Expenditures	Change		
	Mean	Standard deviation	r
Total	$1,368,521	$2,937,471	.238*
Welfare	332,645	1,612,552	.118
Police	54,298	123,283	.426**
Corrections	13,636	86,772	.090
Natural resources	16,926	72,678	.092

*$P < .01$.
**$P < .001$.

The correlations between manufacturing gains and categories of expenditures also are shown in Table 5. It is apparent that police activities are more associated with manufacturing gains than is welfare, even though the latter accounted for a much greater portion of the increases in total expenditure. Corrections, welfare, and natural resources expenditures all have insignificant correlations with net gains in manufacturing. The finding with regard to welfare expenditures is inconsistent with the expectations that capital migration will be positively associated with human resource maintenance activities in the public sector. However, this result probably is due to the fact that educational expenditures are not included.

Table 6 shows that mean net gains in FTE (full-time equivalent) personnel within county government and the distribution of these gains among the various functional categories. Education clearly accounts for the vast majority of gains, 59% in our sample. If public welfare, hospitals, health, and library personnel are added to education to form what may be called the human resources maintenance function of the public sector, one observes that 73% of the net gain in personnel is due to this functional area. Social control allocations may be observed by adding police protection and corrections. Together they account for 6% of the net gain in personnel, which is in close agreement with the gains in fiscal expenditures attributable to social control. Parks and recreation plus natural resources allows one to create an approximation to the maintenance of the physical environment function, and as with expenditures this activity is responsible for 1.3% of the average net gain. Except for administration, the remaining categories form a meaningful functional activity that may be labeled maintenance of physical infrastructure which provides the human resource base of the community as well as the private sector with streets and roads, sanitation, fire protection, housing, and utilities. These activities account for 8.1% of the net gain in personnel.

Table 6. Change in County Government FTE Employees and Their Correlations with Gains in Manufacturing, 1967–1972

Functional category of employees (FTE)	Change		Percentage of total	r
	Mean	Standard deviation		
TOTAL	167.32	236.14	100.00	.422**
Human resource maintenance				
Education	98.99	145.52	59.2	.276**
Hospitals	16.29	52.06	9.7	.426**
Health	4.30	41.14	2.6	.114
Welfare	3.69	15.99	2.2	−.020
Library	.56	6.43	0.3	.062
Social control				
Police	8.98	17.18	5.4	.643**
Corrections	.90	4.40	0.5	.171
Physical infrastructure				
Fire protection	5.02	8.08	3.0	.314**
Highway	4.19	19.54	2.5	.268**
Housing	1.86	6.53	1.1	.085
Sanitation	1.49	10.45	0.9	.030
Utilities (except water)	1.34	8.43	0.8	.028
Water	−0.33	7.97	−0.2	−.069
Natural environment				
Parks and recreation	1.44	8.89	0.9	.056
Natural resources	.61	6.39	0.4	.288*
Administration				
General control	3.42	16.90	2.0	.210*
Financial	3.24	8.98	1.9	.327**

*$P < .01$.
**$P < .001$.

Obviously, the largest gains are in the functional area of human resources maintenance. Administration accounts for 3.9% of the gains in personnel.

Using net gains in personnel as an indicator of public sector efforts to cope with manufacturing allows one to assess the human resource maintenance effort including education as well as public welfare. The relevant correlations are reported in Table 6, column 4. Here it is clear that growth in educational personnel is correlated with manufacturing net gains ($r = .276$). Again, welfare allocation gains are not associated with net gain in manufacturing ($r = −.020$). Police has the strongest correlation with growth in manufacturing ($r = .643$).

As can be observed by inspection of Table 6, there are eight categories of personnel gains having positive associations with net gains in manufacturing. In order of magnitude they are: fire protection, education, highways, natural resources, and administration/general control. Again, the evidence of correlation is positive, but weak. This is especially so when one recognizes these coefficients as the upper limits of causal effects.

Interpretation of Causal Order

The most parsimonious method for examining the goodness of fit between our theoretical model and the empirical evidence is path analysis. Indeed, the multiplier model can be viewed as an elaborate causal or path model which one can describe by a set of structural equations. However, as already stated, the model we are examining is very reduced in form. The portion of the complete flow model being estimated is presented schematically in Figure 1.

The possibility of spuriousness in the zero-order correlation coefficients has been dealt with in two ways. First, level of manufacturing in 1967 has been explicitly introduced as an exogenous variable and allowed to be correlated

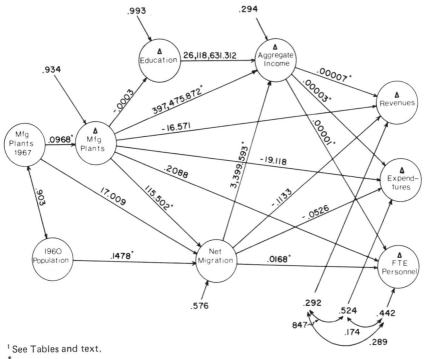

[1] See Tables and text.

[*] Significant Paths.

Fig. 1. Path diagram of new industry effects on the public sector, 1967-72.[1] (Coefficients are in unstandardized metric)

Table 7. Regression Estimates of Effects of New Industry[a]

x_i \ y_j	Δ Mfg. (1)	Δ Education (2)	Net migration (3)	Δ Income (4)	Δ Revenue (5)	Δ Expenditure (6)	Δ Personnel (7)
Constant	4.255	1.215	-132.219	-34,717,386.720	-1,317.826	-473.690	2.945
1. 1960 population			.148 (.030) .610				
2. 1967 mfg. plants	.0968 (.0232) .357		17.009 (17.800) .122				
3. Δ Mfg.		-.003 (.001) -.056	115.502 (29.430) .225	397,475.872 (114,259.395) .107	-16.571 (22.753) -.023	-19.118 (13.092) -.081	.209 (.922) .011
4. 1960 educ.		-.006 (.006) -.096					
5. Δ Education				26,118,631.312 (17,608,654.554) .041			
6. Net migration				3,399.593 (365.053) .469	-.113 (.099) -.080	-.053 (.058) -.114	.017 (.004) .439
7. 1959 income				.516 (.052) .478			
8. Δ Income					.00007 (.00002) .341	.00003 (.00001) .548	.00001 (.00000) .619
9. 1967 revenue					.682 (.063) .721		
10. Expenditure						.522 (.067) .528	
11. personnel							-.045 (.031) -.158
R²	.128	.013	.669	.913	.915	.725	.805
Adjusted R²	.120	-.003	.660	.910	.912	.716	.798
F-Ratio	17.416	.797	18.677	305.179	311.179	16.524	119.515
DF	1/119	3/118	3/117	4/116	4/116	4/116	4/116

[a]Each column entry for the variables in columns 1–7 list three numbers. They are, respectively, the unstandardized regression coefficient, the standard error of the estimate within parentheses, and the standardized regression coefficient.

with 1960 population size as a second exogenous variable. The second control for spuriousness due to scale of the local systems is executed by making the 1967 level of each endogenous variable explicit in the structural equations for the estimation of change. For example, the estimation for change in education is:

$$\Delta \text{ Education} = a + b_1 \text{ Education 1960} + b_2 \Delta \text{ Manufacturing} + e$$

The coefficients indicating the effect of initial level on change in each endogenous variable are omitted from Figure 1, but are given in Table 7 where the multiple regression estimates are shown in detail.

If the theoretical model is correct, one should find the zero-order correlations between net gains in manufacturing and public sector changes reduced, if not completely eliminated, by the intervening causal processes described in Figure 1. That is, changes in the size, quality, and economic affluence of the human resource base, as measured by net migration, education, and aggregate income, should permit a strong interpretation of the processes linking private sector capital migration and public sector response.

Moreover, one should be able to observe that the indirect paths from manufacturing to public sector changes should be statistically significant, or at least some of them should be and thereby indicate the processes which account for the explanation of the zero-order correlation. Specifically the theory posits that growth in manufacturing will result in population increases, due mainly to greater net migration, and that incomes paid to these added families will raise the aggregate income. In addition, it is expected manufacturing firms often pay wages above the local average. This immediate, short-run effect should be observable in the coefficient of the direct path from change in manufacturing to change in aggregate income. A similar but indirect, long-term effect of manufacturing on income is anticipated as the local employment opportunities expand to include higher-skill jobs, producing gains in educational attainment and consequently higher wages. This indirect effect should appear in the coefficients of the linking of change in manufacturing to change in education, and change in education to change in aggregate income.

Net migration and changes in aggregate income are the critical variables in the explanatory model, especially the latter. Increased disposable income spent locally on capital investments and consumable items generate an expanded tax base which permits gains in revenues. But some of the greater disposable income generates increased demands for public sector services. Thus, (1) one should expect to find significant coefficients on each of the paths from change in aggregate income to all public sector changes; and (2) the "costs" of population increases are expected to appear indirectly in the path coefficients from net migration to change in aggregate income and from change in aggregate income to the public sector changes.

In view of the fact that the covariation of manufacturing growth and public sector change was quite limited, one must anticipate rather large coefficients of nondetermination for each endogenous variable.

Finally, because of the nature of budget-making processes within the public sector, it is reasonable to expect some correlation among public sector changes to remain after the effects of changes in export base and human capital resource are removed. Hence the model makes this expectation explicit by allowing correlated residual variances among the public sector changes.

Reference to the beta coefficients in Figure 1 reveals an extremely good fit between the theory and the empirical estimates. The direct paths from manufacturing growth to public sector changes are all reduced to non-significance.[21] Three paths to aggregate income gains from manufacturing growth were predicted, one direct and two indirect. The direct path is significant, indicating a short-run effect on gains in disposable income. The indirect effect via net migration also is significant. More plants mean new jobs which attract inmigrants whose incomes contribute to the aggregate of family income. One should note this does not necessarily translate into a *per capita* gain in income. The indirect path via increases in educational attainments of adult males is inconsequential. There is no effect of manufacturing growth on gains in educational level.

Gains in aggregate income have a positive and significant effect on all three public sector changes. Because of large differences in the scale of aggregate income and the public sector variables, the beta coefficients are small in absolute numeric value, but they are of consequence. The partial F-ratios for the coefficients of change in income in the regression for change in revenues, change in expenditures, and change in FTE personnel are 18.858, 20.875, and 22.502, respectively.

The effects of net migration on revenues and expenditures are entirely indirect via gains in income, as predicted from theory. However, there is a direct effect as well as an indirect effect of net migration on gains in FTE personnel. While direct effect was not anticipated, it probably is due to the fact that growth in educational activity is included in the FTE personnel but not in the other public sector change. As a public good, educational expenditures are likely to increase as a function of population growth independent of the contributions those additional people make to the tax base.

Thus we observe that the total effect of manufacturing growth on public sector changes is mediated by net migration and gains in aggregate family income. Accordingly, we derive two empirical generalizations from the analysis. First, the total effect of growth in manufacturing in nonmetropolitan counties between 1967 and 1970 was positive but quite limited. No more than 17% of the public sector change can be attributed to manufacturing. Second, the total effect of manufacturing is mediated by net migration and gains in aggregate family income. This finding is generally consistent with logical derivations from the export base and multiplier theory of economic change.

CONCLUSIONS AND IMPLICATIONS

The analysis permits some tentative conclusions. To the extent that a net gain in manufacturing activity has a causal influence on the public sector, it does so through its influence on population size rather that by way of intermediate effects on (1) quality of the labor supply or (2) returns to labor. From the perspective of the public sector, these findings seem to mean that net gain in the number of manufacturing plants is but one factor among many to be dealt with either as a source of demand or a revenue base.

Public officials in communities with new industry are able to raise more revenues (or at least a little more) than those in communities without new industry. This is consistent with recent case studies. Unfortunately, we are unable, with data currently available, to examine the mechanisms used by local officials in order to extract these added revenues. We cannot know whether the additional funds come from increases in assessed valuation of real property (commercial or residential), greater local consumption, or greater intergovernmental transfer payments. But we can be confident that a small part of it derives from an increase in the aggregate income. Indeed, it appears that the most probable explanation for the observed positive effect of new industry on revenues is population growth, since gains in industry are associated with population growth which generates an increase in aggregate income which, in turn, creates more revenue.

From the public sector perspective, people cost money and more people cost more money. Examination of expenditures and personnel allocation indicates that maintenance of the human resource quality and social control account for most of the added costs. Surprisingly little is due to increased expenditures on maintenance and expansion of the physical infrastructures. But no category of expenditure or personnel allocation has a very strong relation to net gains in manufacturing. To the extent there is such a relation, it too is explained by the causal path from population to income to public sector variables.

From the standpoint of public policy which views manufacturing as the primary policy instrument for revitalization of nonmetropolitan communities, one may interpret these findings as supportive or as disconfirming. On the one hand the data show the effects of manufacturing to be inconsequential for changes in the public sector. There is very little relief from fiscal burdens on the public sector attributable to net gains in manufacturing. The essence of this interpretation is that manufacturing is irrelevant to public sector changes and therefore logically cannot be regarded as an effective policy instrument.

On the other hand, one may point to the weak positive effects and the fact that these effects can be understood and explained by the causal processes implied in the export base multiplier model as support for manufacturing as a proper policy instrument. The essence of this interpretation is that manufacturing is an appropriate intervention but has been used too sparingly and hence shows only limited results. What is needed is more manufacturing, not less!

At this stage in our analysis, we are not prepared to accept either interpretation as the correct one, or even the most compelling one. Rather, it appears to us that these findings suggest the need to expand the number of policy instruments used to increase the capital flow into nonmetro communities. The logic of the export base multiplier theory seems reasonably consistent with the empirical facts. And the small effect of manufacturing per se might be strengthened if more plants were added to these social systems. However, the fact of the matter is that manufacturing is not a growth sector in post-industrial societies. Thus, the most compelling interpretation is (1) acceptance of the logical structure underlying the mechanism for achieving a policy of increasing capital flows to nonmetro areas in order to stimulate local economies, and (2) expanding the instruments of capital input. One may wish to consider the wisdom of the policy, but that discussion requires evidence beyond the scope of the present analysis.

NOTES

[1] Commission on Population Growth and the American Future, *Population and the American Future* (Washington, D.C.: U.S. Government Printing Office, 1972); Walter Isard, *Methods of Regional Analysis: An Introduction to Regional Science* (New York: The Technology Press of M.I.T. and John Wiley, 1960); John Maynard Keynes, *The General Theory of Employment, Interest and Money* (New York: Harcourt, Brace & World, 1965); Wilbur R. Thompson and John M. Mattila, *Econometric Model of Post-War State Industrial Development* (Detroit: Wayne State University Press, 1969); Charles Tiebout, "Exports and Regional Economic Growth," *Journal of Political Economy,* Vol. 54 (1956), pp. 160–165; and David M. Smith, *Industrial Location: An Economic Geographical Analysis* (New York: John Wiley, 1972).

[2] Justifications for this point of view are presented in several recent publications including Gene F. Summers et al., *Industrial Invasion of Nonmetropolitan America* (New York: Praeger, 1976); Gene F. Summers, "Small Towns Beware: Industry Can Be Costly," *Planning,* Vol. 42 (1976), pp. 20–21; Gene F. Summers and Jean M. Lang, "Bringing Jobs to People: Does It Pay?" *Small Towns,* Vol. 7 (1976), pp. 4–11; Gene F. Summers, "Industrial Development of Rural America: A Quarter Century of Experience," *Journal of Community Development Society,* Vol. 8 (1977), pp. 6–18; and Eldon D. Smith and Gene F. Summers, *How New Industry Affects Rural Areas,* (Mississippi State: Southern Rural Development Center, 1978).

It is our opinion that as social scientists we have a responsibility to empirically examine implications of a theory which encourages public policy architects and community development agents to regard new manufacturing as the best, perhaps only, policy instrument for improving the conditions of life in nonmetro communities. Failure to do so provides a passive endorsement of policies and practices whose consequence may be a lesson in futility that could have been avoided.

Our acceptance of the challenge of this responsibility for assessing and reporting the implications of theory often has been interpreted as "opposition" by the proponents of rural industrialization. We do not accept our role as that of the "loyal opposition." Rather, we affirm our commitment to demythologizing views of the world as an essential element in the difficult task of shaping policies and actions which are as consistent as possible with the realities that confront us.

[3] Summers et al., op. cit., note 2, p. 76.

[4] While there is an extensive literature developed around this concept, the elements essential for an understanding of it may be found in a series of articles by Richard B. Andrews appearing in *Land Economics,* Vols. 29–31 (1953–1956), all titled "Mechanics of the Urban Economic Base," and in subsequent publications by Walter Isard, op. cit., note 1; Edgar Z. Palmer et al., "The Economic Base and Multiplier," Business Research Bulletin No. 63 (Lincoln, Nebraska: College of Business Administration, University of Nebraska, 1958); Ralph W. Pfouts, ed., *The Techniques of Urban Economic Analysis* (West Trenton, N.J.: Chandler–Davis Publishing Co., 1960); and Charles M. Tiebout, *The Community Economic Base Study* (New York: Committee for Economic Development, 1962).

[5] In early formulations, the "basic" industries were limited to extractive industries and manufacturing, but more recent treatments permit the inclusion of recreation, government, and education. It appears to us this is still too restrictive if one accepts net flow of money into the local economy as the criterion. Indeed, it is precisely this restrictive use of the concept and the attendant classification of industries into basic and nonbasic which encourages exclusive reliance on manufacturing as the vehicle to bring capital into the local economy. More careful attention to the process, and less concern with the classification of industries, permits consideration of a wider range of mechanisms for achieving the desired outcome of greater cash flows. These include improving the efficiency of existing firms, expanding the markets of existing firms, formation of new firms, importing firms within "growth sectors" of the national economy, and greater shares of state and federal funds. The feasibility of such an expanded conception is being studied currently by Professor Glen C. Pulver, Department of Agricultural Economics, University of Wisconsin–Madison (personal communication).

[6] Summers et al., op. cit., note 2, pp. 72–105.

[7] Ibid., pp. 62–71.

[8] Ibid., pp. 78–85.

[9] Ibid., pp. 89–92.

[10] Ibid., pp. 92–102.

[11] Ibid., pp. 92–97.

[12] Ibid., pp. 92–107.

[13] Charles B. Garrison, "Economic Impact of New Industry on Small Towns," unpublished doctoral dissertation, University of Kentucky, 1967; Charles B. Garrison, "New Industry in Small Towns: The Impact on Local Government," *National Tax Journal,* Vol. 24 (1971), pp. 493–500; Ronald E. Shaffer, "The Net Economic Impact of New Industry on Rural Communities in Eastern Oklahoma," unpublished doctoral dissertation, Oklahoma State University, 1972; Ronald E. Shaffer and Luther Tweeten, *Economic Changes from Industrial Development in Eastern Oklahoma,* Bulletin B-715 (Stillwater: Oklahoma State University, Agricultural Experiment Station, 1974); Ronald E. Shaffer and Luther Tweeten, "Measuring the Net Economic Changes from Rural Development in Oklahoma," *Land Economics,* Vol. 50 (1974), pp. 261–71; and Dwight G. Uhrich, "Economic Impact of New Industry on the Brookings Community: 3M, A Case Study," unpublished master's thesis, South Dakota State University, 1974.

[14] Shaffer, op. cit., note 13.

[15] Summers and Lang, op. cit., note 2, p. 11.

[16] For the rationale and explanation of this procedure, see George Bohrnstedt, "Observations on the Measurement of Change," in E. F. Borgatta, ed., *Sociological Methodology* (San Francisco: Jossey–Bass, 1969), pp. 113–133.

[17] See Lauren H. Seiler and Gene F. Summers, "Locating Community Boundaries: An

Integration of Theory and Empirical Techniques," *Sociological Methods and Research,* Vol. 2 (1974), pp. 259–280.

[18] The creation of this file was supported by the Wisconsin Experiment Station, College of Agricultural and Life Sciences, University of Wisconsin–Madison and the North Central Regional Center for Rural Development. The data file contains approximately 1,000 variables for each county. A list of publications and unpublished manuscripts bases on analyses of this data file is available upon request.

[19] The random sample of 276 counties was reduced to 240 due to the removal of metro counties and the fact that 12 counties were missing expenditure data in 1967 and 8 in 1972. In addition, one county had no county government.

[20] FTE employees are full-time equivalents, i.e., 100 FTE employees does not necessarily mean 100 employees, since some positions may be part-time.

[21] In order to be regarded significant, a coefficient must be at least twice the magnitude of its standard error. We have chosen to display the unstandardized regression coefficients in Figure 2 because of their greater meaning subatantively. Thus, each added manufacturing plant is estimated to have added 115.5 persons to the county population as a consequence of net migration from 1965–1970, *net of* the effects of numbers of plants in 1967 and county population in 1960. Population and 1967 level of manu-facturing makes equivocal their coefficients with respect to net migration.

PART III

CONCLUSIONS

Chapter 12

IMPLICATIONS FOR NONMETROPOLITAN DEVELOPMENT POLICY

H. L. Seyler and Richard E. Lonsdale

INTRODUCTION

The topics examined in this book clearly suggest a number of important policy implications bearing on the future of nonmetropolitan America. Authors have treated a rather broad spectrum of issues associated with the phenomenon of nonmetropolitan industrialization, both its rationale and impact. In all instances, an overriding theme has been the economic and social change, indeed the transformation, that has taken place.

The changes experienced across nonmetropolitan America have occurred in the absence of any integrated national policy. Though there is a great variety of federal programs designed to improve conditions in all or a selected group of nonmetropolitan areas, with each program having certain foci (e.g., alleviating poverty, reducing unemployment, assisting smaller communities, etc.), no grand strategy has emerged as in many other modern industrial societies. Federal programs in the U.S. have been, at best, loosely coordinated with state and local development efforts.

That so much change has taken place without a general policy to guide it leaves observers understandably concerned about the future of nonmetropolitan America. What can the people in this part of the country, representing almost a third (31%) of the U.S. population, expect in the coming years? What are the long-term implications of the topics treated in this book? Obviously, more attention should be given to the coordination of development efforts and the establishment of policy objectives. The purpose of this concluding chapter is to discuss five general areas in need of careful consideration and evaluation in formulating any kind of policy conceived to affect nonmetropolitan industrial development. In effect, these represent five areas where future research could be appropriately focused.

THE NEED TO VIEW NONMETROPOLITAN INDUSTRIALIZATION
AS A PHASE IN NATIONAL
ECONOMIC DEVELOPMENT

The dramatic expansion of manufacturing activity in nonmetropolitan areas can be viewed as an inevitable outcome produced by a number of interrelated components of the modernization process. It would seem to be a normal stage or phase in the development of a modern nation's space economy. Other economically advanced industrial societies seem to be experiencing the same general phenomenon. The forces combining to promote it include the transportation and communications revolution which has reduced the friction of distance, improved capital mobility, changes in industrial organization, the diffusion of urban values to the countryside (especially by television and the automobile), the real and perceived social and economic problems associated with larger urban concentrations (the "urban crisis"), geographic differences in wage rates, the declining demands for farm labor, growing public concern with rural-to-urban migration, increased public awareness of regional poverty problems, and a host of other influences. Governmental policy can moderate or eliminate some of these conditions (e.g., legislate standard wage rates, selectively enhance the attraction of some areas through infrastructural investments, etc.), but for the most part these influences acting in concert seem to be a product of the modern post-industrial, high-technology society.

Coincident with the above trends has been a strong tendency of community leaders, development agencies, and some analysts to treat new manufacturing employment as the logical catalyst to induce and sustain the forces of economic transformation. As Heady has stated:[1]

> Rural industrialization is a big hope for those communities which have the characteristics favoring it. We can find many outstanding examples where the initiation of a new plant by an outside firm caused a turnaround in the employment and income decline of a rural community. To an extent, national leaders equate rural development with rural industrialization.

Such has been a pattern of thinking, and not without a logical basis. As noted by Lonsdale, manufacturing is the one kind of basic ("community forming") employment that many communities can logically expect to attract.[2] Though not a growth sector in the aggregate, manufacturing has locational flexibility and decision makers have shown a willingness to elect nonmetropolitan locations.

Beyond manufacturing, and excepting governmental facility location and primary activity intensification, the service sector can provide impetus for growth and development. However, settlements in many nonmetropolitan areas are disadvantaged with respect to this sector. They lack the size, relative location, or site amenities to compete successfully for business or personal service firms with areally extensive and noncontiguous markets. Unless there is an arbitrary decision by federal or state government to locate a major public facility which may act as a magnet for other private sector expansion, the service sector in these areas often depends upon growth in another sector, such as manufacturing, for entry-level thresholds to be met before any growth can ensue.

It remains to be seen how much greater a share of the nation's manufacuring employment can be garnered by nonmetropolitan areas. Haren and Holling cite data on p. 16 showing a 23.5% share in 1962 and a 28.8% share in 1978, with an absolute gain of over 1.8 million. Based on population, nonmetropolitan areas are already almost as intensely industrialized as the nation as a whole. Can nonmetropolitan America, with about 31% of the national population, acquire yet higher shares—35 or 40%—of the manufacturing employment? Are U.S. metropolitan concentrations emerging as largely service centers amidst a sea of locationally dispersed manufacturing?

If this kind of locational redistribution of industrial activity is inevitable in an advanced society, then surely this recognition should be incorporated into the deliberations of economic and social planners at all levels. It seems increasingly evident that one cannot plan economic growth or social change without a clear appreciation of the forces altering the geographic distribution of economic activity. And it is just as critical whether planning emphases are focused on adjustment to, or redirection of, the current phase of an unfolding process of dispersal.

What about the effect of other influences now emerging or on the horizon, e.g., the energy situation, control of plant emissions, and the rising "flood" of imported goods? Will these forces serve to reduce or even curtail the locational redistribution of American manufacturing? One could reason that (1) it has been partially due to "cheap energy" that the revolution in transportation transpired permitting industrial dispersal, and (2) the kind of "filtered-down" manufacturing operations described by Erickson and Leinbach as characteristic of nonmetropolitan areas involve the very kind of goods that often lend themselves to production overseas and importation into the U.S. despite tariffs and quotas. On the other hand, the lower value of the dollar on international money markets serves to improve the potential for filtered-down operations in the U.S. to meet foreign competition.

These are complex questions which have a great bearing on both the short- and long-run course of nonmetropolitan industrialization.

THE NEED FOR A CLEARER UNDERSTANDING OF DEMOGRAPHIC TRENDS AND THEIR ROLE IN PRODUCING AREAL ECONOMIC CHANGE

Perhaps the most fundamental and important change in nonmetropolitan America is the celebrated "demographic turnaround," i.e., the historic reversal of the long-standing net out-flow of people from nonmetropolitan areas. Many explanations have been offered and many factors considered. The role of manufacturing in fostering this process warrants a comprehensive research effort. Two chapters in this volume treat the theme, but the relationship is still unclear.

Data provided by Haren and Holling suggest that manufacturing has provided much of the new basic employment in nonmetropolitan areas since 1962, and assuming an employment multiplier effect, it would seem to have initiated a good measure of increased nonagricultural employment. Furthermore, since the impressive upswing in manufacturing activity immediately preceded the drop in nonmetropolitan out-migration, it is not illogical to link the two. Evidence presented by Kuehn is generally consistent with this reasoning.

A more sceptical view is provided by Heaton and Fuguitt who note that "... manufacturing may have received more attention than it merits as a solution to the problems of nonmetropolitan population decline." They feel that manufacturing will have an even less significant impact in the future as the services sector assumes a greater role in the nonmetropolitan employment picture. A recent paper by Smith and Pulver supports this contention.[3] Such judgments may confuse cause and consequence, given earlier remarks about the difficulty of expanding service activities in less-urbanized areas.

Differences in the interpretation of the link between population and industrial growth, in part of the product of divergent research designs and assumption, serve to emphasize the pressing need for more work in this area if the implications for development policy are to be understood. Particularly, there is a void in our awareness of gross inflows and outflows of migrants in response to different types and levels of industrialization, or the absence of it.

There are other aspects of demographic change which have important policy implications. Focusing primarily on gross inflows, Kuehn observes that new and return migrants assume jobs to such an extent that hiring of longer-term residents (that could reduce unemployment) obtains at lower levels than local officials had hoped. On the other hand, Kuehn notes that such inmigrants (who tend to be younger, better educated, and more experienced or trained) can serve to "... revitalize human capital in rural areas." What is the long-term significance of the return of younger former residents? How important are factors other than job availability, such as preference for a more rural life-style, in sustaining this inflow? What social and economic impacts will the inmigrants bring to host communities as they respond to enhanced employment opportunities in the industrial sector? What are the demographic trends as regards women and minority participants in the industrialization of nonmetropolitan areas?

Contrary to what some might expect, Kuehn found that return migration was more important for areas at greater distances from metropolitan concentrations. Perhaps manufacturing development in more distant, smaller places permits people to realize their locational preferences, bearing in mind the growing popularity of small towns in residential preference polls.

Are the more recent migration trends sustainable? The psychology may be critical; if industry continues to expand in nonmetropolitan areas on the expectation that labor will continue to be available, it could become a self-fulfilling prophesy as workers move in (or return) to take advantage of the new jobs. Can the "return to the country" movement be sustained without a continuation of industrial dispersal? What would happen to migration patterns if nonmetropolitan manufacturing jobs plateau or decline? Is the "demographic turnaround" merely a passing reaction to the "urban crisis," soon to dissipate as urban problems are ameliorated? In his framework chapter introducing the impact analyses above, Seyler reports a growing feeling that the country is amidst a pervasive deconcentration process that will obtain into the indefinite future. In pondering the multifaceted demographic implications of industrial dispersal, and its implications for developmental policy, it is remarkable how little we really know.

THE NEED TO ASSESS LONG-TERM IMPLICATIONS
OF INDUSTRY MIX

Traditionally, certain kinds of industrial operations have been more favorably disposed toward nonmetropolitan locations, a fact widely recognized and well documented. In general, such industries have tended to be labor-intensive, low-profit margin, and slow-growth in character, with textiles, clothing, food products, metal fabrication, and electronics assembly being representative examples. Not surprisingly, labor has been the most important locational consideration in the triple sense of availability, cost, and attitude. As Erickson and Leinbach noted, such operations tend to be in the mature phase of the product cycle where production processes have been "routinized." Operations often require little in the way of goods and services from the local region, and the income and employment multipliers are accordingly minimal in many instances. Not all nonmetropolitan industries fit such a profile, but historically most have shared these characteristics.

Can nonmetropolitan manufacturing employment continue to increase if the heavy dependence on slow-growth industries is maintained? Thus far it has, in part through the acquisition of an ever enlarging share of the nation's slow-growth industry. But, long-term prospects seem to be limited unless one assumes an unending birth, maturation, and dispersal process at a national scale. If one assumes no change in industry mix and a decreasing pool of maturing industries, the potential for continued growth in nonmetropolitan areas seems bleak in the long run. Reinforcing this possibility is the fact that some slow-growth industries have proven to be particularly vulnerable to foreign competition, with electronics assembly being a celebrated example. Therefore, the character of the industry mix provides grounds for questioning the capacity of nonmetropolitan areas to sustain manufacturing expansion. Such pessimism is found in some of the statements of Haren and Holling.

The challenge, as has been noted, is to attract higher-wage, higher-technology industries earlier in their production cycles. Professional industrial development people claim this process is already under way and has been for some time.[4] Firms in the somewhat more "intermediate" wage and technology categories (i.e., somewhat more in the growth phase of the product cycle) are becoming increasingly common in nonmetropolitan areas. Examples include electrical and nonelectrical machinery, fabricated metal products, transportation equipment, paper products, chemicals, and construction materials. Many of these industries are not in the low-wage category. They can locate in nonmetropolitan areas and offer a wage sufficiently above that prevailing locally to attract the amount and qualities of required labor. In support of this position, Heaton and Fuguitt found new higher-wage industry was attracted to both higher- and lower-wage areas. When a new plant is introduced in a lower-wage area, especially one with a tighter labor market, existing lower-wage firms can be hurt as a result (e.g., textiles, clothing, electronics assembly, and furniture operations). But, in effect, the process could serve to upgrade the local industry mix, improve wage and skill levels, increase the multiplier effect, and strengthen the tax base. Indeed, it is to this proposition that proponents of nonmetropolitan industrialization tie their case.

Some areas are more likely to experience the upgrading of the local industry mix than others. Such an eventuality seems more probable in those nonmetropolitan areas near larger urban centers and along interstate highway corridors. Conversely, many "less-attractive" areas may not experience an upgrading and be pleased indeed to attract any kind of industry (consistent with the "half-a-loaf" principle). In the future, therefore, it should become increasingly difficult to characterize nonmetropolitan growth potential as if there were a common industry mix. Policy formulation will have to reflect the probable impacts of differing industrial composition if developmental objectives are to be met.

THE NEED FOR BETTER METHODS OF ESTIMATING COSTS AND BENEFITS OF INDUSTRIAL GROWTH

There are serious discrepancies between expectations painted by advocates of industrialization and the growth and developmental changes that have actually occurred in nonmetropolitan areas. The discordance is at least partially attributable to the environment of change. Most models describing social and economic processes are more accurate when applied to larger aggregates. Unusual, individual cases become the exception supporting a general rule. Transferring growth and change models developed for a national, metropolitan, or large regional context to nonmetropolitan areas involves a shift to much smaller aggregates. An inevitable consequence is a loss of descriptive or predictive efficacy. Shaffer makes the point with his incisive remark about the absence of a multiplier that accurately and generally characterizes employment, sales, or revenue changes accompanying industrial growth in nonmetropolitan, and especially rural, settings. Smaller, less economically diverse area economies simply lack the potential for the large multiplicative effects of round-by-round interindustry linkages observed in larger population and activity concentrations. Extensive commuting and income leakages compound problems of projecting general growth impacts.

Based on Shaffer's overview of general economic impacts, it is safe to conclude that 100 new manufacturing jobs will yield less impressive changes than suggested by Lindsey's study of a set of nonmetropolitan communities.[5] To promote more realistic expectations of change related to industrial growth, a family of multifactor models are required to assess or project probable benefits or costs. Such growth models would generally be applicable for classes of places with similar size, economic profile, relative location, and areal settlement pattern.

Developmental changes following industrial growth also diverge from expectations advanced by industrialization proponents. Just as growth impacts are limited, social spillover effects of industrial expansion seem to be restricted. Seyler's analysis indicates household income levels change insignificantly with growth in manufacturing employment. Since his study examined but one region of the county, and considered manufacturing in the aggregate, additional research is necessary before a conclusive statement is warranted. In particular, assessments of the effects of industry mix are essential if the validity of benefits from industrial upgrading is to be appraised. The frequency with which many of the "intermediate" stage industries appeared in the Plains suggests that expected income gains from industrial upgrading has not occurred, but the record is incomplete.

Kuehn and Shaffer both find that upgrading of skill levels, at least in the short-term, seems to be a feature associated with new or return migrants rather than generally improved vocational opportunities for longer-term residents. The combined effects of inmigration and appropriation of jobs by commuters from the outside lessen the potential job enrichment for community residents.

Both Kuehn and Shaffer observe that many inmigrants, including returnees, accept lower incomes upon assuming a manufacturing job in nonmetropolitan areas. There is also a suspicion that many of these inmigrants possess skills and experience in excess of that required in their new jobs. Taken together, these factors have to dilute the developmental impacts of industrial expansion. On the one hand, underemployment or inefficient use of human resources can obtain; on the other hand, households enjoy lowered incomes.

Turning to public sector changes where growth and developmental elements converge, Summers and associates find that industrial expansion is neither boon nor bane for nonmetropolitan communities. An increase in the number of industrial plants does not mean that important improvements will necessarily follow in the public sector. Though revenues may increase, so do demands and costs of providing public services.

A final developmental facet should be addressed as well, for it is one factor that is persistently inserted in any discussion of the merits of nonmetropolitan industrialization. The less tangible improvements in well-being, or quality-of-life, are often seen as inevitable and almost quintessential benefits enjoyed by residents of less-urbanized areas. Dispersal of manufacturing to non-metropolitan areas, it is argued, permits more people to realize their residential preferences and partake of the good life. Citing polls and the evidence of striking reversals in population growth patterns, advocates of non-metropolitan development frequently and too uncritically conclude that personal welfare is elevated for those affected.

Research in support of this position is wanting when an important distinction is rendered. There are peoples' perceptions of their well-being, and more objective indices describing it. A recent study determined that subjective appraisals of components of well-being by residents of nonmetropolitan areas were not consistent with widely accepted, objectively derived indices.[6]

When another perspective is added, the welfare benefits of nonmetropolitan development become more clouded. There are many alternative settings for the growth of population and economic activity, including manufacturing. Many metropolitan areas offer an array of living arrangements, or life-style possibilities, some of which are virtually identical to those found in non-metropolitan areas. Low density settlement, lack of serious congestion or pollution, and low incidences of social pathology are features of many, certainly smaller- to intermediate-sized, metropolitan areas. Thus, if area development policy is based on the realities that describe welfare, including quality-of-life, variations over the nonmetropolitan landscape, more objective cost and benefit appraisals are required.

THE NEED TO PROVIDE ASSISTANCE TO COMMUNITY LEADERS AS THEY ATTEMPT TO COPE WITH A CHANGING ECONOMIC MILLIEU

It is appropriate to quote a statement by King that "The key to rebuilding rural America is leadership; the key to rural industrialization is local leadership."[7] Similar statements have been made by many observers familiar with the problems communities face in the area of economic development and new job creation. Federal agencies may provide sources of funding, and state governments may offer programs of community assistance, but in the final analysis the critical actions necessary to meet problems of community development originate with creative leadership at the local level.

Under the general label of "community leaders" are here included persons responsible for local governance, planning, utilities, public education, police and fire protection, chamber of commerce activities, and others involved with business or industrial development. In larger nonmetropolitan communities there may be a number of people on the public (and sometimes private) payroll carrying out their responsibilities on a full-time basis. But in smaller communities many of these tasks are borne by individuals on a part-time basis while they maintain their regular job as merchant, rancher, or town banker.

Local problems of economic development can be highly complex and extraordinarily time consuming. They might involve community improvement, acquisition of land for industrial parks or sites, the organization of local "community action" groups, the laborious preparation of applications for financial assistance to various federal agencies, complying with federally mandated regulations, carrying out programs once funding is secured, etc., to name a few. The number of federal agencies and state offices with which community representatives must deal has multiplied in recent years, as has the complexities that must be managed when seeking funds. Successful communities are rewarded with town beautification projects, new housing for the elderly, a new golf course and public swimming pool, an industrial park, improved water and sewerage systems, and other features to make the community a better place to live and more competitive in attracting new industry or encouraging the expansion of existing firms.

Meanwhile, industrial firms seeking nonmetropolitan locations are becoming more demanding in what they expect from a community. They want assurances concerning local housing availability, utilities, and water supply. With tighter labor markets, they want more accurate estimates of labor quantity and qualities. Because of environmental and zoning issues, they may only consider those communities with already approved industrial sites or functional industrial parks. Because of a desire to start operations in a short time, firms may only consider those communities with buildings ready to occupy.

How reasonable is it to expect the typical nonmetropolitan community to possess the amount and quality of leadership to perform these increasingly demanding tasks? For the larger town and smaller cities who can afford it, the problems can be resolved by hiring new, full-time personnel charged with the responsibility for carrying out specific projects. For other places this may not be possible or practical. Smaller communities have to redouble their efforts and determination and rely on the effectiveness of unpaid (or modestly paid) community leaders. For the local merchant giving of his or her "free" time to serve as mayor or director of the local development corporation, no matter how valiant the effort, the tasks may be overwhelming or at the least very stressful.

Without doubt there is a need to assist community leaders in meeting the burdensome complexities of their tasks. Many kinds of assistance are currently provided in the form of seminars, handbooks, extension-type activities, advice from state development agencies, and the like. But here again smaller communities are at a disadvantage as the more specialized professionalized staffs of larger places are both more knowledgeable of these resources and far more likely to maintain fruitful liaison with assistance agencies. For those smaller communities that manage to tap into the assistance network, knowledge of how to do something does not spare community leaders from the time-consuming task of executing development programs. No solutions to this dilemma are suggested here. It would seem naive to hope that federal programs of assistance and regulation could be recast in a manner designed to minimize the demands on local governments or community action groups.

The question of community leadership has some troubling implications for nonmetropolitan development policy. If communities with more effective local leadership (for whatever reasons) have an advantage—and are able to widen that advantage—over other communities, should this be accepted by regional planners as a kind of natural selection process? After all, it could be reasoned that much of the American economic landscape has evolved in such a laissez faire environment. Or, in an effort to minimize regional welfare differentials, should state or federal government take steps to encourage more effective community leadership? The ability and commitment of local leaders to meet the challenges of the times will continue to have an effect on industrial location decisions. Any policy that seeks to direct or redirect industrial dispersal in nonmetropolitan areas must reflect the realities of highly variable community leadership.

SUMMING UP

With all of the equivocations appropriate throughout this book, one thing cannot be disputed. Nonmetropolitan communities will have to cope with changes that have been initiated or amplified by an industrial redistribution that is transforming the American landscape. To the degree that change can and should be managed, attention to the five areas we have discussed will be relevant to the design and execution of area development policy. If, and as, we move toward a national, goals-oriented plan, some kind of balance will be struck between national economic efficiency and regional or locational equity in economic well-being. When aggregates are examined, current trends are reversing some of the long-standing inequities in the distribution of population and industry. Though not treated in this book, there is at this time insufficient evidence to judge whether deconcentration supports or reduces national economic efficiency.

When we turn to inequities in economic well-being, evidence presented in this book is far from conclusive. Appraisals of selective impacts of industrial dispersal indicate general growth and developmental changes are not impressively positive. But neither are they markedly negative for nonmetropolitan areas. Thus, preceding chapters do not provide a basis for advocating a policy framed to promote continued dispersal, nor one designed to arrest or reverse contemporary trends. This chapter, and the book as a whole, was not conceived to serve such an end.

We have, however incompletely, attempted to extend the documentation about the nature of nonmetropolitan industrialization, and to selectively assess changes in related social and economic components. Rather modestly, we intended our findings and interpretations to contribute to a reasoned weighing of the benefits and costs of alternative developmental policies and programs for nonmetropolitan areas. Furthermore, we hope to have provided an enlarged information base for those involved with area or community development ventures.

NOTES

[1] Earl O. Heady, "Rural Development and Rural Communities in the Future," in L. R. Whiting, ed., *Rural Industrialization: Problems and Potentials* (Ames: Iowa State University Press, 1974), p. 141.

[2] See Chapter 1 of this book.

[3] Stephen M. Smith and Glen C. Pulver, "Nonmetropolitan Industry: A Shift in Job Creation Strategy for Rural America," *A.I.D.C. Journal,* Vol. 13 (1978), pp. 7–22.

[4] Based on comments made at the American Industrial Development Council Institute, Norman, Oklahoma, in August 1977; and comments by officials of the Nebraska Department of Economic Development in 1978.

[5] Fred D. Lindsey, *What New Industrial Jobs Mean to a Community* (Washington, D.C.: Chamber of Commerce of the U.S., 1962).

[6] Patricia A. Lambert, "Comparisons of Social Well-being Components and Perceived Quality of Life Indicators in Rural Kansas Counties," unpublished master's thesis, Kansas State University, 1977.

[7] W. Wilson King, "Preface," in L. R. Whiting, op. cit., note 1, p. ix.

SUBJECT INDEX

193